Australian Railwayman

Previous books by Ron Fitch
Making Tracks (1989)
Railroading at its Wildest (1993)

A northbound Ghan at Marree. The tank in the
foreground was supplied with water from an
artesian bore. (*Photo:* The Port Dock Station
Railway Museum)

Australian Railwayman

From Cadet Engineer to Railways Commissioner

Ron Fitch,
OBE, PhD, ME, FIEAust, CP Eng, FCILT

ROSENBERG

First published in Australia in 2006
by Rosenberg Publishing Pty Ltd
PO Box 6125, Dural Delivery Centre NSW 2158
Phone: 61 2 9654 1502 Fax: 61 2 9654 1338
Email: rosenbergpub@smartchat.net.au
Web: www.rosenbergpub.com.au

National Library of Australia Cataloguing-in-Publica-
tion data:

Fitch, R. J. (Ronald John), 1910- .
Australian railwayman.

Bibliography.
Includes index.
ISBN 1 877058 48 3.

1. Fitch, R. J. (Ronald John), 1910- . 2. Railroad
engineers - Australia - Biography. 3. Railroads -
Australia - History. I. Title.

385.092

Abbreviations

AFULE Australian Federated Union of
           Locomotive Enginemen
CAR Central Australia Railway
CR Commonwealth Railways
NAR North Australia Railway
SAR South Australian Railways
TAR Trans Australian, Railway
WAGR Western Australian Government
       Railways

Cover design Highway 51 Design Works
Set in 10 on 12 point Times New Roman
Printed in Singapore
through GComm Print & Publish

Contents

Dedicated to all those people who made it possible:
family, teachers, tutors, superiors, colleagues, mentors
and workmates

SAR twin 600 class locomotives being attached to the inaugural westbound Indian Pacific at Broken Hill, 24 February 1970 *(Photo:* W.A. Bayley)

Author's Note

The publicity that followed my being awarded in 2002 — and at the not-so-young age of 92 years — a Doctorate of Philosophy by the University of New South Wales prompted suggestions from a number of sources that I write my memoirs. It was apparent therefore that those sources were not aware of my two earlier books — *Making Tracks* (1989) and *Railroading at its Wildest* (1993) — and understandably so in view of their being now out of print. Bearing in mind too that not only have there been enquiries from time to time for those two publications, but also that I would be the only person still living who had played some part in a number of incidents recounted in them, it was felt that the preferred course would be to write my memoirs, which, while including the essential content of the two books — but in a different format — would also contain new material, both of a personal nature as well as in the railway context.

Australian Railwayman is the outcome.

The author wishes to record his appreciation of the assistance given him in many ways by Nicholas Pusenjak and Graham Watson of the WA Railway Historical Society and Ron Fluck and Bob Sampson of the Port Dock National Railway Museum.

520 class locomotive, Duchess of Gloucester, heading an ARHS special train near Eden Hills, South Australia, April 1970 (*Photo:* Ian Hammond)

Kalgoorlie, Western Australia, departure of the first eastbound Trans Australian, 25 October 1917 (*Photo:* Westrail)

1   A Lifetime of Memories

On 20 February 2003 I had the honour of being guest speaker at the Annual Dinner of the South Australian Division of the Institution of Engineers Australia, where I outlined the experiences and objectives which, in my opinion, resulted in my working life being one of unforgettable pleasure and pride. Those objectives included the following:

- Do not let them break your spirit, no matter what.
- Tell the truth as you see it, irrespective of its palatability or likely acceptance by those to whom it is directed.
- Learn to live and work under harsh conditions, and to respect the men and women who are prepared to accept such a challenge, at times in some of the most inhospitable environment on earth.
- Get to know your staff and treat them as one of the team. After all, the man at the coal face is equally entitled to our regard.
- Always do your homework.
- Don't talk down to anyone, however humble.

In retrospect — and thanks to my parents; to my two sisters and brother, who subjugated their personal desires to the whims of their younger sibling; to my wife Doreen, with whom I shared 60 wondrous years and who, through marriage, became what one of my colleagues described as a 'dedicated railwayman'; to our family of whom we were both immeasurably proud; and to a number of people in many places and of many callings — my entire life did in fact become both unforgettable and a source of pride.

My 46 years' long railway career — which consisted of 27 rewarding years literally on the wallaby, working in the field, at times under primitive conditions, and of 19 as an administrator with its managerial and political overtones — would have been somewhat unique in the Australian context, and almost incredible in the wider one. Indeed, after having learned something. of my working life, Geoffrey Kichenside, Railway Books Editor for David & Charles, said, 'It is really railroading at its wildest', a description deemed appropriate for the title of my second book.

It started in Western Australia in February 1927 and ended in South Australia in March 1973. It encompassed three railway systems totalling 16,267 route kilometres or over 38 percent of Australia's mainland routes, and extended from the Indian Ocean in the west to the New South Wales and Victoria borders in the east, and north to the Red Centre, as well as the isolated systems from WA's Port Hedland to Marble Bar, South Australia's Eyre Peninsula, and the Northern Territory's Top End.

Climatically, it contrasted between persistent summer temperatures as high as 48 degrees and winter ones near freezing point; and between areas with an annual rainfall of 1500 mm (where one became adept at sheltering in the nearest hollow log or burnt-out tree trunk when out on surveys) and those with as little as 180 mm, all of which might be precipitated in a matter of minutes.

It was a career that involved 21 different postings — 17 of them by direction and only four by choice — and which necessitated 26 changes of domicile, 13 of them after our marriage in 1936. Indeed, in the nine years to 1945 we shifted house 11 times, the individual occupancies varying from three days to two years. Our first marital home was a three-roomed hessian house on a construction job. Such a nomadic life was not conducive to the wellbeing of one's household furniture which, in addition to the inevitable damage occasioned by those 13 transfers, also suffered from a number of movements in and out of storage while we were on temporary secondment elsewhere. Two of the latter were in dirt-floored garages. Nevertheless, one piece of congoleum floor covering 36 inches (91 cm) wide and costing three shillings a yard (38 cents a metre) served in the hallways of six successive houses, subject of course to appropriate surgery on the occasion of each shift.

In those days, one did not demur when transferred to meet departmental requirements. On the contrary, as young men we sought country service whenever possible; and, even when a particular move might have been the last thing that we would have wanted, we accepted it as one of the inevitable demands of a railway life. Nor was the notice of transfer always adequate; sometimes as little as 24 hours. Once I received such short notice to move from Kalgoorlie to Geraldton — a shift of over 1200 kilometres — and, on the day that I reported there, I was given just one day to move again, this time to Wurarga, a tiny and virtually uninhabited siding 183 kilometres inland.

For several years during the Depression I lived in a tent and cooked my meals over a fire in the open, using a tin billy can, a home-made gridiron and a camp oven, and subsisted over an entire summer on a diet predominated by tinned meat, potatoes, onions and bread and jam.

Tableware consisted of an enamelled mug and plate, knife, fork and spoon. Should a meal extend to a second course, some intermediate washing up might be called for, a procedure that, on one occasion, I carried into the family home. I had returned there for the Easter break, and, having finished one course, unthinkingly picked my plate and cutlery, washed them at the kitchen sink, then dried them and returned with them to the table where the family looked on, incredulous and silent. However, my lapse did not match that of one of my former university colleagues who forgot where he was and followed the time-honoured bush custom of throwing the dregs of his teacup over his shoulder before seeking a refill.

Among other things, my career has included carrying my swag and attempting to snatch a few hours' sleep in a galvanised-iron or weatherboard rest house, or on the floor of a remote railway shelter shed, shearers' quarters, or a guard's van; even just under the stars, cushioned against a spinifex bush.

Not infrequently, it has meant working up to 15 hours a day for ten days straight or working around the clock repairing washaway damage and being too tired to shave or even bathe. One just flopped down and slept, oblivious to one's own revolting malodour.

Other memories include travelling a distance further than from London to Rome to the scene of a derailment, and the same distance back again after the damage had been repaired; travelling on a gang section car at night on an unfenced railway with the ever-present risk of collision with a camel, a wild bull or a kangaroo; riding a section car over washouts up to 15 metres long and three metres deep, trusting that the sleepers would hold the rails to gauge and not have us catapulted into the hole; wading waist-deep through a flooded creek and holding one's swag head high to keep it dry; and, finally, having the sometimes dubious privilege of travelling on a number of trains worldwide, some named, some nicknamed and some that should never have been allowed on the track at all!

But perhaps the most rewarding experience has been the opportunity to work with, to live under the same conditions as, and to get to know and to establish lasting friendships with a number of railwaymen of all grades and in all places.

The story goes back to the time when neither roads nor footpaths were bituminised, and stationmasters would provide home-made whisks — fashioned out of strips of cloth attached to a truncated umbrella handle — with which intending passengers could remove the dust from their shoes before entraining. Station platforms too were paved with unsealed laterite gravel, and one of the porter's rostered duties was the daily hosing down of the surface to allay the dust.

It also goes back to the days when passenger carriages were illuminated by peanut-oil lamps, often with excess oil swirling around the bottom of the glass bowls and having a mesmeric effect on the passengers; and when smoking compartments were strictly a male preserve equipped with cuspidors set into the floor between facing seats in the forlorn hope that the expectorators were possessed of a good aim.

It was a time when steam locomotives hauled both suburban passenger and country mixed trains at the incredibly slow start-to-stop average speed of 27 km/h; and when small kerosene headlighted coal burning locomotives not only fouled the atmosphere with belches of black smoke, but also imperilled the passengers' eyesight with showers of cinders, as well as constituting a threat by the starting of bushfires during the dry season. Then, in later years, when heavy furnace oil supplanted coal as the fuel, an oily flocculence took over from the cinders and, while not endangering one's eyesight, one's clothing did suffer.

In those early days, engineering practices too were primitive, being essentially of the pick, shovel, wheelbarrow and Clydesdale vintage. Prewar, the tracklaying 'machines' consisted of 52 pairs of bare hands and one draught horse, the latter to haul the trolley carrying the rails and sleepers to the railhead as it crept forward; while the lifting and lining of the track — and to a standard not exceeded by today's sophisticated equipment — relied on the eyesight and the muscle power of the workmen. Australia did not receive its first track tamping machine — a primitive one by current standards — until 1949, and, even then, the lifting and lining of the rails remained a manual operation.

Survey instruments were also archaic. For 22 years I used a Cooke Troughton and Sims theodolite branded 1897, and with a sighting range in summer limited to about 400 metres, an incredibly short distance in today's climate of laser technology.

The period also saw the achievement of a unified rail gauge from Brisbane to Perth but, sadly, and as a result of interstate parochialism and Commonwealth intransigence, it also witnessed the passing-up of a heaven-sent opportunity to correct the nation's century-old rail gauge problem. Indeed, the author would be the only person still living who was associated with the standardisation project as far back as 1929.

The privilege of having witnessed and participated, either significantly or insignificantly, in those developments has been enhanced by a number of personal experiences not often available to any one person.

In the strict railway context, they would include my rise from engineering cadet on one railway system to chief civil engineer on another and, finally, to Railways Commissioner on a third.

Another would be my participation in three Royal Commissions into railway matters; the first, behind the scenes and being responsible for the preparation of data; the second, sitting as the Commonwealth's nominee on a Royal Commission of three; and the third, the Aunt Sally at whom most of the arrows were directed.

A fourth matter in this context and, unfortunately, not the happiest one, was related to political overtones and pressures. This included Commonwealth–State negotiations, the opportunistic use of the railways as a political football, progressive inroads into their autonomy, and their conversion from an instrument of national development into one of political expediency.

However, it was the personal experiences that made my life so memorable. The most gratifying features included, firstly, my years in charge of unemployment relief works in Western Australia during the Depression, living in camps under conditions identical with those under my direction; and secondly, establishing a rapport with my workmates of all grades, getting to know them personally, living and working with them in some of the most remote parts of the continent, enduring the same inconveniences and hardships as did they and their wives, and accepting their hospitality tendered with dignity and as hosts of equal standing. This bond has not diminished, but rather has it strengthened, in retirement, to the stage that all traces of subordination have disappeared. Indeed these things remain with me as the most satisfying and rewarding features of my working life.

In June 1934 I was posted to Williams, on the railway from Collie to Narrogin and located 161 road and 293 rail kilometres from Perth, there to undertake the third of my six unemployment relief jobs with which I was associated during the Depression; and it was here that I met Doreen.

Together with her parents, she had come to live there following her father's transfer from Perth by the then Postmaster General's Department. However, after winding up the Williams job early in 1935, I resumed my nomadic way of life, moving successively to Meekatharra, Allanson and Cue, 1065, 117 and 950 kilometres respectively from Williams. As a consequence, our courtship soon developed into a long-distance affair, restricted to a twice-weekly exchange of letters and occasional meetings. However, on Boxing Day 1936 we were married by the Rev. George Tulloch at Perth's Saint Andrew's Presbyterian Church, then began our wedded life in the three-roomed hessian house in Cue.

Geoffrey Kichenside was right. Truly, it was railroading at its wildest — but, at the same time, most rewarding. I have been fortunate in having family members, teachers, tutors, coaches, supervisors, colleagues and friends who made substantial contributions to my upbringing, education and development, and to whom, together with my workmates of all grades and in all places, I shall be eternally indebted. For these reasons and more it is felt that, for both historical and personal reasons, the story should be told.

2   A Railway Family

My parents were married in Kalgoorlie on Western Australia's Eastern Goldfields, and my elder sister Winnie and brother Harry were born there. My other sister Jean was born in the Perth suburb of Subiaco; yet the youngest child of Henry John Lesingham Fitch and Sarah Ann Fitch (nee McArthur) was born on 8 June 1910 at Surrey Hills, an outer Melbourne suburb. It took me 50 years to discover why.

In 1960, my mother's younger sister Jean, then married to George Moss and a resident of Numurkah in rural Victoria, wrote to say that she was about to celebrate her golden wedding and that I, two months old at the time, had been the youngest guest at the wedding. It then all became clear to me. My mother, who always maintained an undisguised bias in favour of the McArthur clan and the State of Victoria, would have been determined to attend her sister's wedding, irrespective of the effort, inconvenience and cost.

Indeed, it did involve a week-long sea voyage between Fremantle and Port Melbourne for a family of four, together with a six-month-old foetus who had no option but to go along for the ride, and on the return for a family of six, the father having followed the others to Victoria a couple of months later — and the foetus having in the meantime matured into a male child, later to be baptised Ronald John Fitch.

His birth certificate states that his arrival was supervised by a midwife, but he has been given to understand that it was touch-and-go whether in fact he did not utter his first wail in the spring cart transporting mother and emergent infant from her parents' home in Nunawading to the midwife at Surrey Hills.

Oddly, somewhat similar circumstances surrounded the arrival, 36 years later, of our younger son Phillip. In his case, the taxi transporting Doreen to the King Edward Memorial Hospital in Subiaco arrived with only minutes to spare. Had the taxi taking her to the hospital been two or three minutes later in arrival, his place of birth might well have been recorded as 'Railway Road, Subiaco', or 'Yellow Cab, registration unknown.' Within a couple of minutes, a nurse came down the stairs, removed her surgical mask and said to me:

'You've just had a baby boy.'

To this I replied: 'It can't be mine. I've just brought my wife in.'

Her response was: 'It's yours all right.'

Railway-wise, I really never had a chance. I was always destined to follow that path and become the ninth in the Fitch family railway hierarchy of ten.

It all started in Victoria where I had three uncles and two cousins who were stationmaster, train controller and engineman with the Victorian Railways while another cousin, a civil engineer, commenced his railway career there before moving to the Commonwealth Railways.

To this list should be added another uncle who had been a guard with the Western Australian Government Railways and who prompted my father — who had migrated to WA during the gold rush of the 1890s — to join the WAGR, which he did, first as a porter, but eventually spending all but two of his 42 years' service as a signalman. To complete the decuplet, my elder sister Winnie married George Renshaw, also a railwayman, whose service with the WAGR included that of porter, stationmaster and clerk.

With such a family background and its aggregated contribution to the Australian Railways in excess of 400 years — as well as the strong affinity that prevailed between my father and me — my gravitation towards a railway career was never in doubt. Not for one moment have I regretted it. Finally, in 1969, our elder son Russell married Jill McCusker, younger daughter of the New South Wales Commissioner of Railways, Neal McCusker, and his wife Rene.

Both of my parents were born in Victoria. My mother, the third of five children born to braw Scottish immigrants, Duncan and Mary McArthur, first saw the light of day at Nunawading on 9 January 1872 while my father's birth at Homebush on 27 November 1874 was the eighth in 14 years to George Augustus and Eliza Jane Fitch. Indeed, in subsequent years, the number of Fitch offspring rose to ten. George and Eliza were also immigrants, from Essex and London respectively, although Eliza, whose maiden name was Tijou, was understood to have been a descendant of émigrés from France during the Revolution.

Duncan McArthur was an orchardist; while George Fitch, initially a mariner, had settled at Homebush where, when not procreating, he operated a puddling machine in which gold bearing ore was washed to separate the metal from the mullock.

Henry John, who first met Sarah Ann while working as a butcher at Nunawading, followed the gold rush to Western Australia in 1895, but instead of proceeding directly to the Eastern Goldfields he spent some time working as a labourer on the reclamation of the Perth Esplanade adjacent to the Swan River. Later, he prospected for gold near North Dandalup, south of Perth, and at that time a gazetted goldfield. However, finding nothing more than a few colours at North Dandalup, in 1897 my father moved to Kalgoorlie — at that time only four years old and more of a camp than a town — but instead of succumbing to gold fever, on 10 November 1897 he joined the Western Australian Government Railways.

The railway to Kalgoorlie had been opened only nine months earlier and further gold discoveries saw the start of ten years of frantic railway construction, not only to serve the Golden Mile itself but also Kanowna, Leonora and Laverton, as well as from Coolgardie to Norseman; in all over 550 kilometres.

Only two days before my father joined the WAGR, the lines from Kalgoorlie through Boulder to Lakeside, and from Golden Gate through the mining leases to Kamballie were opened for traffic. Five years later, a loop line from Kamballie through Brown Hill and back to the Hannan Street station near Kalgoorlie was completed, thereby encircling the Golden Mile, reputedly the richest square mile of land in the world.

With his lifelong friend and workmate Charlie Jenkin, Harry Fitch was one of the first signalmen at Golden Gate, where he served under Harry O'Connor, later Chief Traffic Manager and one of the finest railwaymen in the history of the WAGR.

Fifteen months after joining the railways, Harry Fitch played a small part in an incident involving the Premier of Western Australia, Sir John Forrest.

At that time, the mining ordnances provided that, on being granted a mining lease, it was incumbent on the lessee to indicate the line of lode so that others could prospect the area for alluvial gold. One company, the Ivanhoe Venture, did not do so, the general opinion being that no such lode existed and that the company was in fact engaged in alluvial operations. When the Minister for Mines, Edward Wittenoom, promulgated a regulation limiting alluvial mining to ten feet (3.05 m) from the surface, this aggravated the situation and there was widespread discontent among the alluvial diggers.

In February 1899, Sir John, accompanied by a large party, had gone to Kalgoorlie by special train for the official opening of the Kalgoorlie—Menzies railway. A crowd of angry miners soon congregated outside his hotel, demanding the repeal of the regulation, and when Sir John Forrest left his hotel he was jostled by the crowd and forced across the road towards the station. The main doors had been closed to hold back the mob, but the weight of numbers forced them

Kalgoorlie, Western Australia, Hannan Street (the main street) 1896, three years after the discovery of gold (*Photo:* Library Board of Western Australia)

open and the Premier was swept across the platform and down on to the track. In the railway yard was a local passenger train awaiting 'line clear' before departing for Boulder, and Sir John boarded it. So too did the miners, although their anger had abated by that time.

As the rostered guard had been booked off for crib, the stationmaster instructed my father to take the train out to Boulder forthwith. So Fitch assumed the role of guard and gave the right of way to the driver. One of the guard's duties on those trains was to collect the tickets from the passengers, so my father went through the train to do so. The first man that he approached said: 'I don't have to pay. I'm the guest of Sir John Forrest.' This stratagem was taken up and passed along the train faster than could my father walk through it.

Having established himself in the railways at Kalgoorlie, Henry John sent for Sarah Ann, whose transition from the softness of a Nunawading orchard to the sun, sin and sand of Kalgoorlie must have been a shattering experience. So too would have been her lonely journey by ship to

The Golden Mile, Western Australia, February 1899. Ministerial train that took the official party to the opening of the Kalgoorlie–Menzies railway, taken against the backdrop of the Golden Mile (*Photo:* State Library of Victoria)

Hannan Street, Kalgoorlie, c. 1900 (*Photo:* Library Board of Western Australia)

Fremantle and then by train to her destination.

They were married on 16 May 1901 by the Reverend Alexander Crowe, doyen of the Presbyterian Church in Western Australia, and whose ministrations to the roaring camps will never be forgotten. The bridal pair were attended by my father's sister Madge Fitch and his cousin Frank Bedgegood.

For a short time they lived in the then highly respectable Hay Street before moving some distance away to Piccadilly Street. It was a timely shift because Hay Street soon developed into, and remains to this day, the local red light district. Indeed, 30 years on, when posted to Kalgoorlie for the first time, I was embarrassed when, in all innocence, I sought to locate my parents' first marital home.

Living conditions on the goldfields were rugged. Houses were constructed of either hessian, canvas or galvanised-iron; while the primitive sanitation, the scarcity of water, the heat, the flies and the dust all helped to create a climate ripe for a typhoid epidemic, something to which my mother fell shortly after the birth of my elder sister Winnie.

Prior to pioneering the Mundaring water scheme reaching Kalgoorlie until 1903, most drinking water had to be brought in by train.

Being a railway employee, my father was in the privileged position of receiving a free ration of 25 gallons (about 115 litres) of water each week. Anything beyond that had to be bought.

In 1907, the family moved to the Perth metropolitan area, and after a short time in East Perth, settled at Subiaco, five kilometres west of the city, and where the family roots remained for the next 98 years. It was at Subiaco in 1908 that my sister Jean was born, and no doubt so would have I but for the fact that my mother was determined to attend her sister Jean's wedding.

My youthful development and, ultimately, my rewarding career and adult life were the outcome of a happy and secure, if somewhat spartan, family life, together with the fact that, being the youngest of four children, I was accorded preferential treatment not only by my parents, but also by my siblings. My brother Harry, six years my senior, took me under his fraternal wing, fostering and encouraging me in all things — educational, sporting and recreational. At the same time, Winnie, eight years older than me, mothered me in many ways, while Jean and I, being only two years apart, had many things in common, especially during our teens and beyond, when our scholastic, sporting and social activities ran parallel and brought us even closer together.

The author's father, H.J. Fitch   The author's brother, H.D. Fitch   The author, c. 1968

My mother carried with her to her death on Christmas Day 1942 strong and unbreakable traces of her strict Scottish Presbyterian upbringing, particularly those of highland frugality. Indeed, she seemed to enjoy saving money, and would frequent the city's department stores' half-yearly sales with an avid determination to achieve the best possible purchases, and then return home and balance the contents of her purse to the nearest penny. Once, she made vinegar from our home grown grapes, while on another occasion she went so far as to manufacture her own laundry soap.

She was also a combination of contradictions. Deeply religious, highly principled and ever willing to help a lame dog, not only was she possessed of Victorian prudery and Scottish Presbyterian bigotry, but she could also be somewhat harsh in her dispensation of family discipline. Her medicine chest seemed to be limited to two items; senna tea and castor oil. We children were obliged to swallow a cupful of the former every Saturday morning irrespective of our level of continency; and she would prescribe a tablespoonful of castor oil for every complaint or accident, be it a splinter in the finger, a sprained ankle, whooping cough or tonsillitis — at times even as a punishment for some juvenile misdemeanour — and after having forced down that revolting purgative, we children were subjected to the added torture of

having to lick the spoon lest one trace remained uningested. And she did this despite the fact that she could never bring herself to swallow even one teaspoonful of the nauseous stuff!

My mother held an abiding abhorrence of alcohol which, it seemed, arose from her father's reported fondness for a wee dram or two. Perhaps therefore she would have been appalled had she realised that her home-brewed vinegar most surely would have failed the breathalyser test.

No doubt a by-product of her Calvanistic upbringing, she was also possessed of a phobia in respect of Roman Catholicism. Had she known that, 27 years after her death, Phillip — our younger son and her youngest grandchild — would marry Susan O'Driscoll according to the rites of the Roman Catholic Church, and that their three children would be confirmed to the same faith, it is not unlikely that her ashes would have turned over in Caledonian displeasure in their niche at Perth's Karrakatta Cemetery. On the other hand, had she been able to observe that union resulting in a happy, well adjusted and successful family, there is reason to believe that those crematorial rotations might have stopped.

In the light of her puritanism, her discipline, her intractability in some matters, and her driving ambition that her children would succeed, in retrospect I feel that, as a child, I held her in some awe. Nevertheless, she was a loving and caring mother, who literally worked herself to death for her family; and who, with my father, provided us children not only with a happy and stable home life, but also with opportunities not normally available to others of our relatively humble origins.

On a lighter note, I never forgave her for the fact that, at a time when the wearing of lace-up boots was more or less mandatory in the boyhood arena — and when even lace-up shoes were considered effeminate — until I was about seven years of age she persisted in fitting me with bar-type shoes normally worn by girls. My embarrassment was compounded by the added indignity of being obliged to wear large lace collars. I did not dare question my mother's authority to clothe me as she thought fit, but her actions did foster something of an inferiority complex which stayed with me long after I had reverted to the masculinity of lace-up boots and had shed the lace collars.

My father, while possessing similar characteristics in respect of hard work, thrift and an ambition to do the best for his family, was ever ready to encourage us in our endeavours and to console us in times of failure, yet tempering praise lest it lead to swelled-headedness.

As a railway signalman, he worked shifts to a roster covering 24 hours a day, seven days a week, for 50 weeks of the year, for his entire 42 years' railway service. Those shifts were initially of eight but latterly of six hours duration, but without a meal break. In addition, over the last 11 years of his career, he conducted, in his own time, classes and correspondence courses in railway safe-working procedures. Yet, despite all this, he found time to be a home gardener, as well as taking a personal interest in and attendance at our church, school and sporting activities.

He was an impressive figure and his integrity unchallengeable. The University of Western Australia offered bursaries to undergraduates, on the application form for which was a declaration to be signed by one's parents stating that, without the bursary, the student would be unable to enrol. After reading the declaration, my father said:

'I can't sign that! You are going to the university in any case.'

I became aware soon after enrolling that many a parent of financial standing far higher than his had signed it without compunction.

Perhaps because I was the youngest of four children, my father and I seemed to develop a close relationship which resulted in our spending a lot of time together — in the signal cabin with him of a Sunday, at sporting fixtures or camping and fishing. Is it any wonder that I worshipped him, and that my railway career was pre-ordained from an early age?

3   Home Town Memories

I was conceived in Subiaco in 1909, born in Victoria in 1910, and crossed the interstate border on the Long Straight near Deakin on 26 May 1949 and became a naturalised South Australian; yet my whole life — and, in particular, my first 39 years — were indelibly linked with the Perth suburb of Subiaco, and with two addresses in Nicholson Road only three allotments apart, namely Numbers 196 and 202. Not only were they my homes for the first 21 years, but also family's direct association with them continued until 2004, when my elder sister Winnie, then 102 years old, vacated it.

I may have ended my permanent attachment to the family home in 1931 when I set out on my wanderings around the WAGR, but, until 1936, it remained my family and city base. Even after our marriage in that year, Doreen and I lived, more or less temporarily, in six different houses in Subiaco, and for tenures ranging from three days to four years. The extreme briefness of the three-day tenancy was forced on us by the invasion of an army of fleas.

Growing up in Subiaco

My parents built their first home at 196 Nicholson Road in 1907, and lived there until 1917, when they shifted to Number 202, a property that they had built originally as a rental investment. At that time, and indeed until the 1920s, Nicholson Road was remote from almost everything and I must assume that my parents built there because of the relatively cheap land prices.

Apart from the Shenton Park Hotel and a small and not overly well stocked convenience store at the corner of Derby Road and Gloster

202 Nicholson Street, Subiaco, the family home for 87 years

Street, and owned by a middle aged bachelor, Bill Eaton, who used to decorate its interior with tassels alternating between religious messages and pendants of saveloys, intended for sale but prone to contamination by house flies, there was no other commercial establishment within half a kilometre. Indeed, Subiaco's business and commercial district was located at the northern end of Rokeby Road, almost one and a half kilometres distant.

So too did access to public transport involve a tedious trudge along unsealed and un-footpathed dusty roads. The nearest tram service to the city necessitated an uphill drag of a kilometre to Rokeby Road while, until Daglish was opened in 1924, the nearest railway stations — Subiaco and West Subiaco (the latter subsequently renamed Shenton Park) — were, respectively, over two kilometres and one kilometre distant. We four children were obliged to tackle the trek between home and the Subiaco station twice each school day during our periods at the Perth Boys' and Perth Girls' Schools. Even our primary school years at the Subiaco school involved daily walks of over one kilometre there and one kilometre back.

Electric power did not reach our house until 1917. Prior to that, we had to rely on kerosene for lighting and wood fuel for heating. The lighting could be something of a hazard. I can recall one occasion when the dining room curtains caught fire after the Millar table lamp had been placed too close to them. Deep sewerage too did not arrive until the mid-1920s.

However, in spite of these somewhat primitive conditions, we had a lot of fun. The Shenton Park swamp has since been transformed into a beautiful lake and park, but in our youth it was the scene of many a juvenile activity: canoeing in home-made non-buoyant and capsize-prone craft; catching tadpoles, frogs and tiny fish; and the baking of potatoes in their jackets in swamp-side fires, both potatoes and matches having been surreptitiously purloined from home.

The area behind the hotel, and extending south to Keightly Road, had once been the site of a dairy. However, in my time it was both vacant and unfenced, and, in deference to its former function, was nicknamed Cow Dung Flat. It was here that we practised kite flying, subject to our being able to endure the pain of the double-gees — known elsewhere as three-cornered jacks — that infested the area, and constituted a perpetual threat to our bare feet.

Following World War I, the area experienced massive changes. Cow Dung Flat was subdivided and war service homes built there while, in Nicholson Road, four new shops — two grocers, one butcher and one hairdresser-tobacconist — were opened, although the last named really provided the facade for a starting-price bookmaking enterprise. Concurrently, a former timber yard became the site of an open-air cinema which later went indoors and became the Shenton Theatre.

Roads were then sealed, footpaths provided, and bus services introduced between Perth and Fremantle and between West Subiaco and Perth. The early vehicles were primitive by current standards, the original ones being charabancs rather than buses, but they were the forerunners of an extensive and efficient transport service From

that time onwards, the city of Subiaco expanded and developed a high degree of civic pride which it has maintained to this day.

My formative years in Subiaco also spanned World War I and, although I was only eight years of age when it ended, I was old enough to comprehend the final stages leading to victory. I still recall hearing the pealing of the local volunteer fire brigade's bell announcing wartime successes and, in particular, news of the Armistice, when I raised objections to being wakened to be informed that the war was over. Then, two or three days later, we assembled in the school yard to welcome home Cliff Sadlier, our very own Victoria Cross winner.

I could go on forever reminiscing over my 39 years' continuous and my 95 years' total association with Subiaco, but these comments might provide some indication of the atmosphere in which I grew up; stringent by today's standards, but rewarding and constructive enough to have given me a worthwhile start in life. I might have been an expatriate since 1949, but it still ranks with Adelaide as being what Peter Allen called 'Home'. So too does the Subiaco Football Club retain a place in my football heart.

The Subiaco Football Club

Even today, I have memories of being seated between my mother and father and watching a maroon-guernseyed and white knee-length trousered man being carried shoulder high from an oval by two similarly attired individuals. I was informed subsequently that the year was 1915; the location Perth Oval (Loton's Park); the occasion, Subiaco's third premiership; and the shoulder-hoisted player Herb Limb, who in the last moments of the match and over his head, had kicked the winning goal. From that moment on, I became imbued with an intense loyalty to the club that remains with me to this day — although, for the past 50 years it has been shared with South Australia's Glenelg Football Club.

Compared with the gladiatorial amphitheatre that engulfs it today, the Subiaco oval of my early days was inconceivably modest. Until the brick grandstand was added in 1924, the only building on the site was a small timber framed structure housing primitive facilities for players and with a partly roofed viewing area on top. In the early days there existed an additional structure not associated with football. At the north-eastern corner, outside the playing area, was a large picture screen upon which silent films were shown on summer evenings, the patrons reclining comfortably on the oval itself.

Minors were admitted free to home matches, the gates to the 'outer' spectator area being opened to them following the start of play, a gesture that proved to be a valuable incentive to youthful enthusiasm. As youngsters, we held the players in boyish adoration. Indeed, one of our boasts — entirely fictitious — was that we used to carry the players' bags through the turnstiles, and so get into the grandstand area free of charge and in the company of one of our heroes.

On one occasion my day was made when a delivery van, owned by the city firm Robertson and Moffatt (later Ahearns Ltd) and driven by Wally Steele, the club's rover, suffered a puncture outside our home. I was honoured with the privilege of lending him a hammer from my father's tool kit. From that time onwards, that hammer assumed an aura bordering on sanctification.

It had been a long held dream that, one day, I might don the Subiaco guernsey, and in 1929, three months before my nineteenth birthday, I was given that chance. It was a disaster! I was summarily dropped to the reserves; but later that year my football career was resurrected when I regained my place. My playing days at Subiaco ended following the 1931 grand final — in which, incidentally, we were courageous losers to East Fremantle — when I was transferred by the WAGR to Kalgoorlie, a move that heralded the start of my railway peregrinations.

In an endeavour to engineer my return to Perth, Walter Richardson — Club Patron, Mayor of Subiaco and local Member of Parliament — approached me saying that, as Jack Scaddan — a former President of the Club and a long-time supporter — was Minister for Railways, it would be a simple matter to arrange the move. Lionel Boas, a former committeeman and player, made the same suggestion to my father. Between us, we rejected both approaches, arguing that, there being a depression at the time, I was not going to

jeopardise my career in that way.

My subsequent football career included two seasons with Kalgoorlie City in the Eastern Goldfields League, and two with Williams in the Great Southern Association based on Narrogin, the latter broken by a one year interregnum while I was at Meekatharra. At that time, the standard of football on the Goldfields closely approximated that of the Perth League. Many players from Perth, rendered unemployed by the Depression, had migrated to Kalgoorlie seeking work on the mines. My team, Kalgoorlie City, included 14 former League players. Indeed, four of my former Subiaco team mates — Arthur Ballantyne, Len Lowry, Bert Nissen and Arthur Barrett — were among those with whom or against whom I played during my two seasons there.

In those days, the game was played, not for money but for pleasure and satisfaction at having achieved a certain level of proficiency. Unbelievable as it may appear in today's climate of professionalism and players of millionaire status, at that time, with one exception, we even had to pay our own way to matches. The exception was the Fremantle Oval, when we were reimbursed two shillings (20 cents) to cover the train fare. Being a railway employee, I was entitled to half fare, which represented a saving of ten cents per match. Over my three years with the club, I played at Fremantle on six occasions, which meant that, overall, I profited by a total of 60 cents during my football career!

Contact with the Subiaco Club was not renewed until I returned to Perth in 1944; and, as a committeeman and selector, I maintained my active association with it until my move to South Australia in 1949, but my interest never waned.

However, the Fitch connection with the club continued on for many years. Shortly after graduating in medicine, Ken Fitch — son of my brother Harry — became its long term medical officer, a service for which he was elected a life member in 1970.

I was privileged to be guest of the club at the 1961 preliminary final (unfortunately lost by Subiaco) and again in 2002 — while in Perth to attend sister Winnie's 100th birthday as well as the University Engineers' Club Committee's

80th Anniversary Dinner—when I was shown over the modernised Subiaco Oval complex, and entertained at lunch.

Before concluding these comments on my football life, I should recall two unconnected but in their own way instructive episodes.

The first: Playing in the 1933 grand final for Kalgoorlie against Boulder we were trailing by one point when, with only minutes to go, I was awarded a free kick that even I knew that I did not deserve. Nevertheless, I drop-kicked for goal, but it did not quite make the distance and we lost the premiership by that one point. After the game, the Club President said to me. 'I'm glad you missed that goal. There would have been a riot had you kicked it.' To this day I suffer nightmares over that kick, and regret that I did not try a torpedo punt. It might have made the distance.

That premiership match also heralded the breaking of my pledge. It was the custom in Kalgoorlie that, after a game, players, officials and close supporters adjourn to a local hotel to partake of a celebratory or consolatory drink, depending on the result. Mine was normally of the non-alcoholic type, but after our win in the previous week's preliminary final I was urged to break out. This I did not do, but said that, should we win the grand final, I would have a shandy. My one point loss in that match should have freed me from that promise, but when somebody put a glass of beer in my hand I relented and drank it. This must have given rise to something of a sensation, because for the next week or two I could not walk down Hannan Street without friend, foe or stranger stopping me and saying: 'They tell me that you broke out last Sunday.' I just could not live it down. However, such debauchery was short lived. It lasted for that one drink, following which I reaffirmed the pledge.

The second: When playing my first game for the Williams Club in 1934, I was amazed when, as the siren sounded for the half-time break, every player on both sides — except me —rushed off the ground and into the dressing shed, emerging a moment later with a jacket over his football togs and into another shed, there to partake of afternoon tea! I could not believe my eyes; but, on reflection, was not that what true sport is all about? It is, and rightly should be, only a game and not the media controlled and advertisement saturated gladiatorial circus that it is today. The men with whom and against whom I played that day were mostly farmers who, after spending their Saturday morning on the tractor, had returned home, showered and lunched before leaving for an afternoon's enjoyment chasing the football around the local oval.

Both Subiaco and I have come a long way since that day in 1910 when, two month's young, I came there for the first time, to become the sixth and youngest member of a family whose roots, established there three years earlier, remained in Nicholson Road for 97 years. But that association lives on. Nina Fitch — daughter of Ken and great-grand-daughter of H.J. and S.A., and also born and bred in Subiaco — still lives there, not in the former family home, but in Cullen Street nearby. The dynasty must surely reach its centenary; most likely even exceed it.

4   School Days

Memories of this period are dominated by four things: the embarrassment that I suffered following the maternal edict that I wear bar-type shoes and lace collars; a proneness to accident; happy and fulfilling school days; and a moderate success in the sporting arena.

In respect of accidents, I was just plain clumsy. It all started at about three years of age when I opened up my forehead following on a spontaneous head-on attack on the timber framing of a house under construction.

This propensity towards self destruction did not diminish with the passage of time. Over, the next 30 years — and apart from innumerable injuries arising from my bull-headed and accident-prone attitude towards sport — I endured a damaged ankle while dry sledding down the bank of the Swan River at Guildford, a broken arm after falling off some school playground equipment, and a badly injured knee following the derailment of a rail motor trolley. Nor did it stop even then. At age 93, a slip after showering resulted in my taking a running dive at the bathroom wall; the outcome, a fracture to a neck vertebra!

My formal education started in 1916 at the Subiaco Primary School; for the first two years in the 'infants' section under Headmistress Heslop; the next two in the 'intermediate' section under Mrs Coe; and finally, the last three years in the main school under Headmaster Bob Llewellyn.

An English lady, Miss Heslop, possessed, even for those days, such strange views on infant discipline that we novice pupils were in constant fear of her. On the other hand, both Mrs Coe and Mr Llewellyn had a different attitude to us; in particular Bob Llewellyn who, although subject to occasional choleric outbursts, wholeheartedly encouraged and supported us in every way, both in and out of school hours.

In 1922, I moved to the Perth Boys' School where, apart from the outstanding headmastership of T.C. Chandler, I had the good fortune to be introduced at the outset to W.J. Skipworth, a teacher who had the greatest impact on my development both in and out of the classroom, and with whom I maintained a personal association that lasted for over 20 years. In that same year, I was awarded a scholarship to the Perth Modern School, a government high school, entrance to which was, at that time, attained through a competitive state-wide examination.

T.C. Chandler (*Photo:* Library Board of Western Australia)

Teaching staff, Perth Boys' School, mid-1920s. T.C. Chandler and W.J. Skipworth are 4th and 5th from the left, front row, while H.C. Coombs (later Governor of the Reserve Bank) is on the far right of the back row.

Scholastically, I can lay claim to a unique and unbreakable record; that of enjoying the shortest ever pupilage at that elite and prestigious institution. It lasted precisely one day! I was not expelled, but left of my own accord. On my first day there at the start of the 1923 school year I was curtly told by Headmaster Joe Parsons — a man who, from my brief encounter with him, appeared to lack any trace of humanity towards his pupils — that I had 'loafed all last year' and relegated me Year 8. So I went straight back to Perth Boys', there to be welcomed with sympathy and understanding by Tommy Chandler and Bill Skipworth, and where I remained until completing Year 10. My return to Perth Boys' turned out to be to my advantage. It was from there that I was awarded a Coombe Scholarship.

In 1921, Sir Thomas Melrose Coombe, a prominent theatre owner in the city, endowed three scholarships for boys attending government schools in Western Australia who were sitting for the Junior Certificate public examination from Year 10. The scholarships, which were valued at

£50 ($100) per year for two years, were intended to meet the fees and other costs associated with enrolment at one of the four public schools in Perth, namely Hale (formerly High) School, Scotch College, Guildford Grammar School and Aquinas (formerly Christian Brothers') College. They were awarded on the bases of scholastic attainments, sporting achievements and personal qualities; perhaps akin to a mini Rhodes Scholarship.

In 1924 I was awarded one of the Coombe Scholarships and enrolled at Hale School for the two years leading to the Leaving Certificate Exam. (Incidentally, the 1922 the inaugural Coombe Scholar, Bryce Johnson, also from Perth Boys', sponsored an annual prize for students of the school at Junior Certificate level, based on the combined vote of masters and pupils. In 1924 I was fortunate enough to be awarded that prize also.)

Like other private schools at that time, attendance at Hale was normally within the reach of only those whose parents were in the higher financial bracket, and in a number of cases, where academic achievement was not always either the demand of the parents or the ambition of the son. However, not all pupils lacked scholastic ambition and during my two years at the school three boys were awarded university exhibitions, while I was also offered one, but did not take it up because its acceptance would have restricted my course of study to agricultural science.

As a scholarship holder coming from a humble family background, during the initial stages of my sojourn at Hale I was the recipient of some snobbish condescension from a handful of boys who I felt were superior to me only in matters of financial and social standing. Fortunately, however, and particularly after I had achieved some success in the sporting arena, I was widely accepted and shed my feeling of inferiority. I must stress also that not once did the staff, from headmaster down, display anything but a fair and encouraging attitude towards me.

These reminiscences of my childhood would not be complete without some reference to my youthful sporting activities, and to my early introduction to the railway world.

The former included cricket, gymnastics, YMCA rules basketball (now supplanted by the game invented in 1891 by James Naismith) and tennis, as part of the social life of the Subiaco Presbyterian Church. However, the more propitious phase began at Perth Boys' School in 1922 and continued at Hale School, at which I was fortunate enough to make the cricket, football, athletics and life-saving teams while, in respect of gymnastics, I was leader of the squad at Perth Boys' and the recipient of the silver medal at Hale. Of these activities, three highlights remain with me to this day.

The first: Having been a member of the Perth Boys' School football team which, in 1924 — and indeed over several preceding years — did not lose one match. One of our opponents, Midland Boys', managed to score in only one of the three matches that we played against them. In one of those matches the final tally was 42 goals 20 behinds to nil. However, I very nearly achieved notoriety in that I came within a whisker of permitting Midland to score. After having played

in the centre for the first three quarters, the coach relegated me to that of full back for the fourth. Confident that the ball would continue to be confined to the other end of the oval, the two back pocket players and I proceeded to sit down on the turf and paid little attention to the play — until, on looking up, I noticed to my horror that an opposing player had rushed past us, bouncing the ball on his way to the undefended goal. Fully conscious that, should he score even one behind, I would be summarily dropped from the first 18, I caught up with him and brought him down with a rugby tackle. His free kick was immediately captured by one of our players and my football bacon was saved.

The second: After representing Perth Boys' as a member of two unbeaten relay teams, at Hale School in 1925 I captured the Under 16 years Athletics Championship — and, with it, the Headmaster's Cup. When I later represented the school at that year's Interschool Sports Meeting I broke the record in the 440 yards Under 16 event but still came only second to Guildford Grammar's outstanding Tony Taylor.

The third: My ephemeral career with Hale's first eleven. A somewhat bungling wicket keeper and a rabbit with the bat, I was called upon to fill the gap when Reg Sewell, the regular keeper, fractured his leg. In this stand-in position, I achieved the rare distinction of collecting a black eye when I put my eye rather than my gloves in the line of flight of the ninth ball of the last over of the day. As there was not any no-ball recorded, and the eight-ball over has long since passed into history, perhaps my accidental achievement will stand as an all-time record.

Railway Indoctrination

In respect of my juvenile indoctrination into the railway mystique, the story goes back a long way; indeed, it started at the age of about six or seven years.

Probably because I was the youngest of four children, my father, then a signalman in Perth, periodically took me to work with him of a Sunday. There, I was privileged to observe the trains at close quarters and, as a special treat, to participate in a very small way — indeed insignificantly and merely tokenistically — in some of their oper-

Interior of Signal Box B, Perth, where I spent many an out-of-school hour and where my father worked for nearly 20 years, collecting two hernias on the way (*Photo:* Westrail)

ations. The signal cabins which I visited included three in Perth, two at Fremantle and single ones at East Perth and Midland Junction.

Train movements over the single line of railway between East Perth and Rivervale were controlled by the electric staff system of safe working. Trains were permitted to enter the section only when the engine driver was in possession of a train staff, a metal rod fitted with distinctive rings peculiar to each individual staff section and which, when not in use, was secured in an electrically locked frame located at each staff station. To avoid the possibility of two trains meeting head-on on the single line, only one staff at a time could be removed from the frames, and then only when the signalman at the opposite end activated an electrical relay. Communication between the two signal cabins was maintained by a system of bell codes, spelled out by means of a morse type key on the staff frames; and all messages were preceded by 'Call attention', which consisted of just one short ring. When spending a Sunday with my father in the East Perth signal cabin, on occasions I was honoured with the privilege of 'calling attention' of the signalman at Rivervale.

Then, at Fremantle, after a passenger train had arrived from Perth, the steam locomotive would run around the carriages in readiness for its departure on the return journey. To indicate to the engine driver that the track had been set for the reversing movement, a green flag would be displayed by hand from the signal cabin. Sometimes I held that green flag, but always under strict paternal supervision.

The Melbourne Road level crossing in the middle of the Perth station yard has long since disappeared, but when in use the heavy wooden gates protecting the crossing were opened and closed by rotating a large wheel in the adjacent signal cabin, known as Box A. I was allowed to pit my juvenile muscle power against the inertia of the gates. Invariably, the gates won.

Nevertheless, these excursions were not per-mitted to interfere with my Sabbatarian obligations. I was always deposited on a train that would get me to Sunday School on time.

The greatest thrill was the model railway. In the safe-working classroom at the Railway Institute, there was a double track model electric railway, about 20 metres long, together with crossovers and switches, as well as four stations — Calm, Cool, Collected and Eureka. On this model railway, safe-working students used to practise train working, under simulated conditions.

For 12 years, my father doubled as both signalman and safe-working instructor and, conditional on my promising to sit through a seemingly interminable and boring lecture without fidgeting, I would be taken to the Railway Institute to observe the model railway in operation.

Was it any wonder therefore that I was predestined to follow a railway career? Once or twice after graduation I did consider breaking away in search of higher remuneration — particularly in the mining industry — but my efforts were unsuccessful, and in retrospect fortuitously so. I would not have been happy in any other calling, but there was a somewhat piquant twist to the story.

As a schoolboy, I had no specific plans for the future except a desire to undertake some form of tertiary study. However, towards the end of my matriculation year my brother Harry, a pharmacist, suggested that I follow his profession and become apprenticed to him.

At that time, pharmacists' hours ranged from 8.30 am to 8.30 pm on weekdays and from 6.30 pm to 8 pm on weekends and public holidays; so, with perhaps a touch of bravado, I declined the offer, saying: 'When I get a job, it is going to be a nine to five one.' Little did I realise at the time that, eventually, I would opt for one with interminable hours, more akin to 9 am one morning to 5 am the next — and even beyond that!

Fortunately, my father came home from work one day and said: 'The Railways are advertising for engineering cadets. You are putting in for one.'

The rest is history.

5   Academe

My introduction to the University of Western Australia was somewhat unorthodox. When I passed the Leaving Certificate (Year 12) Examination and matriculated in 1926, I was still six months under the minimum age for entry to the university. The headmaster of Hale School wanted me to repeat my final year and went as far as to offer my father reduced school fees should I do so. However, on the day before the start of the 1927 school year I learned that I had gained a civil engineering cadetship with the WAGR, and in the light of this I applied to be admitted to the university. The application was approved.

In 1927, and except for the engineering faculty and the biology and geology departments — which were located at Crawley, some five kilometres west of the city — the university was still housed in its original buildings, ones which surely must have dumbfounded, indeed demoralised, not only the foundation academic staff but also their successors. An assortment of dilapidated and unpainted weatherboard or galvanised-iron single-storeyed structures, squeezed cheek by jowl into a city block in Irwin Street and extending from Hay Street to Saint George's Terrace, housed the administration block, library, common rooms, lecture theatres, and the physics, chemistry and agricultural science laboratories. The entire agglomeration was nicknamed — affectionately or derisively, depending on one's point of view — Tin Pot Alley.

The headquarters of the Engineering School were located at Shenton House at Crawley's Matilda Bay. Its facilities could best be classed as being in the lower order of primitive!

Tin Pot Alley, the Perth campus (*Photo:* The University of Western Australia)

Shenton House, built mid-nineteenth century, was a two-storeyed brick building, with pokey little rooms which barely accommodated the generally less than 20 undergraduates attending lectures at the one time; while an enclosed verandah served as the drawing office. However, in 1927 a separate two-storeyed brick building — consisting of upper and lower halls and three small rooms — was built adjacent to provide a lecturer's study, two common rooms and the new drawing office. Use of the lower hall seemed to have been confined to the Annual Engineers' Ball and, pending construction of its boatshed, it housed the Rowing Club's racing eight, the *Everard Darlot.*

The Engineering School, Matilda Bay, 1927 (*Photo:* The University of Western Australia)

Winthrop Hall, Crawley, 2005 (*Photo:* The University of Western Australia)

Crawley, the School of Civil and Mechanical Engineering, 2005 (*Photo:* The University of Western Australia)

To all intents and purposes, laboratory facilities did not exist, a number of galvanised-iron sheds, standing knee-deep among the wild oats in the grounds adjacent to Shenton House, merely posturing as such. Fridays were designated 'Heat Lab', when all students from second to fifth year donned working clothes and spent the day trying to create some order out of the chaos. Part of the author's contribution to this activity was to spend every Friday for two academic years threading two inch pipes! Then, in our fourth year, when the civil engineering syllabus covered reinforced concrete design, we used to spend one afternoon each week hand-mixing concrete and laying down floors in the tiny rooms that passed for laboratories.

For some inexplicable reason, a year or two earlier the university had acquired two ancient Babcox and Wilcocks steam boilers from the abandoned Subiaco power station and the undergraduates assisted in their laborious transportation to Crawley, there to be bricked in and re-established. During my five years at the university, those wood burning boilers were fired only once, and then for no apparent reason.

The Engineering School was an accredited testing authority, its principal function in this regard being to test locally manufactured cement. Initially, the testing equipment was antediluvian, stress being applied to the test specimen by means of a flow of small shot, the weight of which, at the moment of fracture, was converted into pounds per square inch. This was replaced in 1930 by a more up-to-date machine which, on one occasion, was the source of some embarrassment.

For some years, it had been the custom, during the Christmas–New Year break, for the Engineers' Club to organise a reunion of former engineering students. Club president at the time, I hosted the 1930 reunion and, to provide evidence of at least some modernisation, invited the visitors to inspect the new testing machine. But, during a demonstration of its capabilities, one of the operating valves became unstuck, leaving Andy Bowden — Lecturer in Charge of Mechanical Engineering — drenched by a strong jet of mineral oil.

My first year at the university coincided with the revelation of the Hackett bequests and, with them, the eventual transfer to Crawley of those activities still housed at Irwin Street; the construction of the magnificent new buildings; and the demise of Tin Pot Alley. However, construction took time and throughout my years at the university we engineering students were obliged to commute between the two locations by means of a small four-wheeled electric tram devoid of any braking system other than a primitive hand-operated one and which used to buckjump its way at hourly intervals along Mounts Bay Road to Matilda Bay and on to Nedlands Park. Not only was a great deal of time wasted in commuting, but at times the lectures themselves were interrupted

Sir John Winthrop Hackett, its first Chancellor, died in 1916, leaving the bulk of his estate to the university. The magnitude of the bequest was revealed in 1926 and, during the next six years, the Winthrop and Hackett Halls and Saint George's College were built, studentships and bursaries established, and the office of permanent Vice Chancellor created.

The foundation stones for the Winthrop and Hackett Halls — the accepted designs for which were awarded in open competition to the Melbourne architectural firm of Alsop and Sayce — were laid in April 1929 during Graduation Week. John Winthrop Hackett, son of the benefactor — who was on his way to Oxford and later to a distinguished career with the Airborne Division of the UK Armed Forces and to a knighthood — was present at both functions. The two halls were officially opened by Miss Patricia Hackett on 15 April 1932, again during Graduation Week and at which ceremony the author received his bachelor's degree.

The engineering undergraduates played a small but significant part, ensuring that the splendour of the opening. ceremonies was not blemished in any way by a little bit of unfinished construction. Shortly before the big day — and after the contractors, A.T. Brine and Sons, had stated that they would be unable to construct the reflective pool planned to abut the north wall of Winthrop Hall — the undergraduates from Shenton House took matters into their own hands, cut lectures for some ten days and set to work building it. They completed their part of the project on the eve of opening day, and thanks to Oliver Dowell, the head gardener, visitors to the opening ceremony were greeted by a pool complete with flowering water lilies and landscaped surroundings.

It was my good fortune, not only to have been present at the laying of the foundation stones but also to have obtained admission to the official opening of Winthrop Hall. I was privileged too in attending the first Graduation Ball held in Winthrop Hall. To the latter function I escorted Leah Cohen — a delightful and young second year Arts student — after both of us had been stood up by our regular partners.

It would be appropriate at this juncture to recount that, as a preliminary to that first Graduation Ceremony of Winthrop Hall, the engineering undergraduates conducted their own unofficial and ribald opening.

The stage was set up as a consulting engineers' drawing office, whose specialties were flagrantly and suggestively displayed as 'PILES, TRUSSES AND DERRICKS'. However, not being able to attract clientele, they decided that, while retaining their advertised specialties, they would change their consultancy to that of medicine.

Thereupon in walked a rather bewildered man, who introduced himself as being named Hall, and added: 'I've got the gravel'.

The pseudo-medicos thereupon threw him on to one of the drawing office tables and, using tools more befitting engineering practices, proceeded to open up his abdomen. Then, in rapid succession, were extracted from the patient and thrown to the floor, a sheep's heart and liver, a pig's bladder, a string of uncooked sausages and two — and, in the interests of anatomical correctness, only two — tennis balls.

The man's abdomen was then sewn up, again using engineering techniques; and, after having been put back on his feet, was told:

'We can't find any gravel,' to which he replied:

'Of course you can't. It's in the truck outside.'

University of Western Australia Engineering School, 1931. Staff (seated, left to right): P.H. Frankael, O.F. Blakey, A.T. Bowden, W.R. Baldwin-Wiseman. Final year students (standing, front row, left to right): Fitch, Haynes, Munro, Coxon, Perry, Temby, Graham, Blatchford, Corbet (and Fry and Manners, second row, left-hand side). The author was looking away from the camera to hide a black eye he had collected a few days earlier in an inter-faculty football match

As he was leaving, the man was asked his first name, to which he replied 'Winthrop'.

Thus was Winthrop Hall unofficially opened, the dramatis personae including Jim Utting and Harry Hopkins as the surgeons and Eugene O'Driscoll as the patient.

In my days, the engineering course was light on engineering theory but heavy on the humanities. This might well have been attributed to H.E. Whitfeld — foundation Professor of Mining and Engineering, and later the university's first permanent Vice Chancellor — who, despite his engineering background, appeared to have had a distinct leaning towards the arts. This was apparent in 1932 when he arranged for Associate Professor Wood of the Classics Department to deliver an oration entirely in Latin. Few if any undergraduates present had any idea of what he was saying. Indeed, one is led to conjecture what was Whitfeld's reaction when, at the opening ceremony, Patricia Hackett, lauded the University's decision to adopt 'Seek Wisdom' as its motto rather than one couched in either Latin or Greek.

The engineering curriculum naturally included a number of essentially science subjects, such as mathematics, physics, chemistry, geology, and astronomy and geodesy. At the same time, three arts subjects were added, and most of us took English literature and two courses in economics. Consequently, the content of our five years' study could be summarised as comprising 21 engineering, 9 pure science and 3 arts courses.

Some of the subjects were, in fact, inconsequential; among them, military engineering, delivered by an army engineering officer; railway civil engineering by W.E. Wood of the WAGR, and which appeared to concentrate on the lecturer's self-aggrandisement (of which more later); and works management and law for engineers which at least covered some worthwhile tips arising from Frank Blakey's construction experiences prior to his appointment to the university, as well as instruction in elementary bookkeeping.

It could also be said that the two courses in surveying in the civil engineering syllabus and supervised by G.M. Nunn — a retired licensed surveyor whose standard reply to any query from a student was 'Don't be a fool' — were of minimal value. Surveying I barely gave us sufficient time to set up and check our theodolites, while the second course, which included astronomical and geodetic surveying, was little better. Fortunately however, comprehension of the fundamentals of the latter was assisted by Professor Ross' lucid lectures in astronomy and geodesy, which we undertook a year later. Overall, I graduated virtually surveying-ignorant, and had to learn in the field by trial and error — particularly the latter — a situation which, in the early stages of my career, resulted in a number of morale shattering cock-ups.

The five years' study at the university were undertaken under conditions no less primitive than were those experienced during most of my working life.

We left it underqualified in pure engineering theory, a state of affairs for which Professor Blakey expressed his regret during a conversation some years later. Nevertheless, any deficiencies in that regard were more than compensated for by the breadth of the curriculum and the humanity of the academic staff. As a result, we received an education that enabled us to take up whichever branch of civil engineering became available to us, be it mining, local government, highways, harbours, water supply and sewerage, drainage and irrigation, or railways; and when, due to the economic circumstances then prevailing, work was where you could find it. It did none of us any harm.

Being pitched into the depressed workforce immediately after graduation was less of a trauma because of the hands-on and blue collar nature of studies. In my case, its very nature set the pattern for most of my working life.

During my undergraduate days, the academic staff at Shenton House consisted of P.H. Frankael (electrical); A.T. Bowden (mechanical); O.F. Blakey (civil and structural); W.R. Baldin-Wiseman (hydraulics); and, for a short period prior to Blakey's arrival, W. McLagen (drawing); while W.G. Townsend was testing officer.

Frankael, nicknamed 'Tater' — who joined the Engineering School as lecturer in 1916 and was appointed Associate Professor in 1926 — was of Danish descent and had studied in Germany. He continued to lecture from a German textbook; and this, together with his marked European accent, taxed our comprehension of the subject. Fortunately, however, for us civil engineering students, the two courses in electrical engineering we were obliged to undertake were relatively elementary. The source of his nickname mystified me until, one day, in the course of a lecture, he pronounced the Greek letter 'theta' as 'tater', and it all became clear to me.

P.H. Frankael had the students' interests at heart. He condoned, indeed supported, their irreverence and freely participated in their activities, both inside and outside the lecture theatre.

A gold medallist from the Edinburgh University, Andy Bowden was appointed Lecturer in Charge of Mechanical Engineering at Crawley in 1926 and raised to Associate Professor in 1937. On study leave in the UK in 1939, he remained there to assist the war effort.

On his arrival at Crawley in 1926, he must have been stunned, even demoralised, at the paucity of facilities at the Engineering School. Nevertheless, he carried on, not only with his lectures but also in his attempts to make something out of the collection of second-hand and nondescript items of machinery that postured as the mechanical laboratory.

At the same time, he pursued his belief that Charles Ackroyd-Stuart rather than Rudolph Diesel should be credited with the initial concept of the compression-ignition engine. However, I am unaware if Bowden's theory was ever published; and, if so, of its acceptance or rejection.

Andy Bowden established a rapport with his students that extended to chess evenings with them. In the early 1960s, when he and his wife revisited Australia, his former students accorded them celebrity status after an absence of contact extending over nearly 30 years. At a reunion we expatriates living in Adelaide held for them, I remarked to Andy that, despite the primitive conditions under which he laboured at Crawley, perhaps his stay there might have had some rewarding features. His reply was to the point:

'It was a privilege.'

To those of us who knew him, studied under him and remained in touch with him after graduation, Frank Blakey was the best thing that happened to the Engineering School in our day.

Graduating Master of Engineering from the University of Queensland, Othman Frank Blakey spent a few years in structural design before being appointed Lecturer in Charge of Civil Engineering at Crawley in 1927. This background, together with the fact that he continued with some design commitments after taking up his post — indeed he was responsible for the steelwork design of at least two Perth city office blocks — meant that we were lectured by one qualified in both theory and practice, as well as providing us with the opportunity to visit work sites.

The scope of his teaching was broad. Over our five years' course, he lectured or supervised in ten courses — in materials and structures, in engineering design, in drawing, and in works management and law for engineers. He went even further, and freely gave of his private time assisting individual undergraduates.

But it was his consideration and concern for the welfare of his students that drew us to him. He understood our irreverence, wholeheartedly supported our activities and went out of his way to facilitate them. One example of this was his gesture in designing the Rowing Club's boathouse.

Until the growth of numbers rendered it impracticable, it had been the tradition that, at the end of their final year, fifth year students be entertained by Frank and his wife Barbara at a formal dinner at their Nedlands home. Both retained a keen interest in the former students and their friendly approach was reciprocated, graduates seeking out the Blakeys whenever and wherever their paths crossed, be it in Australia or overseas.

Towards the end of 1951, when Frank and Barbara were returning to Perth from a sabbatical, George Manners — who graduated with me in 1932 before moving to Victoria — organised a reception for them which was attended by almost every expatriate graduate from Crawley who was living in Victoria and could possibly make it. I too found reason to make a lightning trip from Port Augusta — where I was stationed as Chief Civil Engineer for the Commonwealth Railways — to Adelaide to meet them and to accompany them on that section of their transcontinental train journey. Frank died some months later and I am glad therefore that I had the privilege of those few hours on the train with him.

W.R. Baldwin-Wiseman — 'Baldie' to us students — came to Western Australia in 1929 from the UK where he had graduated in civil engineering, later serving in the British Army with the rank of captain. After demobilisation, he specialised in hydraulics.

At Crawley, Baldie proved to be a lucid lecturer on the subject, and in our final year he tutored us in water supply and irrigation, this course being undertaken while seated around his study table. A charming man with old world mannerisms, his lectures used to be punctuated with stories of his experiences as a technical witness in civil cases involving water supply matters, and in the course of which he was apt to describe the presiding judge as 'a dear motherly old soul', a term that could well have applied to Baldwin-Wiseman himself.

Our studies also brought us into contact with the departments of English, mathematics, physics, chemistry, geology and economics — of which the principals were W.L.F. Murdoch (English), A.D. Ross (mathematics and physics), C.E. Weatherburn (applied mathematics), N.T.M. Wilsmore (chemistry), E. deC. Clarke (geology), and E.O.G. Shann (economics).

For different reasons, we undergraduates got on well with four of the six, while our rapport with the other two could best be described as equivocal in one instance and distinctly frosty in the other. Perhaps the relationships could be epitomised in the following terms.

Murdoch: Perhaps Australia's greatest essayist and undoubtedly a much loved institution at the university, was noted for his humour and for his strong support of students' rights. Indicative of his humane approach to the student body was the fact that he was credited with being the librettist of one of the songs rendered with gusto by them during Graduation Day preliminaries.

Ross and Weatherburn: Both were noted, not only for the clarity and content of their lectures, but also for their humanity and their approach to the students. Ross' delivery was marked

by distinct though not distracting traces of his Scottish accent, which, when associated with a noted sibilance, gave rise to his nickname of 'The Whistling Baritone'. On the other hand, Weatherburn's relationship with engineering students was enriched by the fact that his twin sons, Keith and Don, were undergraduates along with us.

De Courcey Clarke: We brash students took readily to 'Corkie', regarding him as one of us! Prior to his appointment to the university he held field positions with the New Zealand and Western Australian Geological Surveys and this, together with his academic qualifications and his down-to-earth and friendly approach, made study under him something of a pleasure.

Edward Owen Giblen Shann, whose third Christian name was paraphrased to 'Giblets' by irreverent students, was a courteous, overtly friendly man, but behind it all one could sense a strong streak of cynicism, perhaps even smugness. Moreover, it was evident that he resented the presence of the engineering students at his lectures and tutorials. In his *Campus at Crawley* (1963), Fred Alexander suggested that Shann 'had a fondness for social forms and for a certain parade of professorial dignity'

N.T.M. Wilsmore might have been an outstanding scientist, but any trace of a congenial relationship with his students simply did not exist; nor did his general attitude towards them foster anything but a feeling of awe, indeed trepidation. Lacking any apparent suggestion of humour, his lectures, after filtration through his rather copious yet straggly beard, were barely audible to any but those seated close to him. His irascibility even led to dispute and conflict with some of his professorial colleagues.

The initials of his first names of Norman Thomas Mortimer provided undergraduates with a heaven-sent opportunity for caricature, the letters being amended to 'NTP', an abbreviation of the well known scientific term 'normal temperature and pressure'.

One should not conclude this thumbnail sketch of Wilsmore without reference to his demonstrator and alter ego, Percival Babington. 'Babbie' tried hard to emulate his professor in all things, even to the sporting of beard, and attempted to adopt an attitude towards the students more in keeping with that of a lecturer than of a demonstrator.

Today, more than 70 years after graduation, and a working life that ranged from inexperienced mistake-prone greenhorn engineer to Railways Commissioner, I feel that I can look back objectively and assess the nature of my university years.

Despite some deficiencies, all-in-all, it was appropriate. The course was light on theory. Worthwhile laboratory facilities simply did not exist, and not until the construction of Winthrop Hall and associate buildings was there any trace of the academic aura that pervaded Oxbridge and Ivy League campuses.

However, those primitive conditions, as well as the very nature of the course, had their advantages. It was significant that, with only one or two exceptions, the foundation professorial staff stayed with the university. Possibly, they too became enamoured of the pioneering atmosphere surrounding Tin Pot Alley and Matilda Bay. Together, they constituted a solid and humane team of mentors and advisers.

From an engineering undergraduate point of view, the primitive conditions and the pioneering nature of the practical work — both of which often necessitated compromise in a number of ways — were a ready made prelude to our immediate post graduation period, when we were pitched headlong into the Depression and then on to World War II. Indeed, every one of us started our professional careers with activities that concentrated on pick and shovel, and not on design in the drawing office.

So also did the consideration of the humanities equip us for those prewar years. Indeed, the hands-on and personal contacts constituted one of the most satisfying features of my whole working life.

Our course of study was appropriate to the conditions then applying and it did none of us any harm. Personally, my five years at Tin Pot Alley and Matilda Bay were the introduction and forerunner to a rewarding professional life.

However, lest it be assumed that the university lacked any academic excellence, it should be pointed out that, of the students attending between 1927 and 1931, 11 eventually rose to professorships. At the same time, another graduate rose to governorship of the Reserve Bank of Australia.

The Big Strong Silent Men
Any reminiscences of Tin Pot Alley and Matilda Bay would not be complete without reference to the Engineers' Club. My election to its Presidency in 1931 remains to this day the highlight of my university life.

Its alternative nomen, 'The Big Strong Silent Men', derives from the chorus of the Engineers' Song which, it is understood, originated at the University of Southampton and was adopted by the engineering undergraduates at Crawley. The chorus went:

For it is now as it was then,
The engineers they knew things.
They are the big strong silent men
Who do not talk but do things.

Initially, the song consisted of three verses and chorus, but following the construction of the reflective pool adjacent to Winthrop Hall, a fourth verse was added to commemorate the achievement.

The song was treated by the engineers with reverence befitting an anthem, and they invariably stood during its rendition, but their singing of the last line of the chorus was usually threatened by members of other faculties, who used to drown us out by chanting: 'Who talk but never do things.'

In my time the club was the strongest individual student body on campus, but this standing was challenged by the Blackstone Society, which came into being following the establishment of the Law Faculty in 1928.

Apart from our innate and brash sense of superiority, our strength could be attributed not only to our relative isolation at Crawley, but also to the fact that, in four of the five years' course, our attendance in any one academic year was limited to only two terms, the other six months being spent working in the field.

The arrival of the law students provided us with a worthy opponent against whom we could indulge in some good natured but lusty rivalry which, at Graduation Ceremonies — at that time held in Government House Ballroom — used to develop into a free-for-all in which the casualties arising from such disturbances were generally confined to the folding chairs hired for the ceremony. However, the transfer of the Graduation Ceremonies from Government House to Winthrop Hall heralded the end of such confrontations and interfaculty rivalry in recent years has, in the main, been diverted to the sporting arena.

We freshers were introduced to the club — to which all engineering students attained automatic membership — in 1927 when the President, Dave ('Ponkey') Grey, told us that, when established in 1921 it went by the questionable title of 'DBA', but a year later and to relieve its treasurer of the embarrassment caused by the connotations associated with that three-lettered title, it was changed to the more respectable one that it has borne ever since.

Although lacking participation by second and fourth year students, who did not resume until second term, club members were regular contributors to Graduation Day processions through Perth streets. Those with which the author was associated included, in 1927, and as leading float in a sequence depicting the evolution of the automobile, 'Boadicea's Model De-Luxe', a draught horse drawn chariot concocted out of a cutaway section of a 400 gallon square iron water tank mounted on steel wheels and driven by kangaroo skin clad undergraduates. Sadly, over the years, a great deal of such irreverence seems to have disappeared.

Another example of our tendency towards madcapery took place during 1929 Graduation Week, when despite a complete lack of knowledge of the rules of the game, we challenged the girls to a hockey match. Probably because my sister Jean was an All-Australian and a State player, I was unanimously elected centre forward, while the perilous position of goalkeeper was decided by the drawing of lots!

My understanding of the laws of the game was limited to a rough conception of the offside rule, so when Jack Horrigan, our right inner, dribbled the ball downfield towards the goal I knew just enough to keep behind him — that is until their goalie came out to tackle him. At that point I ignored the offside rule as well as respect for feminine frailty, and, with football

tactics in mind, delivered her one of the best hip-and-shoulder tackles in my repertoire. The umpire ignored the infringement; Jack Horrigan scored; the unfortunate goalie was taken away for medical attention; and the engineers won the match one-nil!

The annual Engineers' Ball was the club's most important public function, and its standing on the university's social calendar was rivalled only by that of the more formal Graduation Ball. Indeed, following the 1931 ball, Mrs Clarissa Fox, wife of Associate Professor Fox of the Philosophy Department, wrote to the club saying how much she had enjoyed the evening, and finished with the comment: 'It is a pity that other University functions are not conducted as efficiently and as well as yours.'

The balls were famous for their decorations, the preparations for which became virtually a full-time activity for all engineering students except those in first year during the week leading up to it, something encouraged by the Faculty staff, who not only condoned the cutting of lectures but made available any equipment that we might wish to use.

Apart from its outstanding decorations, the 1929 Ball saw the birth of the Engineers' Club shield. Its general concept evolved from mutual discussions, while the artwork was left to George Manners and Don Munro. The motto, 'They do not talk but do things' was translated into Latin for us by the Classics Department, correctly, we trusted.

Profits from the balls were donated to the Engineering School Library, which was administered by the club. Any such profits were deemed to be free of State Amusement Tax provided that they met or exceeded a specified proportion of the costs. The club was never called upon to pay any tax, but in most years it took a measure of creative accountancy to avoid doing so.

During my undergraduate days the engineers were dominant in rowing and rifle shooting, but not so in other sports. This lack of success could be attributed to the fact that the academic year for engineering students was limited to two terms. However, in cricket and football, they were runners-up on some occasions, one of which remains embedded in the author's memory. It

Keynote Speaker, 80th Anniversary Dinner, University of Western Australia Engineers' Club, 16 February 2002 (*Photo:* Naureen Taylor)

happened in 1931.

At that time, I was playing weekend football with Subiaco, where it became my habit to collect a black eye each Saturday afternoon. But on this particular occasion I had survived a torrid match against Claremont without even a scratch, an achievement that evoked congratulatory comment from team-mates, coach and training staff alike. However, the next day, when playing for Engineering against Science — which was captained by Dick Lawn of East Perth and later coach of Claremont — I tackled Chris Kuhlman, a diminutive opposition wing man, and delivered him a crashing blow to his left elbow with my right eye; the outcome, the mother and father of all black eyes!

That incident also had another overtone. The annual group photographs of the Engineering School were scheduled for the following week, and, for photogenic reasons, I was obliged to look away from the camera in both the group and the committee shots.

Even though the engineering course denied us full participation in University sporting activities, in 1927 I was awarded, along with some others, half-blues for cricket and football.

At that time blues were only awarded to inter-varsity competition, in which Western Australia's participation was restricted to rowing and rifle shooting. However, with the broadening of inter-varsity participation, as well as the entry of university teams into local competitions, awarding of blues covered a wider field of sports and those for half-blues rose from inconsequential performance to worthwhile standards of achievement.

Apart from a dinner in Adelaide in 1963 to mark the University's 50th Anniversary — and attended by WA expatriates, their wives and partners, and at which the Engineers' Song was treated with traditional respect or derision depending on one's faculty affiliation — and casual meetings with former students of our vintage who might be passing through, my departure from WA in 1949 meant that I had little contact with the university or the Engineers' Club until 1998, when Dr Emma Hawkes of the History Department sought photographs and archival material to assist in her research of the Engineering School. Her request led to correspondence with her and with the club's office bearers. This relationship lasted for four years and culminated in 2002, when I was able to combine a trip to Perth to celebrate my sister Winnie's 100th birthday with attendance at the University Engineers' 80th Birthday Committee Reunion Dinner, which was held in Currie Hall on Saturday 16 February. It was a magnificent function, attended by about 200 former committeemen and their partners, and having been President in 1931 I was invited to head a list of eight speakers, each one reminiscing on the decade during which he was at the school.

To this day, my association with the Engineers' Club remains one of my lifetime highlights. So too was the Committee Reunion Dinner — held 71 years after I had left Matilda Bay, where I was able to recount some of our earlier experiences and misdemeanours—and which gave rise to the reminiscent nostalgia that will remain, with me for ever.

The Frail Age Degree

My flirtation with academe did not stop in April 1932. Indeed it continued until October 2002, but not without two substantial interregnums. Including the graduation ceremonies themselves. The saga extended over 76 years, but academic activity totalled only 17, with hibernation periods of 14 and 45 years' duration.

During the first of the latter, I undertook studies conducted by the WAGR and qualified in the specific railway subjects of safe-working, timekeeping and preparation of timesheets, the internal combustion engine, timetabling and rostering, and permanent way and platelaying; and subsequently became both instructor and examiner in the last named subject.

Then, in 1947, Professor Frank Blakey asked me to deliver a series of lectures in railway civil engineering at the University of Western Australia, in the course of which a number of basic but curly questions were hurled in my direction by the students. At about the same time, the professor mentioned that he would like to see more masters degrees conferred and, to this end, would welcome applications from bachelor graduates of some years' standing.

With these things in mind, I proposed to the Faculty of Engineering that I submit for consideration for the degree of Master of Engineering a thesis titled 'The Basic Relationship Between Roadbed, Rails, Axle Loads, Speeds, Grading and Curvature; Their Influence on the Maintenance and Operation of Railways; Together With Their Application to the Western Australian Government Railways'. The proposition was accepted and, on 14 July 1948, after 18 months' research — which involved a number of studies into the fundamentals of railway engineering and their influence on operations — I submitted a thesis consisting of 146 pages of text, 51 tables and 36 graphs. It was accepted by the examiner and the degree conferred on 21 April 1949.

This might well have been the end of my academic aspirations. However, after my retirement in 1973, and having laboured for nearly 16 years over the writing, rewriting and the suffering of innumerable rejections of my first book, *Making Tracks* (1989), and another four on its less rejection-prone successor, *Railroading at its Wildest* (1993), I felt that I had run out of feedstock for another to complete the trilogy. Nevertheless, I felt that, after 22 years out of the

saddle and with my lifelong love for the railways undiminished, I might undertake an academic appraisal of the performance of the South Australian Railways from 1900 to 1970 — and that included my 19 years with the system. With this thought in mind, in June 1995 I approached seven Australian universities, but was rejected by all but the University of New South Wales, which, through Professor John Black of the Department of Civil and Environmental Engineering, accepted my proposal. When I mentioned to my daughter Rosalind that I was giving some thought to the writing a PhD, she clapped her hands with delight and called it a 'frail age degree'.

On 20 September 2001, after a period of six years during which my activities were devoted almost entirely to the study, I submitted the thesis for assessment. It was titled 'A Critical Study of the Operational and Financial Performance of the South Australian Railways 1900 to 1970' and consisted of two volumes: the first, 290 pages (about 92,000 words) of text and 111 tables; the second, appendixes comprising 107 statements, 37 graphs and 11 maps. Nine months later, on 24

PhD graduation ceremony, 29 October 2002, with Professor John Black

June 2002, I was advised that the three examiners had recommended the awarding of the degree of Doctor of Philosophy.

Despite the problems associated with the project, and to which reference will be made in some detail, I enjoyed every moment of the six years' study, although I did not seem able to convince anyone that the years spent on the project were anything but a chore. However, it was a period of intense pleasure. It provided me with an opportunity to turn my lifetime love for railways into something of academic relevance, as well as constituting a wonderful form of retirement therapy, and especially so following Doreen's death early in 1997.

The problems to which I have referred were those of communications and access to statistics vital to the project.

Due to the fact that, as an external student, I was working alone in Adelaide, nearly 1200 air kilometres from Sydney. Indeed, personal contact with my supervisor, Professor John Black, was limited to only one meeting, in Adelaide in September 1997, at which stage I was approaching the halfway point in the study. Consequently, communication between us was confined to the telephone and the word processor. Thanks to the efforts of John Black, Derek Scrafton — who acted as his Adelaide deputy over the final couple of years — and Anne Gordon of the University of New South Wales' Student Research Administration, these problems of distance were resolved.

However, the greater hurdle proved to be that of assembling statistical data upon which to base a study of the financial and operational performance of the South Australian Railways over the 70 years under review. It seemed that, in 1975, upon taking over the non-urban activities of the SAR, Australian National had either mislaid or destroyed reports, documents and other information pertaining to the former State system; and, after intense but fruitless search and enquiry I was obliged to borrow SAR Annual Reports and other papers from the Port Dock Station Railway Museum and photocopy them. In all, over 2000 documents were involved in this operation and, in addition, it was necessary to resort to the museum's records for rollingstock details, passenger fares, and parcels and freight rates. Indeed, but for the assistance freely given by the museum, I would not have been able to assemble the data essential to the study. Nevertheless, these impediments did not in any way dampen my enthusiasm; on the contrary, the seeming attempt — either intentional or accidental—by Australian National to remove from the records any trace of the former system only accentuated my determination to pursue the project to finality.

My graduation in Sydney on 29 October 2002 was given widespread publicity. This was no doubt prompted by the fact that, at 92 years of age, I was probably oldest PhD graduand in the world and the University of New South Wales justifiably sought to capitalise on this. Personally, I shunned the idea, but in the light of the university's support and encouragement I felt the least that I could do would be to go along with the idea and cooperate.

In doing so, I tried to make something positive out of the hype that followed my graduation and attempted to use my fortunate circumstances as an incentive to others by saying that the best advice that I could give any retiree would be to get out of your rocking chair and do something that would keep your mind active. It hasn't got to be academic or laborious; just something that you want to do, and would find pleasure in doing at your own pace and in your own time.

Subsequently, steps were taken to inquire of Guinness World Records Ltd, and on 2 March 2005 I received a certificate stating that: 'The oldest person to be awarded a doctorate (PhD) is Ronald J. Fitch (Australia) at the age of 92 years 144 days. Ronald J. Fitch received his doctorate by the Faculty of Engineering at the University of New South Wales, Australia on 29 October 2002.'

Naturally, this gave source to a degree of satisfaction, especially to the fact that age should not be an impediment to achievement, and I shall look forward to the day when my name is replaced by that of some other retiree.

So ended my forays into academe. For the most part they were vital preludes or an ongoing supplement to over 40 years' rewarding working life; and finally crowned by six years' labour of love.

6   Western Australia, 1927–49

To Western Australia must go the doubtful honour of having tried to rid the British Empire of its Heir Apparent 16 years before he, as King Edward VIII, abdicated.

It happened near Wilgarup in the South West on Monday 5 July 1920. Five days earlier, after a stormy crossing of the Great Australian Bight, the 26-year-old Prince of Wales had disembarked from HMS Renown at Albany into a rain sodden 'Golden West'. He had then travelled to Perth by train, and had spent three days in the city before leaving for the timber country on the Sunday evening.

Next morning, His Royal Highness inspected tree felling, log hauling and saw milling at Pemberton; and, in the afternoon, had commenced his return journey, which was to take him to Bunbury and then on to Perth. At 2.44 pm, when the train was in the vicinity of Wilgarup and travelling at about 25 kilometres an hour, the three trailing vehicles were derailed, of which two — the Royal and the Ministerial

Derailment of the Royal train near Wilgarup, 5 July 1920 (*Photo:* Library Board of Western Australia)

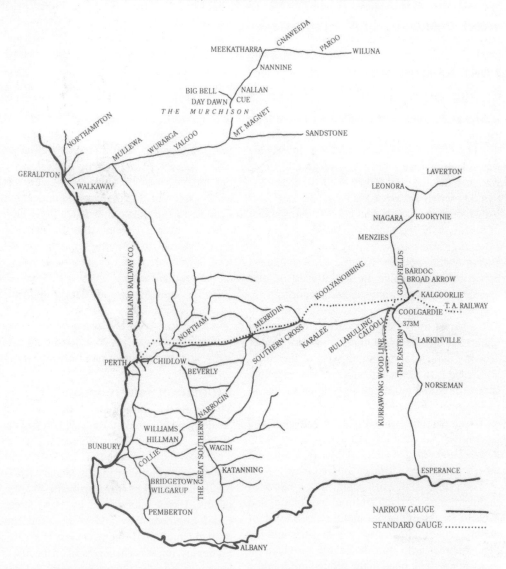

carriages — finished on their sides down a 1.5 metre embankment. The Prince was found unhurt, sitting amid the wreckage and smoking a cigar.

The feeling of relief at the Prince's escape from injury was clouded by an equally deep one of embarrassment following the incident. Colonel Pope, the Commissioner of Railways, refuted allegations that the Royal train was too heavy for the light track over which it travelled. However, it is understood that John Pidgeon, Deputy Chief Engineer Way and Works, was adamant that the line was not sufficiently robust and that the heavy train should not run on it. Pidgeon was overruled, and it was thought that the circumstances surrounding this and the derailment affected his health and accelerated his death a short time later.

There were some conflicting reports concerning the conditions prevailing at the time. One stated that, a few minutes before the accident, Colonel Pope made his way forward to instruct the locomotive crews to increase speed because they were running behind schedule. On the other hand, 12 years after the incident I was told by the fireman of the second of the two locomotives hauling the Royal train that a railway official had told them to slow down because the Prince wanted to have a cup of tea. He also told me that, only a short time before the accident, they had been obliged to check the train speed to avoid a bull that had strayed on to the unfenced line. Indeed, his driver had barely commented on their good luck when the derailment occurred.

As was customary in such cases, a pilot train ran ahead of the Royal one, ostensibly to test out the track. But, in this instance, the weight of the supercargo that had attached itself to the Prince was such that the pilot train was the lighter of the two. The whole episode must have been an ordeal for Colonel Pope, who had been Commissioner of Railways for less than 12 months.

Naturally, the mishap provided overseas journalists travelling with the Royal party a heaven-sent opportunity to indulge in sensationalism. For example, *The Times* published this report:

'The Prince had a narrow escape in an accident to the Royal train today, happily, being entirely unhurt. He left Perth last night to visit the timber growing districts in the south west of the State. He visited Pemberton and witnessed a tree felling competition this morning, proceeding thence to Bridgetown.

'When nearing Bridgetown his carriage, the last on the train, and the carriage next to it were derailed and dragged about 200 yards, tearing up the track. The two carriages toppled over.

'The Prince climbed through the window of the overturned carriage smiling and joking, and insisted on regarding the incident as a topic of humour, chaffing the railway authorities and the State Premier with him on having provided an incident not mentioned in the official programme as a dramatic surprise to relieve the monotony of his task.'

Another incident — probably the WAGR's most traumatic moment — took place less than one year prior to my joining the service. During the second half of July 1926, the State was subjected to intense downpours of rain which resulted in a total of 35 reported railway washaways. Indeed, the track damage was so severe that, on 20 July, all country trains except those to and from Bunbury were cancelled.

The main drama occurred at Fremantle on Thursday, 22 July, when the abatement of the normal westerly winds, coupled with a strong ebb tide, resulted in the release of pent-up flood waters in the Swan River estuary. The torrential outflow into the Fremantle harbour washed out nearly 30 metres of the embankment immediately north of the dual-track timber railway bridge linking North Fremantle with Fremantle. Then, shortly after midday, two 15.2 metre spans of the bridge collapsed, severing both main lines.

The collapse meant that the 19 kilometre direct rail link between Perth and Fremantle was cut, leaving only the 62 kilometre circuitous route via East Perth, Armadale and Jandakot, which was used for freight traffic, while passenger trains were diverted from North Fremantle to the north wharf, where a ferry operated to Victoria Quay on the southern side.

Bridge repairs were started immediately and on 17 October — less than 12 weeks later — single line working was restored. Complete reconstruction was not completed until 22 April 1927, an interruption of precisely nine months.

An Inauspicious Baptism

My official introduction into the Western Australian Government Railways on 15 February 1927 was not without its moments. The first had a touch of piquancy about it.

Following the publication in January 1927 of the previous year's Leaving Certificate Examination results, I was interviewed by H.A. Cresswell, Chief Engineer Way and Works (subsequently retitled Chief Civil Engineer) and H.W. Rockett, his deputy, but was unsuccessful on the first count. However, one the three appointees did not take up his position and I was offered the vacancy. At the same time, a fourth cadetship was created.

The reason given for my not having gained one of the original positions was that, although passing the Leaving Certificate Exam in seven subjects, I had not gained any distinctions. It transpired, however, that none of the first three appointees had done so, while Wally Metcalfe, who was appointed after me, had been awarded two distinctions. Apart from one which appeared to have had some political overtones, one wonders what criteria were applied in the selection of the

Collapse of Fremantle railway bridge, July 1926 (*Photo:* Library Board of Western Australia)

original appointees; and, in respect of my results, the fact that I was also offered a university exhibition in agricultural science would indicate that my marks were reasonably good.

Other moments were associated with the first two days of my cadetship.

Obviously, my arrival was not welcomed unreservedly by A.G. Lunt, Engineer in Charge of the Drawing Office, who was well known both for his irascibility and his utter detestation of engineering cadets and junior draftsmen. When the Chief Clerk, Cuthbert Pope, delivered me into his charge, there was no handshake or word of welcome, just: 'I don't know what to do with him. Send him to Stewart!'

So, with that Lunt-inspired feeling of not being wanted or welcomed, to Stewart I was shunted.

Alec Stewart, Lands and Property Officer, and also editor of the staff periodical *The Railway and Tramway Magazine*, was a lovable yet wholly unpredictable character. A crony of 'Dryblower' Murphy, the Perth Sunday Times poet, Stewart, an elderly bachelor with a Groucho Marx gait and a long wisp of hair straggling over his otherwise bald pate, also dabbled in poetry of a sort. When, a few years later, ill health forced his retirement, among his personal papers were found a number of ballads dedicated to Mabel Normand, a star of the silent films and the object of Stewart's adoration from afar.

My second shock on that, my first day, occurred when I heard Stewart, in replying to a telephone caller, say: 'No, I won't be at work tomorrow; I'll be drunk!' To me, 16 years of age, straight from school and from a teetotal household, the impact of such a statement was devastating. It transpired however that he was referring to the men-only and by no means a non-alcoholic Branch Office picnic scheduled for the next day. This function was, together with Lunt's 'welcome', a mind boggling introduction to my railway career. For the record, Alec Stewart did not get drunk at the picnic but some others did. Indeed, one inebriated gentleman unintentionally dived headlong into the Swan River, fully clothed in his three piece suit.

It would be unfair not to observe that, over the years, the picnics became much more circumspect affairs than was that which heralded my initiation into the Branch.

The frostiness that blighted my welcome was probably due to the fact that, at that time, the Branch lacked any academically qualified engineers among its middle and higher echelons. There appeared to have developed a prejudice against university graduates, and this despite provision for such a course of study in the cadetship indenture. Coincident with this bias against academic qualifications, one felt that engineering cadets were deemed nuisances rather than potential assets and, as a result, they received no in-house training whatsoever.

This attitude was not confined to the Drawing Office. With one or two exceptions, it extended to the District Offices. Indeed, after spending a few months attached to the Geraldton office I was farewelled back to the university by District Engineer C.R. May with the comment that, 'It is a pity that you are going to the university because, when you finish, you won't know enough to know that you know nothing'.

Overall, the only accepted qualification seemed to be that of experience. Even three years after graduation and in charge of my third construction job, Chief Civil Engineer Cresswell — tall and distinguished, with old-world mannerisms, and with his pince-nez spectacles protected from damage by a black cord around his neck — continued to greet me with 'Great experience this, Fitch', which I would acknowledge with appropriate deference even though I was doing the job that I had been set to do.

This concentration on experience to the disparagement of qualifications seemed to have also given rise to a sense of impotence in the mid-level grades and the Drawing Office was staffed to a large degree by time servers, a circumstance that offered little encouragement to us newcomers.

Resulting from these attitudes, when in 1931 I completed my five years' study at the University reasonably qualified in theory, I lacked any worthwhile practical background.

Fortunately, that disparagement of academic qualifications changed abruptly when, in 1931, the Railway Construction Branch, formerly attached to the State Public Works Department, was transferred to the Railway Department and amalgamated with the Way and Works Branch to constitute the Civil Engineering Branch. This brought to the Railways a number of qualified engineers and, in particular, J.A. Ellis, the Engineer for Railway Construction, who in the three years prior to his elevation to the position of Commissioner of Railways completely reversed the former Department's negative attitude towards engineering cadets. Some years later, the author was appointed Engineer and Chief Draftsman — virtually Senior Design Engineer — and he could not but notice the substantial lift

in quality compared with that prevailing when he first joined the Branch.

Since my graduation, which coincided more or less with the arrival of Ellis and his team, was followed by the retirement of most of the 'experience above all and to hell with qualifications' employees, I was soon able to overcome the indignity that I suffered as an engineering cadet and establish a rapport with my, superiors, colleagues and workmates.

The Western Australian Government Railways

When I joined the Way and Works Branch of the WAGR in 1927, the system was experiencing a period of prosperity which would have been matched only by the boom years of the 1960s. The second phase of railway development in the State was approaching its peak and the trackage had grown to 6305 kilometres. It started after World War I and arose out of a migration agreement between the United Kingdom and Western Australian governments, and was aimed at greater cereal production as well as mixed farming on small holdings in the higher rainfall belt. The latter, known as the Group Settlement Scheme, was the brainchild of Sir James Mitchell, State Premier and, in later years, Governor.

Funds were made available by the British Government for the construction of railways to serve the new land development, and by the early 1930s 12 lines, totalling 1100 kilometres in length, were completed; from Piawaning to Miling; Norseman to Esperance; Bencubbin to Bullfinch; Amery to Kalannie; Burakin to Bonnie Rock; Narembeen to Merredin; Lake Grace to Newdegate; Lake Grace to Hyden; Nyabing to Pingrup; Jardee to Northcliffe; Busselton to Flinders Bay; and from Denmark to Nornalup. In addition, eight railways were authorised and surveyed but not built. They were from Boyup Brook to Cranbrook; Brookton to Dale River; Manjimup to Mount Barker; Yarramony to Merredin; Yuna to Dartmoor; southwards from Southern Cross; westwards from Salmon Gums; and eastwards from Hyden.

Other railways constructed during this period were those from Meekatharra to Wiluna in the Murchison, and from Waroona to Lake Clifton in the south-west. The latter must have enjoyed one of the shortest lives of any railway in this country. It was opened in August 1922 and ceased to be a government railway in 1924.

Although new construction tapered off in 1933 — the only new line to be built during the next 20 years being that from Cue to Big Bell — a number of regrading and deviation projects were undertaken during the next seven years.

Grade improvements, either by regrading or deviation, were undertaken between Collie and Brunswick Junction, Jardee and Bridgetown, Bruce Rock and York, Merredin and Northam, Merredin and Yellowdine, Wyalkatchem and East Northam, Mullewa and Geraldton, Mullewa and Yalgoo, and between Miling and Clackline. These improvements permitted heavier train loads and more effective working over a total of 1180 kilometres of track. During the same period, the heavily taxed single line sections of the now defunct Eastern Railway were duplicated between Bellevue and Swan View, Tunnel Junction and Mount Helena, and between Spencers Brook and East Northam.

During the 1930s, the WAGR was responsible for two innovations.

The Goldfields pipeline, which conveyed water from Mundaring Weir to Kalgoorlie, paralleled the Eastern Goldfields railway from a point near Mount Helena right through to Kalgoorlie. During early morning of Christmas Day 1931 a severe burst near Meenaar, 132 kilometres east of Perth, washed out the railway formation and it was fortuitous that one of the Kalgoorlie Expresses was not derailed.

Following this incident, and in view of the condition of certain sections of the pipeline, the Goldfields Water Supply and the Railway Departments instituted a joint rail motor patrol ahead of the express trains, which operated in each direction six nights a week. A length of 409 kilometres from East Northam to Lilliginni was patrolled by two men — one Water Supply employee and the other a railwayman — using a Singer motor vehicle adapted to run on the rails. A spotlight was directed on to the pipeline to detect breaks and repairs were made whenever necessary. As the pipeline was reconditioned, so was the length of the patrol reduced, and in April 1935 it was discontinued.

Then, in 1937, Governor class diesel electric rail cars replaced the ambling, uncomfortable and sometimes malodorous mixed trains on the Perth–Katanning, Perth–Merredin, Geraldton–Yuna–Mullewa, and the Bunbury–Busselton–Northcliffe routes. The cars were named after state governors, the flag bearer being the Governor Stirling, after Captain James Stirling, who established the Swan River Settlement in 1829.

A later achievement was the provision, in 1947, of a hot water service, including hot showers, on The Westland, the overnight passenger train connecting at Kalgoorlie with the Commonwealth Railways' Trans Australian. It would have been the first train in Australia to have reticulated hot water to the hand basins in its compartments; and it would also have been the first in the world to provide passengers with hot showers en route. The heating equipment was primitive but effective. At both Perth and Kalgoorlie, a bricked-in 1800 litre square iron tank constituted the boiler; the fuel, inevitable old sleepers. After heating, the water was piped by gravity into insulated tanks under the sleeping cars.

It was reported at the time that Commissioner of Railways Ellis, together with his senior officers, was on hand at the Perth station to witness the departure of the first Westland equipped with hot water. When he entered the shower compartment to test the efficiency of the system the scalding cascade that descended on and drenched the fully clothed Commissioner proved beyond doubt that it did in fact work.

Although the entry of Japan into the war in 1941 resulted in some increased tempo, not at any time was the WAGR called upon to bear a transportation load comparable with that of the

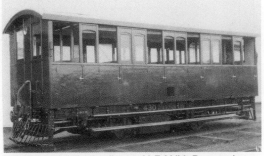

Petrol mechanical rail car, ALBANY–Denmark, 1922 (*Photo:* Westrail)

Dort motor rail inspection car, c. 1925 (*Photo:* Westrail)

Rail car, Port Hedland–Marble Bar (*Photo:* Westrail)

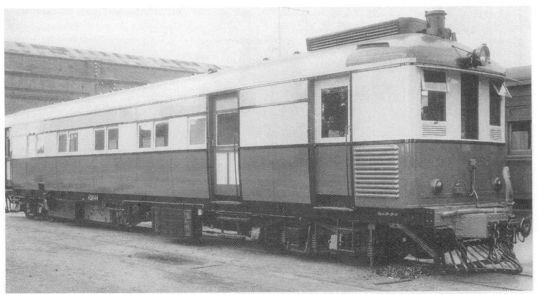

Sentinel Cammell steam rail car, Perth–Armadale, Western Australia, 1930 (*Photo:* Westrail)

Governor class diesel electric rail car, 1937 (*Photo:* Westrail)

Wildflower class diesel electric rail car, 1950 (*Photo:* Westrail)

Singer rail motor inspection car, Goldfields Water Supply pipeline, Western Australia, 1933 (*Photo:* Westrail)

The Prospector, Perth–Kalgoorlie diesel hydraulic rail car on dual gauge track in Avon Valley, Western Australia, 1972 (*Photo:* Westrail)

Australian Railwayman

other mainland Australian railways. The main problems of manpower and material shortages were indeed worse in the immediate postwar period than during the war itself. We did have one or two moments of excitement, however.

The threat of a Japanese invasion was viewed seriously in Western Australia, and preliminary steps taken to prepare the more strategic bridges and jetties for demolition. Early in 1942, when I was stationed at Narrogin, in the Great Southern, it was decided to make such preparations on the deep water Jetty at Albany as well as on the bridge over the Hay River on the Nornalup branch. Holes were bored in the timber piles at the deep water jetty in the two to three fathom range, and in every pile at Hay River, and gelignite charges prepared and stored for positioning and firing were the order to do so given. Railway employees selected to fire the charges were allowed time to practise lighting the fuses under windy conditions. The town jetty at Albany was not so prepared, its general condition being such that, should the enemy disembark there and march off in military order, the whole structure would collapse, thus rendering the invaders responsible for their self destruction.

Similar pre-demolition procedures were observed at Esperance and, when I transferred to the Kalgoorlie office shortly after the fall of Singapore, we had trouble stopping the locals from blowing up the town's two jetties there and then. Apparently they overlooked the fact that, having landed there, the enemy would still be 3000 kilometres away from the nation's centres of population. Fortunately, the jetties remained intact.

Another little bit of excitement occurred on the night of Good Friday 1943, when a military train, carrying General Grant tanks, was derailed on the Eastern Goldfields line about 35 kilometres west of Southern Cross.

Finally, on 17 January 1945, the Fremantle harbour literally caught fire. When a workman using an oxy welding torch on the deck of the vessel *Panamanian* accidentally ignited a piece of sacking and threw it overboard, the heavy concentration of waste oil on the surface burst into flames, endangering the US submarines harboured at Fremantle. Fearing that the incoming tide might carry the flames upstream towards the timber bridge carrying the railway from North Fremantle to Fremantle, the top brass of the WAGR rushed to North Fremantle, but the flames did not reach the bridge.

In hindsight, the censorship applying at the time of the fire was Gilbertian. The West Australian carried large banner headlines concerning the fire, which, it said, occurred at 'an Australian port', together with such detailed descriptions that no reader, least of all the Japanese, could possibly have been unaware of the locale.

The years following the war proved to have been even more difficult than were those from 1939 to 1945.

To all intents and purposes, manpower and materials were nonexistent. But for the displaced persons from Europe, the first of whom arrived in 1948 and were tied to directed employment for two years, the Australian railways would have ceased to function in the early postwar years. Even more critical was the situation in respect of motive power. Wartime deficiencies had resulted in a legacy of locomotives crying out for maintenance. Coal shortages too were such that the train service operated more or less on a day-to-day basis. It was not uncommon for the departure of an important train such as The Westland to be delayed until coal or oil was rushed to the East Perth depot.

The WAGR did its best to obtain additional motive power, even for short-term use, and besides placing orders overseas, acquired 25 Australian Standard Garratt locomotives. The Garratts, which were designed in 1942 by Fred Mills, Chief Mechanical Engineer for the State system who had been seconded to the Commonwealth during the war years, were built as a wartime emergency project, and were aimed at relieving the motive power shortages on the narrow gauge railways of the Commonwealth, South Australian and Queensland systems. Unfortunately, and no doubt due to Mills' attempt to design a locomotive meeting both the axle load and clearance limitations of the various railways in this country, they possessed certain inherent weaknesses. As a result, they were not accepted at the time by the three systems for which they were built. Ten years later, South Australia took a number for use on the Broken Hill line, but then only as an interim measure pending the arrival of units ordered from abroad. Their use in Western Australia was impeded primarily by industrial action and did little to ease the critical motive power situation.

The WAGR also purchased steam locomotives from the United Kingdom, including a number of oil burners destined for the Sudan, but deliveries were so slow that no worthwhile relief was achieved until the 1950s.

There was some consternation when one of the first oil burners exploded in the Perth station. The locomotive, with its train, was standing on the goods track next to the main passenger platform., and as was customary, the engine driver had cut off the fuel supply while stationary. However, when about to rekindle the flame, instead of using a lighted wick attached to a long handle, he attempted to do so by allowing the oil to drip on to the still incandescent firebricks. The explosion that followed almost blew him and his fireman out of the cab. Following this incident, Eric Diffen, an engine driver who had had experience with this type of locomotive when attached to the railway construction unit of the AIF, was able to give some advice to the local drivers in the handling of such engines.

Eric, whom I first came to know when we were both stationed in the Murchison some years previously, was also a part-time aviator and racing car driver. In the Middle East, he had earned such a reputation for careering with apparent abandon over newly laid and unballasted track that at one time he was grounded. I met him again during Easter 1943 when, on home leave, he assisted with track repairs following the derailment of the military special train west of Southern Cross. On that occasion, he greeted me speechlessly, not from emotion at our reunion, but rather as a result of having refreshed himself copiously while his train was delayed at Merredin for several hours.

The postwar years were very trying ones for the railway administration; nor were they made any easier by the Royal Commissions into the Australian Standard Garratt locomotives and the WAGR itself. The latter followed the election of the first non-Labor government in Western Australia since 1930–33.

While in Opposition, H.S. Seward, Member for Pingelly, was a trenchant and unremitting critic of the Western Australian Government Railways. Yet he was not averse to seeking special privileges. It was reported that, during the war years when passenger accommodation was critically stretched, he asked that an entire compartment be reserved for him on Friday evening's Albany train so that he could enjoy his 210 kilometre journey from Perth to Pingelly in VIP luxury. This was denied him.

When the incoming Premier, Ross McLarty, made him Minister for Railways, one of Seward's first actions was to make the railways the subject of a Royal Commission. There was no doubt that the new Minister sought to make the railway administration the scapegoat for the malaise from which the system was suffering, and which had arisen from the wartime and postwar shortages of manpower and materials. The fact that the problems were not unique to Western Australia, but were worldwide, seemed to have been ignored.

Royal Commissions and judicial enquiries provide the politician with a convenient vehicle by which a whipping boy can be dredged up. Western Australia in 1947 was no exception. The Commissioners were A.J. Gibson, principal of a firm of engineering consultants, and D.H.C. du Plessis, Deputy General Manager of the South African Railways. The WAGR was represented by P.C. Raynor, Assistant to the Commissioner of Railways. His contribution was outstanding and his limitless faith in the future of the railways was vindicated in the long term. The employees' interests were watched by T.G. Davies, Secretary of the Western Australian Branch of the Australian Labor Party. Throughout the entire enquiry, his attitude was distinctly pro-railways, and his presence enhanced the departmental case.

Mr du Plessis was a thoroughly competent railway administrator, but he seemed unable to comprehend that industrial conditions, wage levels and employer–employee relations in WA were vastly different from those then applying in his native South Africa. Indeed, some of his criticisms of our costs showed quite plainly that he did not appreciate the fact that workmen in this country received an arbitrated minimum wage and not just a bowl of mealies.

While Gibson might have been an eminent consulting engineer, it soon became patent that, in railway matters, he could claim neither knowledge nor understanding. One particular instance of this was when he was looking into the tracking characteristics of the S class locomotive, a unit designed and built at the Midland Junction workshops. I was instructed to prepare a short length of curved track at the locomotive depot so he could observe the movement of the driving wheels relative to the rails when the locomotive rolled into it. The locomotives were having tracking problems on the main lines at speeds of about 60 km/h; therefore a test run at less than 10 km/h could only be a waste of time.

He then ordered the locomotive on to the main line between Midland Junction and Bellevue and rode on the footplate with a pot of whitewash in his hand. Whenever he felt that there had been an irregularity in the locomotive's movement he proceeded to drop a dollop of whitewash on the permanent way. Later, he walked along the track and inspected its alignment at those spots where he had dropped the whitewash, but all that he achieved was to splatter the permanent way in the manner of a seagull in flight!

Along with other requests for information, Gibson asked that every statistical statement in the WAGR Annual Reports for the preceding 50 years be graphed, his stated intention being to set them out in sequence on a large board and, with the help of a cursor of appropriate size, to study the trends. Assisted by a team of young and enthusiastic draftsmen who worked up to ten hours a day, I produced 12 distinctively coloured copies — measuring 76 x 51 centimetres — of each individual graph. However, I doubt whether Gibson made any use of them. It would have required an area the size of a basketball stadium upon which to set out the graphs in sequence, and a cursor with the dimensions of a gantry crane to have spanned them.

The Royal Commission's report did little more than to condemn J.A. Ellis and his senior officers for the condition of the railways. It ignored entirely the fact that, over the preceding 17 years, the system had suffered from financial, manpower and materials stringencies, as well as a heavy wartime traffic load. It also contained strong implications that the railway administration had been both indolent and indifferent towards the system's welfare.

Indicative of the scathing — and, in the author's opinion, unjustified — comments made by the Commission were the following random excerpts:

'We know of no other comparable railway system in any other part of the civilised world which has been so neglected.'

'After making due allowance for all the difficulties with which the railway management has been confronted over a period of many years, we find it difficult to escape the conclusion that some of the unsatisfactory features and bad conditions which we have found in so many centres could have been avoided, or at any rate mitigated, if greater interest and energy had been displayed by the management.'

'The rank and file of the staff, taking their cue from the senior officers, have become apathetic, and in consequence, efficiency and discipline have reached a low ebb.'

As one who was seconded full time, not only to the preparation of the departmental case but also to furnishing data sought by the Commission itself, and who sat through every one of its public hearings, I can maintain with confidence that the Commission's findings were manifestly unfair.

If any evidence was required to invalidate the Royal Commission's criticisms of indolence and indifference on the part of the senior administration, it would be manifest in the fact that, early in 1949, three senior officers — Chief Civil Engineer S.J. Hood, Chief Mechanical Engineer F. Mills and Workshops Manager W. Raynes — died within a matter of weeks, obviously as a result of the strain of the preceding years. Only one or two years later, P.C. Raynor also died, and this too could well be attributed, at least in part, to the stresses of the previous 20 years.

In 1949, shortly after the issue of the Royal Commission's report, Seward had the Railway Act amended to provide for a Commission of three. Ellis did not seek reappointment and A.G. Hall, formerly Director General of Railways in

Pakistan, was made Commissioner, with C.W. Clarke and P.C. Raynor Assistant Commissioners. Clarke came from the position of Chief Mechanical Engineer for the East Indian Railways. Raynor was the only local appointee, and upon his death R.E.B. Lee, formerly of the Victorian Railways but latterly WAGR Comptroller of Accounts and Audit, was appointed to the vacancy.

The three-man Commission lasted for eight years, a period during which the WAGR suffered from every kind of malady — brought about for the most part by bickering among the three members — and, following the dismissal of one Commissioner and the resignation of the other two, control reverted to a single Commissioner.

Seward lost his seat in the Parliament shortly afterwards. It would have been poetic justice had he stayed Minister for the next ten years. Had he done so, he would have suffered the sorry aftermath of his antipathy to the railways as well as to his subsequent actions.

My part in those 22 years with WAGR from 1927 to 1949 was truly itinerant. Not only did my work take me to such extremities of the railway system as Wiluna in the north, Laverton and Esperance in the east, Denmark in the south and Flinders Bay in the south-west — with rail distances from Perth ranging up to 1141 kilometres in the case of Wiluna and 914 kilometres for Laverton and Esperance — but also did it involve 19 individual postings, 17 of them by direction and only two by application.

The postings were a varied lot, from a minimum of only three days before being re-transferred to a maximum of four and a half years. Locality-wise, they consisted of five terms in Perth, three in Kalgoorlie, two at both Geraldton and Northam, as well as at Wurarga, Meekatharra, Cue, Narrogin, Hillman, Williams and Allanson.

Over the years, one's living conditions were just as diverse as one's employment. Summarised, they included the occupancy of 12 houses, including the family home during my cadetship; six boarding houses or hotels; four tents; and two portable hessian or weatherboard structures on construction sites.

But that does not convey the complete picture. The greater part of one's time when attached to district offices was taken up with survey work, in which case one camped overnight in a survey van, which was a railway vehicle fitted out with such basic items as a water tank, wood stove and canvas stretchers; and which, when shunted off on to some remote siding, provided temporary accommodation for the engineering staff.

When camped in a survey van, ablutionary facilities were usually confined to a tin dish; but at those stations boasting a locomotive water supply we were able to enjoy the luxury of a cold shower, which would be taken in a little windswept cubicle under the elevated tank. Where no such privacy existed, we had to turn on the locomotive water column and, stripped down to our briefs — or, at times stark naked —withstand a deluge strong enough to knock one over. In the winter, such a shower was not a luxury; it was, in the interests of cleanliness, a freezing necessity.

Travel to and from the work site was by motor section car or quadricycle. These were four-wheeled trollies powered by internal combustion engines with magneto ignitions; either twin-cylinder two-stroke Fairbanks Morse, single-cylinder four-stroke Barr and Stroud, or single-cylinder two-stroke water-cooled Groper, the latter the WAGR's plagiarism of America's Casey Jones. All lacked any semblance of protection from the elements; consequently, in the Murchison or Eastern Goldfields — where consistent summer temperatures exceeding or approaching the Fahrenheit century (37.8°C) contrasted with winter ones near freezing point — one suffered from either wind and sun burn or chillblains. On the other hand, in the south-west, one spent the entire winter in a state of semi-frozen saturation.

This method of perambulation was not without its hazards. In those days, centralised train control extended only from Perth to Northam, and for train information elsewhere rail-motor users had to rely on telephonic advice from the nearest stationmaster. Since there was no stationmaster in the 237 kilometres between Kalgoorlie and Malcolm, in the 203 kilometres between Norseman and Esperance, or in the 177 kilometres between Meekatharra and Wiluna, the placing of a rail-motor on the track was often something akin to Russian roulette. Indeed, I had more than one close shave and several of my colleagues were injured, three fatally.

At that time, rail-motors were not equipped with kick or battery starting systems, and the engine had to be started by pushing the vehicle until the ignition responded. But such was their obstinacy that one was forced at times to push them for interminable lengths before they fired. Sometimes the driver would let fly with an expletive in disgust and give it a final push and let it roll unattended, only to find that, out of sheer cussedness, it would fire and career off down the track, leaving him frantically chasing it on foot.

Apart from five periods attached to the Head Office in Perth — of which three were during university vacations — my peregrinations around the WAGR could be epitomised as five postings to the Murchison (including Geraldton); three to the Eastern Goldfields and to the Great Southern; two to Northam; and one to the South West. Some of those postings were years apart, but it is felt that the story could best be told on a locality basis.

Of my terms in Head Office, the first three were drab, unexciting, time-serving, and symptomatic of my introduction into the Department. However, late in 1937, after six rewarding years in the field, I returned to the Drawing Office to be engrossed for three years in civil engineering design, and, in particular, that associated with the grade improvements.

Then, in 1944, after another four years in the field — this time at Narrogin in the Great Southern and my third stint at Kalgoorlie — and following Federal Minister for Transport and External Territories E.J.Ward's initiation of yet another enquiry into rail standardisation — I returned to Perth to prepare, along with two other engineers, Syd Raynes and Clem Robinson, the State's submission. Two years later I became Engineer in Charge of Standard Gauge Design. However, the whole standardisation concept collapsed under the weight of interstate parochialism and my activities were diverted towards special duties before being appointed Engineer and Chief Draftsman, a position which I held until I left the Western Australian Government Railways

in 1949 to take up the position of Chief Civil Engineer for the Commonwealth Railways.

The Depression

Upon the completion of my university studies I was catapulted into the turmoil of the Depression. In the eight years leading to the outbreak of World War II, the greater part of my duties was devoted to unemployment relief works, when I lived, worked and endured the same extremes of climate as did the men on the job.

I worked on six such relief projects. Three were in the Murchison — at Wurarga, Meekatharra and Cue; two in the Great Southern — at Hillman and Williams; and one at Allanson in the South West. It was an experience that I regard to this day as the most satisfying of my working life, and for that reason I feel that, before recounting my activities over those years, I should offer some comment on the Depression itself.

During the 1930s, there was many a teenage boy whose weekly pay had to sustain an entire family. Those boys did not squander their first pay packet on an old bomb or a motor bike; they handed over the whole sum to their parents.

In the blistering summer heat of February 1932, at a spot on the railway to Leonora, I met a boy, who would not have been a day over 18 years of age, who was walking the 550 kilometres from Kalgoorlie to Wiluna in search of work. I was surveying bridges between Paddington and Broad Arrow when I met him. He had already covered nearly 40 kilometres and the fact that he still had over 500 kilometres to go did not daunt him. To face this ordeal, he was wearing a pair of flimsy dancing pumps; his entire possessions fitted quite easily into a child's school case, and he carried his drinking water in a cordial bottle. Nor did he have any blankets. This boy sought a job rather than rely on the 70 cents a week unemployment relief available to him.

A year or so later, at Hillman in the Great Southern, a 19-year-old boy, the sole support of a mother and five siblings, was assigned to my construction job. Small, thin and pale, and looking even younger than his years, he set out to do a man's job.

As an engineering cadet articled to the Commissioner of Railways, my tenure was secure for the time being, but the position became precarious upon the completion of my studies. Twelve months earlier, when the economic climate deteriorated alarmingly, virtually every unmarried employee of the WAGR was retrenched. The same fate could well have befallen me, but luckily I was given an appointment and sent to Kalgoorlie.

My salary of £233 ($466) per annum represented, on a weekly basis, only a few cents above the minimum wage applying on the Goldfields, but at least I had a job. When, a few months later, I transferred to construction, I received less pay than did my foreman or my timekeeper. In fact, my weekly wage rate was lower than that of the labourers, but the saving grace was the continuity of my employment, whereas they worked part time.

The nose dive from the euphoria of 1929 to the depression of 1930 was sudden and dramatic. The State was riding high in 1929, Western Australia's centenary year, but in 1930, everything changed. The season was disappointing; prices dropped and unemployment rose. There was, however, an attitude of determination and self-help. In the face of very little, if any, protest, 'financial emergency' legislation was enacted, cutting all salaries and wages by up to 30 percent.

In the early days of the Depression, there were the inevitable queues for meal tickets, and a daily congregation of unemployed on the Perth Esplanade at the foot of Barrack Street, but these did not last for long. Men rode the freight trains looking for work, and the authorities did their best to turn a blind eye to the practice. When Mick Flaherty, stationmaster at Mullewa, accosted one such freeloader, the man pointed to a railway poster blazoned with the words 'Use Your Railways and Save Your Money' and said, 'That's just what I am doing'. Mick did not have the heart to put him off the train.

The most uncomfortable and certainly the most unpleasant such ride that I saw would have been taken by a train jumper on a goods train passing through the 373 mile permanent way gang camp on the Norseman line. He was travelling steerage, crouched on the lower deck of a double decked railway sheep van, and unable to sit up because of the restricted headroom. Riding first class on the

upper deck above him was a consignment of pigs!

Again, during the same period, I was sitting on the floor of the guard's van of a train on the Kurrawang Wood Line, a private railway providing firewood and mining props to the Kalgoorlie mines. Squatted alongside me was a penniless tramp who had hitched his way down to the line's main camp, hoping to get a job in a cutting gang. He had missed out and was now on his way back to civilisation. Towards sundown, he delved into the sugar bag that held his worldly possessions, and came out with a brown onion. After carefully peeling off the outer skin, he ate the onion, perhaps not with relish but certainly with satisfaction. That, and that alone, constituted his evening meal.

In mid-1932, the Western Australian Government embarked on a massive programme of unemployment relief works, particularly those having a high labour content. More importantly, the accent was also on productivity, and all submissions for funds had to be supported by proof of financial viability.

Works authorised under the plan included irrigation, drainage, water supplies, road construction and railway improvements. Those undertaken by the railways covered track duplication, regrading, ballasting and improvements to locomotive water supplies. During the next ten years, grade improvements were carried out on 11 different lines, and resulted in better train working over a total of 1180 kilometres of railway; while new locomotive water supplies were constructed at 11 locations. It was a far cry from the wanton waste of public funds that occurred some 40 years later, when a number of sinecures that masqueraded as unemployed relief were initiated. The Western Australian scheme of the 1930s was a credit to its originators.

Men were directed to relief jobs without preference; nor did the men themselves seek it. Clerks, accountants, storekeepers, farmers, locomotive engine drivers, tradesmen, labourers, coal miners, timber workers, even starting price bookmakers camped and worked together without embarrassment or resentment. On all the relief works with which I was associated, not once did I detect any lack of harmony among the men; at the most, a petty tiff.

The scheme did not encourage drones. Except for those jobs where specific skills were required, a man was not asked what his trade or calling might be. There were no special dispensations for out-of-work piano tuners or lion tamers. They were sent to wherever work was available; if they declined to go, they forfeited their unemployment payments. And, once on a job, a man could neither leave without justifiable compassionate grounds nor court dismissal by slacking. A clearance certificate endorsed 'work unsatisfactory' meant that the holder was deprived of his relief payments until he convinced the authorities that he was genuine in his desire for work.

Men went willingly to whichever job they might be directed. They would call at the employment office in the city, be issued with a travel voucher and be given less that 24 hours' notice to go to a relief job, sometimes 1000 kilometres distant. In most cases they left their families behind and camped on the site. The greater part of their pay went directly to their wives in the form of an allotment, retaining for themselves only sufficient upon which to live.

Unemployment relief in those days amounted to 70 cents a week for a single man; a married man with one child got $2.10; and one with six dependants or more the maximum of $4.90 a week. In terms of real money, relief payments in the 1930s were only a fraction of those applying today.

Under the relief work programme, labour was engaged on a part-time basis and was designed to give a single man $2.50 each week and a married one $2.00 over and above his relief entitlement. While working, he would be credited with the award wage appropriate to the work that he was doing, and this would be posted to a kitty. From this he would be paid each week an amount equal to his unemployment relief rate plus $2, or, in the case of a single man, $2.50. His working time would be adjusted so as to keep his kitty in credit at all times. On the average, a single man would work one week in three, and a married one correspondingly more depending on the size of his family. One with six dependants would work nearly full time.

My first experience of this type of work was with predominantly single men who, although working one week in three and nominally entitled to a weekly payment of $2.50, were deducted five cents to cover Financial Emergency Tax.

We were authorised to issue ration orders on the local stores, the value of which was deducted from the man's next pay and paid directly to the storekeeper. These ration orders could be issued only one week in advance. At times we were pestered to go beyond that limitation, not infrequently because the obvious intent behind the request was to cash it at the store and spend the proceeds at the local pub. Being only too aware of the hopelessness of their situation, it was at times heartbreaking to have to deny the request; but in this we had to be firm, not only to conform with government policy but also to help the men conserve their meagre finances.

The system of unemployment relief works payment was subsequently altered to permit the employee to receive the full amount earned during his working period and then to stand down without pay for a term which varied in accordance with the number of his dependants. In addition, margins for skill and overtime were paid in full without affecting the relationship between working and standing down periods.

On the whole, it was a better system. It provided a man with a little more money, and in amounts sufficient to allow for the purchase of such things as clothing. On the other hand, it was harder on the man who was unable to husband the few dollars that he did earn.

Towards the close of one job — at Hillman in the Great Southern — we paid off one man, giving him all pay due to him, including pro-rata holiday pay. He would not have been entitled to any further work, or even unemployment relief, for about six weeks. The man was also in receipt of a small pension, which used to be mailed to Darkan, a township about 10 kilometres away. As one such remittance was due, instead of joining that night's train at Hillman he opted to go into Darkan with the local storekeeper, collect his pension cheque and join the train there. Collecting his normal pay, his holiday pay and his pension all at once proved too much for him. He spent the next 24 hours at the Darkan Hotel; and, when he passed through Hillman on the following night's train he had precisely one halfpenny in his pocket.

One would not wish ever to see such circumstances as the Depression of the 1930s descend on us again. There was, however, an independence, a sense of responsibility and an eagerness to work not always apparent today. The professional man would wield a pick and shovel alongside the clerk and the labourer, and not once did I hear anything but gratitude for having at least a part-time job. After having lived with them and having suffered the same inconveniences of camp life, I came to respect and admire the men and women who met the challenge of the Depression years.

The Murchison

My wanderings around the WAGR, and my first glimpse of the Murchison, had their humble beginnings in March 1928 when, during a university vacation, I was transferred to the Geraldton District Office for two months. Following on a small washaway six kilometres east of Wurarga — itself 183 kilometres inland — I went there with the Assistant Engineer, E.W. Morris, to act as his chainman while he took a few levels. Little did I know that, four years later, this insignificant siding would be the locale of my first construction job and the start of six years on the wallaby.

Wurarga's entire establishment consisted of a railway maintenance gang — one married and four single men — and, incongruously, a small dilapidated galvanised-iron building housing a combined hotel, store and post office. The nearest sheep station, Marloo, was over 15 kilometres distant. At the time of this my first visit, the little hotel-store-post office was owned and operated by Mr and Mrs Tom Seaman, an elderly couple who were renowned throughout the Murchison not only for the broad and delightful brogue which they had brought with them from their native Ireland, but also for their extreme kindliness and generosity. No down-and-out ever wanted for a meal when trudging through Wurarga.

Ernie Morris and I were camped in our survey van, while two penniless tramps had dossed down in the shelter shed on the station platform. Towards sundown, Mrs Seaman announced dinner by banging on a piece of iron suspended from the pub verandah. After about ten minutes, she went over to the two men and asked if they had heard the gong. They had, they told her, but they had no money. Mrs Seaman's Hibernian indignation erupted. 'Who said anything about money?' She had sounded the gong just for those two men.

After we had finished our work at Wurarga, we were directed to travel to Wonella — 74 kilometres south of the rail junction station of Mullewa — there to undertake another survey. Next day, having finished that job, we were returning to Geraldton by rail-motor quadricycle when some 50-odd kilometres south of Mullewa we had a close encounter with Number 74, the southbound bi-weekly mixed train. We were congratulating ourselves on our good luck when the quad caught fire.

Morris did his best to extinguish the fire but I, who was in no danger whatsoever, bailed out immediately. From a 40 km/h flying start I described a neat arc before hitting the ground, rolling down the embankment and coming to rest, with little damage to show apart from a bruise or two, and some torn and dusty clothing.

Mullewa

Mullewa, gateway to the Murchison and a frontier town in its heyday, was a railhead for the vast area to the north and a large railway depot. It was the home of the L and C class steam locomotives. Built in the United States by the Baldwin Locomotive Works, they were bought second-hand in 1901 by the WAGR and modified for use on the light tracks of the Murchison. With their high slung boilers, which permitted unrestricted view from one side of the locomotive to the other, and with their distinctive clatter in running, the L and C classes were unlike any others in use in Western Australia. They cost only a few thousand pounds each, even after modification, and at first they performed admirably. But in the 1930s, something happened.

One Monday morning, Norman Long set out from Cue — 422 kilometres and 317 kilometres east of Geraldton and Mullewa respectively — on his motor quadricycle to patrol the 140 kilometres of track north to Gnaweeda. He had not gone very far before he detected a number of rails that were distorted out of line and crippled, something not evident when he was over the same section two days previously. It transpired that, over the weekend, an engine driver, anxious to return home in time to attend a social function, had decided to ignore the speed limit and the excessive hammer blow — the name given to the dynamic force generated by the revolution of the weights built into the locomotive's driving wheels to counterbalance the lopsided thrust of the driving rods — had proved too much for the light rails, then over 30 years old.

In order to reduce this hammer blow, the locomotives were modified to provide for smaller counterbalance weights. New wheels were fabricated and fitted to the engines, but the rail damage increased alarmingly. A highly embarrassed Dick Broadfoot, the Chief Mechanical Engineer, admitted that, somewhere along the line, the drawings had been misread, and the intended cavities in the new wheel forgings had been filled with lead!

It was at Mullewa too that Mick Burleigh operated under franchise the refreshment rooms on the station, as well as the buffet car which, when attached to Numbers 73 and 74 between Mullewa and Caron, used to provide passengers with an unalterable one-course menu of eggs, bacon, sausages and mashed potato, be it for breakfast, luncheon or dinner; just another indication to travellers that they were Murchison-bound.

Mullewa was also noted for two distinct but entirely different characters; Father Hawes and Dr Hobbs.

Trained as an architect prior to his conversion to cloth, and parish priest at Mullewa, Father Hawes was the epitome of spiritual fulfilment. Moreover, not only did he apply his architectural endeavours to the building, with his own hands, of his church at Mullewa, but he also acted in an advisory capacity during the construction of the Roman Catholic Cathedral at Geraldton.

On the other hand, Dr Hobbs was somewhat typical of the Murchison. Mercurial and headstrong, he seemed well fitted for his calling as the only doctor in that vast area. Habitually driving his Chevrolet tourer like a charioteer, he provided a vital service, going anywhere at any time, often over the tracks that masqueraded as roads, and in doing so saved many a life.

During my later sojourn at Wurarga, a station hand working on Yuin station, about 150

Murchison bungarra (*Photo*: WA Museum)

kilometres north-east of Mullewa, was gored by a bull. Taking the matron of the local hospital with him, Dr Hobbs drove to Yuin where, on the kitchen table, he operated on the man. It was a forlorn hope from the start, but he was prepared to do what he could.

The Murchison River and its branches, dry for the greater part of the year, extend inland for several hundred kilometres, and drain an area one half of that of the State of Victoria. The whole region is known as the Murchison. It is fascinating country; undulating with some small ranges of hills, and from the higher ground one can see for enormous distances. Subject to droughts and relying on autumn thunderstorms for its rainfall, it was a legend in the Murchison that we suffered railway washaways a fortnight either side of Saint Patrick's Day, March being the thunderstorm month.

The Murchison was a hot place; indeed, very hot. Meekatharra, 966 kilometres north of Perth and halfway to Marble Bar — the town holding the world record for the greatest number of consecutive Fahrenheit centuries — is credited with an average maximum summer temperature of 36.1°C. And while the winter days might be mild and pleasant, at night the air could become so cold as to make deep breathing a torture.

Apart from its immense sheep population and such feral animals as donkeys, camels and goats — the first two reminders of the pre-automobile methods of transport that opened up the country, and the third as alternative to tinned milk — the

Murchison abounded in euros, kangaroos and bungarras.

The Murchison blue kangaroo was noted for its fur, and I still possess a rug made from skins obtained in 1933. The total cost, including royalties on the skins, tanning, lining material and making-up, amounted to less than $15. After 70 years, it is still the equivalent of at least two ordinary blankets.

Bungarras are large goanna-like creatures, growing up to two metres in length. When they rear up on their four legs they present a somewhat terrifying appearance, but they are harmless and, in their own way, curious and friendly. At Big Bell, out from Cue, I had a pet bungarra which used to come around while I was eating my crib in the shade of a mulga bush. It would stand within a couple of metres of me, stock still and unblinking, even when I threw it a crust, but the moment I looked away it would snap up the morsel and straightway resume its immobile posture. It was not uncommon for prospectors to encourage these friendly creatures around their camps, because they were reputed to be the enemy of snakes. On the other hand, they did constitute a hazard to railwaymen. On warm days, they had the habit of sunning themselves

C.R. Stewart (*Photo:* Battye Library)

over the rails, where their bulk was sufficient to derail a quadricycle.

The sheep, cattle, feral and native animals were outnumbered by the flies. The larger blowflies did not confine their attentions to food and I have seen them alight on a blanket and deposit a dollop of maggots on it. The smaller bush flies were, however, the greater nuisance. From dawn to dark — that is, in summer, up to 15 hours a day — one could not escape them. Even to speak was to invite an incursion into one's mouth, and one's eyes were a perpetual attraction to them. Lacking any repellant, I used to cover my lips with a cigarette paper in an endeavour to obtain some relief.

I revisited the Murchison in 1990 and, 58 years on, the flies were still there; indeed, they seemed to have multiplied.

Gold was found throughout the whole of the Murchison, extending from Yalgoo through Mount Manet to Sandstone, and northwards as far as Meekatharra and Wiluna. Naturally, the discoveries brought with them a period of hectic railway development. The line from Geraldton reached Mullewa in 1894, and its 317 kilometres extension to Cue was completed in 1898; to Nannine in 1903, and to Meekatharra in 1910. The terminus remained there until 1932, when the 175 kilometres extension to Wiluna was officially opened.

In the same year that the line reached Meekatharra, the railway from Mount Magnet to Sandstone was completed, while, as late as 1937, the short branch line from Cue to Big Bell was built.

Although gold made the Murchison famous, it also abounded with other minerals. In the late 1920s, the WA Manganese Company constructed a line front Meekatharra to Horseshoe, near Peak Hill, with the intention of developing the large manganese deposits there. However, the project did not prosper, and when activity waned in the early '30s the State Government, which had guaranteed the company, sought to redeem its investment. Frank Carter, who had followed Cedric Stewart as Resident Engineer on the construction of the Meekatharra–Wiluna railway, was given the job of taking up the Horseshoe line. Most of the materials recovered were stacked at Meekatharra, and, in part, were used in 1936–37 on the construction of the Cue–Big Bell railway.

Wurarga Reservoir, 1932–33, excavation party complete (*Photo:* the author)

(*Right*) Rock after firing with explosives. Tom Butler in left foreground (*Photo:* the author)

Excavation complete (*Photo:* the author)

Wurarga Reservoir complete roofed and full (*Photo:* the author)

The author's living quarters at the reservoir (*Photo:* the author)

Wurarga

In July 1932, one month after my 22nd birthday and less than a year out of the university, I was posted to Wurarga to take on my first construction job.

That job was to construct a railway reservoir in a normally dry creek bed about two kilometres from the siding. Being the only relatively soft digging for some distance around, the creek bed had become the local burial ground and our first job therefore was to shift five graves from the site. As they were over 20 years old, exhumation and reburial presented few problems, but we were lucky.

Only a fortnight prior to our arrival, a member of the permanent way gang, no doubt in a fit of isolation-induced melancholia, had committed suicide by shotgun blast. It had been intended to bury him in the creek bed alongside the others, but because a justice of peace could not be found to witness the burial in this ungazetted cemetery, the body was taken to Yalgoo. We at Wurarga

The Wurarga Hotel (*Photo:* Douglas Baglin)

Wurarga: our alfresco ablutions (*Photo:* the author)

were thereby relieved of what would have been a most distasteful duty.

The nearest settlements to Wurarga — Pindar and Yalgoo — were 50 kilometres to the west and 40 kilometres to the east. Pindar could only be described as a hamlet, but it was the railhead for sheep stations hundreds of kilometres away. It was not uncommon to see 20-strong camel teams resting there after having hauled wagonloads of wool from as far afield as Milly Milly, nearly 100 kilometres to the north.

However, Pindar did have a meagre claim to

Wurarga dam, March 1990. The roof had gone but the flies had not (*Photo:* the author)

fame. Some years later, Bert Simpson — railway station caretaker and general agent during my time at Wurarga — was elected to the Western Australian Legislative Council before going on to become Minister for Railways!

Yalgoo had once been a busy mining centre, but by 1932 it was only a shadow of its former self, its mining activities limited to a few fossickers.

Although not a big job, the climate and the primitive living conditions, together with the absence of any mechanical aids, made the construction of the reservoir as an unemployment relief project a gruelling one. Essentially a pick and shovel operation, undertaken during the hot dry Murchison summer, it exacted its toll on those engaged on it and who lived at bare subsistence level.

The hard sedimentary rock, known locally as Murchison cement, was blasted out in two layers, each six feet (1.8 m) thick. Holes were hand drilled by jumper to a six foot chequerboard pattern and then bulled. This was a process whereby a cavity was blown at the bottom of the drill hole to take a quantity of granulated blasting powder. Two plugs of gelignite were tamped into the drill hole

and then a third plug, fitted with a short length of fuse and a detonator, was lit and dropped into the hole on top of the other two. This was followed by a small quantity of water to act as a seal and limit the upward thrust of the explosion. In this way, a small cavity was created, into which about two and a half kilograms of blasting powder were poured and ignited by a length of fuse without a detonator.

Several holes were exploded simultaneously, resulting in the shattering of the cement. It was then broken into manageable sizes by men wielding 14 pound (6.4 kg) spalling hammers, an operation that demanded superb muscle power. The upper layer was removed by horse-drawn scoops; the lower one shovel-loaded into skips running on a miniature tramway and hauled to the surface by a Lister engine and winch.

In the extreme heat and without any semblance of a breeze to cool things down, working in the excavation was almost intolerable; nor was there any relief at night.

Typical of the stress under which we lived and worked was the case of Jack Dillon, but who had been seconded to the dam construction. Late one afternoon in February 1933, when the summer heat was at its worst, Jack was struck down with acute sunstroke and suffered convulsions. We placed him on a mattress on the back seat of the publican's car and took him to the doctor at Mullewa, a journey over the bush track that passed for the main road of over two hours. Unfortunately, Jack did not survive.

Two other men left the job suffering from heat stroke, and both died shortly afterwards. However, despite the climatic extremes, the rough living conditions and the miserable pay which amounted to little more than the dole, the men stuck it out, indeed with expressions of gratitude at having a job at all.

Most of the men on the Wurarga job were single, and they worked, on average, one week in every three. Their earnings were posted to a kitty, from which they were paid 24 shillings and ninepence ($2.48) each Monday night. After he had paid his food bill, bought a tin of Westward-Ho tobacco — the cheapest available — a packet of Riz-La cigarette papers and a box of matches, a man might have had enough money left to purchase a bottle of the cheapest red wine. The resultant pandemonium in the camp usually lasted until daybreak on Tuesday morning.

The single men were obliged to remain in the camp during their stand-down periods, and this inactivity created problems — often alcoholic ones. Wurarga's only store was also its hotel, and store orders issued to the men against their weekly pay allotments were sometimes redeemed over the bar. We did our best to prevent this happening, but had no right to interfere. Once, I acquired a black eye trying to restrain an off-duty labourer who had over-indulged and was making a nuisance of himself.

If the work at Wurarga was hard, the climate and the living conditions were even harder. During a ten day period in February 1933, unofficially, we recorded nine temperatures of 48°C. Somewhere during those ten days we enjoyed a cool change, when the thermometer plummeted to 43°C! Then, just for variety and to maintain the legend of Saint Patrick, one afternoon about three weeks later we had a thunderstorm lasting less than half an hour and giving a rain gauge reading of 320 points (81 mm). Water flowed waist deep through the camp which, for easy digging, was in the creek bed. It also filled the newly completed reservoir many times over.

The downpour also gave me a few other moments of concern. The creek leading to the reservoir changed from a dry bed to a raging torrent which endangered not only the railway bridge spanning it, but also the embankments on either side. An eastbound goods train had left Pindar for Wurarga, and in the absence of any means of communication with it I set off walking westwards, armed with a guard's hand lamp and stopped the train about one kilometre short of the bridge. Fortunately, both the bridge and the embankments held.

The dry climate and the lack of fresh food caused outbreaks of Barcoo Rot — persistent sores that would not heal, and which became fair game for the flies. A 'refinement' of this complaint was the Barcoo Spews, when the victim became racked with almost continuous vomiting.

The tough living conditions were not confined to the labouring force; they extended to the foreman, timekeeper and me. My living quarters consisted of a small cabin sheathed for the most part with secondhand black railway tarpaulin. It was not even fitted with a glazed window; in its place was a hinged shutter, also covered with black tarpaulin. It was so oppressive inside the cabin that, for the entire summer, I cooked, ate and slept in the open.

Sleeping under those conditions demanded the adoption of fly-avoidance techniques. As soon as dawn broke, one had two options; either dive head-first under the bedclothes or endure persistent attacks from swarms of bush flies.

Food was an even bigger problem. On Tuesday and Friday nights Hermann Goerling from nearby Marloo station, would bring in some fresh meat, generally aged wether, but in the absence of refrigeration or ice, and where the Coolgardie drip safe was a waste of time, it would be putrid by next morning.

My meat safe consisted of a chaff bag suspended from a mulga bush at two points on its seam, and with a piece of flat board inserted horizontally to form a shelf. The meat would be placed on that shelf and the mouth of the bag tied as tightly as possible. Provided that the blowflies were denied access, this contraption acted reasonably well during the winter months, but in the heat of summer it was useless. For the same reasons, butter degenerated into an oily mess and had to be jettisoned

As a consequence, we were obliged to subsist for the entire summer on a diet consisting essentially of tinned meat, potatoes, onions, bread and jam, topped off with black billy tea. Of these, the tinned meat deserves special mention. It consisted of three varieties — roast beef, spiced beef and corned beef — all under the Imperial brand. Remove the label from the tin and it lost its identity. It could all be grouped under the generic description of tinned dog!

However, to say that we lived solely on this diet would not be strictly correct. On rare but special occasions, someone would shoot a kangaroo or a wild goat and it would be a race to skin it, quarter it and get into the camp oven before it succumbed to either the heat or the blowflies.

Then, on Friday nights, we would have a feast. Percy Copley, railway transport clerk at Geraldton, had some crayfish pots, and arrangements were made for him to place two and a half dozen live crayfish in the care of Dave Ferguson, guard of Number 73, the Wiluna-bound mixed train. Dave would put them in the ice van on the train and deliver them to us, alive and kicking, when it reached Wurarga at about 5.30 pm.

After we had eaten our customary evening meal of tinned dog, potatoes and onions, six of us — three members of the permanent way gang, the publican's son, my timekeeper and I — would cook the crayfish and devour the 30 at one sitting. The Geraldton crayfish is not large, but even so, five per head bordered on gluttony.

Our drinking water was railed 79 kilometres from Mullewa. There was small well with a windmill and tank at Wurarga, but the water was undrinkable. However, apart from a tin dish, it constituted our only ablutionary facility. There we would stand, unprotected and open for all to see, and seek to shower under the outlet pipe from the tank. The water was freezing in winter, but in summer when daytime temperatures consistently exceeded the Fahrenheit century, any attempt to shower before 9 pm would have been an invitation to parboiling.

Laundry facilities too were primitive. A four-gallon (18.2 litres) kerosene tin with one side cut out — not detached but rolled in two halves to provide hand grips at each end — was set over an open fire and one's clothes boiled in it. Underclothes, handkerchiefs, work shirts and trousers were laundered in this way, while socks were hand-washed in a bucket.

Recreation at Wurarga was confined to an occasional game of tennis or cricket. There was an earth tennis court adjacent to the hotel, but the only inhabitant energetic enough to use it was Ethel Moore, busy mother of five children and with her husband, Tom, co-licensee of the hotel under a lease agreement with the Seamans, who had retired temporarily to Tardee station.

Cricket matches were played against visiting teams from Yalgoo, Pindar and Mullewa; the location, Renfrey Park. Renfrey was a station hand, and the circumstances leading to his being immortalised in this manner were typical of the Murchison.

It was customary on nearby stations to allow hands who might have been isolated in an outcamp for three months at a time to spend a week at the Wurarga Hotel, where they would soften their cracking hides, relieve their thirsts, have someone to talk to and, at the same time, annoy no one. At the end of the week they would go back to their outcamp, where they would remain quite happily for another three months or so.

During one such sojourn, Renfrey divided his time between sessions at the bar and clearing the mulga scrub from an area adjacent to the pub. It became known as Renfrey Park.

Preparation of the wicket was unique. An area would be selected near the middle of the clearing and hand picked clean of stones. Next, a 44 gallon (200 litre) drum would be filled with water from the well and rolled over to the wicket area, where the bung would be loosened and the water allowed to run out on to the ground. Consolidation would be achieved by re-filling the drum and using it as a roller. Cricket matting would then be laid over the surface.

A wicket prepared in this manner was not without its surprises, especially for batsmen and wicketkeepers. Indeed, the only way by which a delivery could be assured of going where the bowler intended was to make it a full toss. Still, we had lots of fun, local rules providing for an adjournment for refreshments at the fall of each wicket. Incidentally, it was in the course of Wurarga-style cricket that I met Bert Simpson for the first time, he being captain of the Pindar team.

My Wurarga story is a long one and, for a number of reasons, significantly so. It had a profound influence on my working life and my love for the outback; indeed, it set the pattern for my future

Meekatharra, c. 1935 (*Photo:* Library Board of Western Australia)

career, including my safari-like activities in later years — and under different circumstances — as Chief Civil Engineer for the Commonwealth Railways.

As a raw mistake-prone youth, barely 22 years of age, who had been thrown headlong into his first construction job — and called upon to supervise men more than twice his age and many times more experienced, as well as to withstand an unending tirade of criticism from his superior located at Geraldton, and who inspected the project only twice in eight months — it taught me never to let them get you down, no matter what.

It was the first of my eight unemployed relief works — six of them major ones — spread over nine years, and an experience that proved to be the most rewarding of my working life.

Living and working under the same conditions as did the men provided me with the opportunity to get to know them personally, while still maintaining subordination, something that I was able to achieve at all levels of my career — and with gratifying results throughout.

Meekatharra

In May 1935, after a lapse of just over two years

— during which my postings included a second tour of duty at Kalgoorlie lasting six months, and the remainder of the time on the construction of more railway reservoirs at Hillman and Williams in the Great Southern — it was back again to the Murchison, this time to Meekatharra to undertake a relatively minor job of concrete lining a reservoir that had been built a year or so earlier by Frank Carter, Resident Engineer in charge of the final stages of the Meekatharra–Wiluna railway.

My camp at Meekatharra was located some eight kilometres out of town, with transport to and from limited to walking or railway pull-tricycle. Living conditions were similar to those at Wurarga, but this time the weather rendered the tarpaulin covered cabin habitable. However, the flies were inescapable and in comparable numbers.

Rough and ramshackle, all galvanised-iron and gibbers, and, apart from a few hardy pepper trees, devoid of vegetation, Meeka was a frontier town, fascinating and full of surprises. Its main street, wide and dusty, continued northwards, to infinity it seemed, and after passing through the old mining towns of Peak Hill and Nullagine, finished 650 kilometres away at Marble Bar.

Although not truly the head of the line, the extension to Wiluna having been completed a few years earlier, Meekatharra nevertheless remained railhead for the country to the north. It was the southern terminus of the stock route reaching over 1500 kilometres north to the Kimberleys. Naturally, a great number of the beasts were wild and stampedes not uncommon. For this reason, the livestock trucking yards were located about five kilometres out of town.

Each Saturday, after the arrival of Train Number 73 from Perth, road transports would leave Meekatharra with mail and supplies for sheep stations and settlements to the north, and for reasons of safety on this lonely stretch their progress was monitored and broadcast on the regional radio network

When shearing teams hit the town after months in isolation, Meekatharra used to hum. The guns and the chaps might be missing, and horses outnumbered by motor vehicles, but the atmosphere was vintage John Wayne. Many a station hand too, arriving in town after a year in the outback with a large wages cheque and an even larger thirst, would not get past the first pub in the main street until his cheque cut out. He would then return to his station, happy and unrepentant, and work for another 12 months, no doubt hoping that his holiday horizons would extend further afield next time around.

For recreation, the town offered golf and football. The golf course was so strewn with gibbers that a well hit drive could ricochet off a stone and be lost forever or even finish up somewhere behind the tee. The football oval was more or less free of gibbers, but it was also entirely devoid of grass, or indeed of any soft spots. One look at the playing surface and I decided to pass up football for that season.

It was at Meekatharra too that I encountered two men —Dr Esmond Walsh and Tim O'Shea — who, while being at opposite ends of the social spectrum, seemed to typify the Murchison.

One afternoon in 1935, Ted Clifford — an engineer from Geraldton who was spending a few days with me — and I met Tim, an old time survey hand, in the town's main street. He invited us to his room in a local hotel and there, sitting on his bed, set to work with a pocket knife on a pair of dice. He explained that he was due to have a game of hazards that night with a couple of Italian prospectors and that he was doctoring the dice so that they would do just what he wanted them to do.

'Tim, is this game dinkum?' asked Ted.

Highly indignant that such a suspicion should arise, he replied angrily:

'Of course it's dinkum. They'll have loaded dice too!'

On the other side of the coin was Esmond Walsh. I first encountered him in March 1928 when, as an engineering cadet on university vacation, I was temporarily transferred to Geraldton.

Cue, Western Australia, 1937 (*Photo:* Library Board of Western Australia)

Our first marital home, Cue–Big Bell railway construction, 1936 (*Photo:* the author)

Train Number 73 had barely left the Perth station when one of the other occupants of our four berth sleeping compartment asked a personable young man in his late twenties where he was going.

'I'm going to a place called Meekatharra,' the man replied. 'Where's that?'

His name was Dr Esmond Walsh and he had arrived from Adelaide by train that morning. He had called at the office of the Department of Health looking for a position that offered him the opportunity of widening his medical experience and had been offered one at Meekatharra.

Four years later, while having a meal in the railway refreshment room at Mullewa, the same Dr Walsh sat down at my table, lifted the lid from the bread crock and said:

'You can always tell when you are back in the Murchison by the texture of the bread.'

He was returning to Meekatharra after an overseas trip, and, again, we were travelling companions as far as Wurarga.

I met him again in 1935 during my sojourn at Meekatharra, and yet again two years later, when working on the construction of the Cue–Big Bell railway. Well before that time, he had succumbed both to the Murchison itself and to the charms of the local girl who became his wife.

Cue

In 1936, Big Bell Mines Ltd, a subsidiary of the American Smelting and Refining Company, decided to develop a vast low grade gold deposit

Newly laid unballasted track, Cue–Big Bell railway, 1936 (*Photo:* the author)

Earthworks for sunken road (*Photo:* the author)

Big Bell station yard, 1937 (*Photo:* the author)

Wilgie Mia native ochre deposit, Weld Range, north-west of Cue (*Photo:* the author)

located about 30 kilometres north-west of Cue. As some railway construction was involved, after 15 months in the South West, it was back to the Murchison for me once again, this time as assistant to the Resident Engineer, Cliff Goss.

Once a substantial goldmining town, Cue contained some very fine buildings, in particular, government offices. By the 1920s, mining activity had declined to the level of a few one-man shows, but in 1932 the American Smelting and Refining Company became interested in the Big Bell, a mine first developed an about 1904 but which had closed down after World War I. Following four years' exploration, it was decided to re-open the mine as a high tonnage, low grade proposition; and, in 1936, it brought out a number of American experts to fill the executive positions. It also negotiated with the Western Australian Government regarding the provision of a railway from Cue to the mine.

The two parties concluded an Agreement in mid-year, one of the conditions being a guarantee by the Government that the railway would reach the mine by Christmas. The enabling legislation was in no way controversial. However, MPs dallied over all kinds of inconsequential matters and the Bill was not ratified until the middle of October. This meant that we were given only 57 working days in which to build, from scratch, 30 kilometres of railway.

In engineering terms, it was a simple job, but the critical deadline turned it into a high pressure undertaking. Again, it was essentially a pick and shovel operation. We had a couple of dozen horses and one air compressor, but we would have been better off without the latter. It never failed to break down within the first two hours of starting work each day and we then had to rush the faulty part out to Big Bell, where the mine's workshop staff would set about repairing it.

Meeting such a critical time schedule demanded unorthodox procedures; nor did the very hot weather assist. We started work in October and the rails reached the mine on the 56th working day, during a thunderstorm which flooded parts of the as yet uncompleted line as well as delivering electric shocks to some of the men handling the rails. However, that did not mean the end of the project; it took us another eight months to complete it.

For the greater part, we laid the rails directly on the ground, while the embankments were later constructed by running out filling material from bottom dump railway wagons and lifting the track through it to the required alignment level. In a similar manner, the few minor cuttings and bridges were bypassed temporarily, and completed later on.

The remainder of the earthworks — designated sunken road — were to a system devised for such territory as the Murchison where, although dry for perhaps years on end, the flow of water after rain could not be predicted with accuracy. To overcome this, the rails and sleepers were laid on the indigenous Murchison cement in a trench about 350 mm deep and with only 75 mm between the ends of the sleepers and the vertical sides of the shallow trench. After ballasting and lifting, the head of the rail would be at ground level and the track firmly boxed in. Any water that might flow after heavy rain would pass over the sunken track without doing any damage to the permanent way.

We started platelaying with a raw gang, few of whom had ever seen rails laid before, but after one or two days they became so proficient that they would finish their daily allotment of 1.2 kilometres of track and be back in the camp by mid-afternoon. The men's living and working conditions were rugged. Mining activities over the preceding 40 years had left Cue virtually free of vegetation and the men camped in this denuded landscape.

In the mid–1930s, the only mining activity around Cue itself was the State Battery, where ore was crushed and the gold recovered, first by passing the crushed material over plates covered with mercury, then by treating the residues with a solution of cyanide. The noise from the stamps was deafening. However, one became so accustomed to the din that the silence that followed the closing down of the battery at 6 pm of a Saturday was equally deafening.

The town's water supply came from a series of wells at Nallan, 21 kilometres to the north, and it was so hard that it tasted more like fluid magnesia. Moreover, it was impossible to raise a lather in its original form and this led the locals to devise a treatment whereby it could be rendered passable for laundry purposes. Fortunately, we obtained potable water from another source and were thereby absolved of the agony of being obliged to drink this carbonated laxative.

It was at Cue that Doreen and I started our married life.

For the three months before our wedding, I lived in a 10 by 8 foot (3.1 x 2.4 m) tent set on a timber frame, and with a timber floor. Our first marital home was a three-roomed hessian clad house, the standard for railway construction supervisory staff in those days. It was made up of timber framed sections, each 12 feet long by 8 feet high, covered on the outer sides with house canvas and the inner with hessian. Some sections were fitted with windows, some with a door, and one with a galvanised-iron fireplace. Ten sections would be bolted together to constitute three rooms, and set on top of a timber floor 36 x 12 feet (11.0 x 3.7 m), a ranch type roof fixed over it and a wood burning stove set in the fireplace. The exterior panel walls would then be treated with cement wash, and the inner ones with calsomine. The bathroom consisted of an annexe constructed from a sawn timber tent frame, sheathed on one side only with calsomined hessian and fitted with an iron roof. The plumbing comprised a pull-up shower and a galvanised-iron hip tub, while gaps left in the timber floor met any waste disposal requirements.

It was my third encounter with the Murchison, but Doreen's first. Twenty-one years of age, a bride of ten days' standing, and determined to retain her peaches-and-cream complexion, she had pre-equipped herself with a multitude of cosmetics, a wide brimmed hat and a sunshade; but she was unprepared for the ravages that could be wrought by such a climate.

One day, shortly after her arrival, she came back from a sortie into Cue's one shopping street and, with a voice bordering on terror, said: 'I'm getting out of this place!' She had just seen Mrs Gribble, the town's grand old lady, who had first gone to Cue in 1896, and was still there 40 years later. The hot dry climate had left its indelible mark on Mrs Gribble's countenance, just as it did to every old-timer who had spent a lifetime in the Murchison. Fortunately, when eventually Doreen did leave, she carried no visible climatic scars with her.

For many years after we had left Cue, a number of features associated with our life there were the source of humorous and nostalgic reminiscences.

One: An accomplished pianist, Doreen had taken her polished rosewood Brinsmead piano to Cue, and the hot dry climate played havoc with it. Often during the night, we would be wakened by a loud report, akin to rifle shot. It was only the piano's sound board reacting to a change of temperature.

Two: The flue serving the wood stove used to operate in reverse, and the persistent wind, instead of drawing the flames and smoke up the chimney, used to direct them back into the kitchen. It was therefore necessary to keep the stove's sliding doors closed at all times to counter the possibility of tongues of flame and belches of smoke darting out into the room.

Three: Lighting was confined to a petrol pressure lamp which had the frightening habit of engulfing itself in flames on being lit. On more than one occasion, it had to be thrown out the back door lest it explode and set our hessian house on fire.

Four: For similar reasons, Doreen had to do the ironing out-of-doors, just in case the petrol-iron misbehaved in the same way.

Five: The first time that she hung out the laundry to dry in our unfenced back yard — having washed it earlier using a wood fired portable copper and a galvanised bath tub — it was set upon and dragged from the clothes line by a herd of goats that marauded unrestrictedly around the town.

Another memorable highlight from our sojourn at Cue was the town's rather unique picture show, operated by Jack Hince, the local baker and foreman of the volunteer fire brigade.

Because the town's producer-gas engine powered electricity plant could not meet the demands of the cinema as well as the normal Saturday evening load, the picture show had its own generator, powered by a motor car engine. Except for those rare occasions when it rained, the pictures were shown in the open, and to the background noise of the engine and generator. The motor was fitted with a vacuum pump, which fed petrol from the fuel tank to the carburettor. When the vacuum pump malfunctioned patrons were treated to a start-stop show, while the carburettor was re-fuelled by hand.

There were interruptions too when a dust storm blew up. Not only was one's viewing impaired, but also did airborne sheets of dislodged roofing iron constitute a risk to the audience.

Recreation at Cue was relatively plentiful and included swimming in the collapsed workings of the abandoned Great Fingal mine. For want of something better, in hot weather a few foolhardy individuals would clamber down the vertical sides of the cave-in, using only an old wire rope for support. Once down, they would swim in the 90 metre deep water, and then would have to climb the 61 metres up to the surface, arriving there sick from swallowing some of the brine in which they had swum, face and eyes blasted by the blowing sand, and exhausted from the climb. On occasions, I participated in this crazy pastime.

Sadly, mining activity in the Murchison, which had taken a new lease of life in the 1930s, declined with the onset of World War II; and with it, railway traffic waned to such a degree that, after hanging on precariously for a number of years, the lines were closed progressively.

The first to go was that from Mount Magnet to Sandstone, over which the last train ran in 1947. The Big Bell line was next in 1956, and the Meekatharra–Wiluna section a year later. The final blow was delayed until May 1976, when all services between Mullewa and Meekatharra ceased, thus depriving the Murchison of what had been its lifeline for 78 years.

The Murchison was hot, dry and harsh, yet subject to sudden and unpredictable thunderstorms; sparsely populated; supporting millions of sheep and hundreds of millions of flies; the graveyard of many a mining venture; but with a spell all of its own.

The country that I lived in, worked in and grew to know and to love encompassed a relatively broad and varied slice, stretching over almost one half of the continent. It ranged, in Western Australia, from the heavy timber of the South West and the productive wheat and wool areas of the Great Southern, to the hot and dry Eastern Goldfields and Murchison: The Nullarbor Plain spanning two states: in South Australia and the Northern Territory, the old Oodnadatta Track to Alice Springs, Eyre Peninsula, the Riverland and the South East. Of these, I had two favourites— the Murchison and the Oodnadatta Track—but the Murchison holds Number one spot.

It was where I started my adult working life when, as a raw and inexperienced youth barely 22 years of age, I cut my engineering wisdom teeth; where I was initiated into bush life and work; and where I had my first contact with the Depression and the start of many years' association with unemployment relief works.

My own father succumbed to its spell late in life. He was 70 years old when he first saw the

Hannan Street, Kalgoorlie, 1931 (*Photo:* Library Board of Western Australia)

Murchison, yet, until his death eight years later, he went back there every winter.

To me, the Murchison was something special.

The Eastern Goldfields

In November 1931, I was sent to Kalgoorlie, originally for a period of two months but which lasted eight. It was the start of my six years on the wallaby and, incidentally, it meant that I commenced my adult career at the same place as did my father 34 years earlier.

For about 15 years, the goldfields had been moribund, but the economic depression seemed to have inspired a revival in the gold mining industry; and when at Larkinville south of Coolgardie on 15 January 1931, young Jim Larcombe drove his pick into the Golden Eagle, at 35,344 grams the State's largest nugget, it was the 1890s all over again — and this was especially evident in Kalgoorlie.

As a young man suddenly freed from the restrictions of continuous and concentrated study, Kalgoorlie was a wonderful place in which to live in the 1930s. It had changed dramatically since my parents were married there in 1901. Wide bituminised streets, substantial government buildings, a first class shopping district, the creation of a green belt around the town and a tree planting programme within its boundaries had all combined to make it liveable.

At that time, Kalgoorlie was also noted for two distinctly different institutions: Ben Leslie and the Kalgoorlie trams.

The town's mayor of long standing, Ben Leslie was a Colonel Sanders-like character, with his copious white mane and goatee beard, broad brimmed sombrero, shoe-string tie and charming old world mannerisms. Indeed, Thomas Wood, author of that delightful book *Cobbers*, was so entranced by Ben that he suggested he would have been an ideal intermediary at Geneva, where the power of his personality alone would surely have resolved international disputes.

On the other hand, Kalgoorlie's dilapidated electric tramway system was famous for very different reasons. In addition to lines connecting Kalgoorlie with Boulder and the mines at Boulder Block, there were services to the residential suburbs of Lamington, North Kalgoorlie and

The old baths, Kalgoorlie (*Photo:* Library Board of Western Australia)

South Kalgoorlie, as well as along Burt Street, Boulder. Small four-wheeled vehicles relying entirely on a hand-operated braking system literally bucked their way over the routes. Derailments did not mean a thing. The driver would reverse his overhead trolley, drive the tram back on to the rails and resume his precarious journey.

My most memorable ride took place one night when returning to Kalgoorlie from Boulder Block, or the Dirty Acre as it was appropriately nicknamed. After leaving the terminus and twisting along the Boulder Block Road — hemmed in on both sides by geometrically constructed slimes dumps — the driver negotiated the bridge over the

G.W. Fruin

Kanowna town dam (*Photo:* Eastern Goldfields Historical Society)

railway at Golden Gate. He then left the controls and allowed the tram to run unsupervised while he entered the passenger section to collect the fares. This must have been the normal procedure because the miners, who had come off afternoon shift, were quite unperturbed.

Every type of sport and recreation was available in Kalgoorlie in the 1930s, ranging from the legitimate to the illegal and the dicey.

The famous two-up school operated openly — and subject to a certain amount of tolerance by the authorities — at Brown Hill, adjacent to the Golden Mile; while the whippet races, conducted at the Halfway between Kalgoorlie and Boulder, were not without their suspicions. On race nights, some of the notorious electric trams were declared out-of-bounds to ordinary passengers and reserved for the dogs and their handlers.

Between races, the dogs were tethered to iron spikes driven into the ground. While the leashes were short enough to keep them apart, they did permit eyeball-to-eyeball confrontation and the resultant yapping, barking and yelping were deafening. It was common knowledge too that the unbacked dogs were fed a meat pie shortly before starting time, thus ensuring a degree of predictability in the finishing order.

Kalgoorlie could pride itself on the quality of its swimmers, who learned to swim and trained in the town's 25 yard (23 m) pool in Victoria Park.

The Golden Mile, Kalgoorlie, c. 1931 (*Photo:* WA Newspapers Ltd)

The pool lacked any treatment plant and the water, which was changed twice a week, soon turned into a thick brown repulsive brew. The 25 yarder was replaced in 1938 by Western Australia's first Olympic-sized pool, and the former one became an ornamental fish pond.

However, swimming was not confined to the Victoria Park pool. The Kanowna town dam was also a favourite spot, while Lake Gidgie, normally a dry salt pan north of Kalgoorlie, became the lido of the Goldfields after an occasional cloudburst — that is if one overlooked the fact that the the beach was sticky red loam.

This, the first of my three postings to Kalgoorlie, brought me again under George Fruin, one of the most charming of men and a first class railwayman. Our working relationship, which started in Northam in 1929, also included my second term on the Goldfields. It ended in 1942 after spending 18 months together at Narrogin.

My third term, from April 1942 to June 1944, coincided with the sharp increase in east–west military rail traffic that followed the fall of Singapore; this time under Ernie Morris, who some months earlier had been involved in a collision between his rail motor inspection vehicle and a motor truck in which he suffered fractures to both legs. In the early days after his return to work, he could scarcely walk; indeed, just to surmount a simple door step was an achievement. I have never witnessed such an example of unadulterated guts.

From his headquarters in Kalgoorlie, the District Engineer's territory extended 333 kilometres west to Merredin, 338 kilometres north to Laverton and 377 kilometres south from Coolgardie to Esperance. Apart from the Kalgoorlie–Boulder environs, the bustle of the gold rush days had all but disappeared, but — particularly north of Kalgoorlie and south of Coolgardie to Norseman — there remained many nostalgic reminders of the roaring days long since past.

Travelling over the Kalgoorlie maintenance district was a lonely operation. There were only two towns between Merredin and Kalgoorlie; Southern Cross and Coolgardie. The other names on the map — Burracoppin, Carrabin, Boddalin and Moorine Rock — were barely whistle stops.

On the 183 kilometres run from Southern Cross to Coolgardie, there existed only the Karalee and Bullabulling pubs, set down inexplicably in total isolation; three Goldfields Water Supply Department pumping stations; and an occasional permanent way maintenance gang. Travelling over this semi-desert in relative comfort, one could not but admire the prospectors who, in the 1890s, pushed eastwards from Southern Cross over inhospitable and not auriferous country, to discover the Coolgardie and other goldfields.

Perhaps it would be incorrect to describe the Karalee and Bullabulling pubs as being inexplicably located.

They were remote sidings situated 171 and 68 kilometres west of Kalgoorlie, where trains stopped for seven minutes while the steam locomotive took on water. The two places were regarded as oases by the thirsty passengers on the 'Dry' Kalgoorlie Express, especially those travelling from the Kalgoorlie end, where a liberal interpretation of the liquor laws made the consumption of alcoholic drinks a way of life. As soon as the train started to slow down at either siding, the more athletic of the passengers would jump off and run helter skelter to the hotels, both to consume as much liquor as the seven minutes available to them would allow and to buy some bottled beer — a scarce commodity and a form of currency during the war years.

The locomotive drivers were considerate. They would give a long blast of the whistle a minute or two before departure, then move off slowly to enable any laggards to jump on board.

During World War II, the purchase of bottled beer by servicemen was forbidden in Western Australia. However, the regularity with which this edict was disregarded at Bullabulling led the army authorities to station two military policemen at the siding. Neither would have been very proud of his contribution towards the winning of the war in the Pacific.

Two factors must have contributed to the economic demise of the two pubs: one, the advent of diesel locomotive power and, with it, the abolition of locomotive watering; and two, with the standardisation of the Perth–Kalgoorlie railway, its diversion away from the former route eastwards of Southern Cross.

The country north of Kalgoorlie to Leonora and Laverton, although experiencing something of a revival in the 1930s, was still only a shell of its former self. Substantial stone buildings reduced to rubble, mullock heaps, abandoned head frames and shafts in a state of collapse all combined to constitute a mute requiem to the frenzy that followed the original gold finds at Bayleys and Hannans. But it was not always so. At the turn of the 20th century, a daily train served the thriving communities of Paddington, Broad Arrow, Bardoc, Scotia, Goongarrie, Comet Vale, Yunndaga, Menzies, Jessop's Well, Niagara, Kookynie, Malcolm, Gwalia, Leonora, Murrin Murrin, Morgans and Laverton.

Niagara, 183 kilometres north of Kalgoorlie, (and a place more remote and less like its North American namesake it would be difficult to imagine), had been, for over 20 years, nothing more than a heap of rubble. Yet in the roaring days it boasted an hotel on each of the four corners of an intersection. Neither Kalgoorlie nor Boulder could claim such a distinction.

Six kilometres beyond Niagara stood what was left of Kookynie, which at one time had a population of 9000. When Harry Sandercock opened Kookynie's first pharmacy over 100 years ago, he was besieged by prospectors seeking dental treatment, an activity that chemists were authorised to practise in those days. His takings on his opening night from teeth-pulling alone amounted to $18. One hundred years ago, that was big money.

By 1932, however, the town's commercial establishment limited to an hotel and a combined general store, post office and savings bank. Once, camped there in a survey van, I deposited my salary cheque with the savings bank and, over the same counter, bought a shilling's worth of potatoes. The proprietor could not change a ten shilling (one dollar) note!

Gwalia, 256 kilometres north of Kalgoorlie and three kilometres short of Leonora, was, for a short time about 1900 the home of Herbert Hoover, then a young mining engineer and manager of the Sons of Gwalia mine. Thirty years later, he became President of the United States. Incidentally, the mine was still working at the time of writing.

It was on this line too that, as a young man — straight from the university and thrilled at seeing the outback for the first time — I was taught a salutary lesson. Don't talk down to anyone, however humble.

I was camped in the survey van at Broad Arrow and, one afternoon, I was talking to an Aborigine, a gentle fellow — patriarchal, sporting a long dust stained grey beard, and with only a limited command of English. There had been a congregation of Aborigines at Broad Arrow, and when I asked him when he intended moving on he held up one hand with the five fingers extended and, pointing to each one in turn, said:

'This one that way', pointing north, 'this one that way', pointing south, and so on until the fifth finger indicated that he intended patronising the third northbound train, freeloading of course, in an open wagon

That evening, having finished my dinner, I had about one half a saucepanful of tinned dog and haricot bean stew left over, and seeing whom I assumed was the same Aborigine, called out to him:

'Jackie, you likem some stew'?'

The reply came back in perfect English:

'It wouldn't be bad for a change.'

It wasn't the same Aborigine!

This was my first contact with non-urban Aborigines. Later, having worked with them, lived in the same camps as them and messed with them, I developed a deep respect and affection for them.

Around Coolgardie there was Fly Flat where, in 1892, Arthur Bayley and William Ford changed forever the face of Western Australia when they discovered gold — or perhaps where Tommy Talbot found gold but Bayley and Ford lodged the first reward claim. The surrounding country was pitted with abandoned shafts. A few kilometres south of Coolgardie stood derelict headframes at Burbanks and Londonderry, the latter the site of one of the richest, yet short-lived, glory holes in the goldfield's history. Indeed, old workings dotted the landscape for the 85 kilometres south to Widgemooltha.

Nevertheless, during the 14 years which covered my four years' on-and-off association with this district, the Esperance line remained a lonely one. Except for the railway gangs, the only settlements in the 375 kilometres from Coolgardie to Esperance were Widgemooltha, comprising an hotel and a store; Higginsville, with a store; Norseman, a relatively small but not unattractive mining town; and Salmon Gums, like Widgemooltha, with an hotel and a store.

Salmon Gums had been planned as the junction station for a railway to serve a developmental project in the State's south-eastern wheatbelt. Known as the Three Thousand Five Hundred Farms Scheme, it was the brainchild of the Premier, Sir James Mitchell. However, the railway content of the scheme did not progress beyond the survey stage. After investigations had revealed the existence of excessive soil salinity, and Philip Collier, who had succeeded Mitchell, found it a ready made excuse for abandoning the scheme.

Salmon Gums could, however, claim the distinction of being the home town of Emil Nulsen, licensee of the local pub and MLA for the vast electorate of Kanowna, who held the Railways portfolio for a number of years.

Activities in a District Office centred around the continued maintenance of and improvement to existing tracks and structures, as well as carrying out of the lesser capital works, including relaying and reballasting. Major works projects were undertaken by separate units and, when completed, handed over to the relevant District Engineer.

The duties of the Assistant Engineer in a District Office were essentially those of supporting — and, where necessary, understudying — the District Engineer. This included a large measure of surveying, as well as supervision of capital works. However, in emergencies, such as washaways and derailments, he would have added responsibilities.

In those days, the District Engineer's Office was located in the railway station building and opened out on to the passenger platform. On my first day there, in November 1931, I was confronted with the sight of a herd of goats foraging down the station yard from east to west, devouring all manner of things peculiarly digestable to them. I was to learn that this invasion was a daily habit and strictly to the same time table; 2.50 pm precisely. It kept the station yard free from scrap paper, and it was rumoured that mayoral connections with the herd kept them out of the municipal pound.

For about 40 years, the WA Goldfields Firewood Company operated a small but efficient 1067 mm narrow gauge railway, commonly known as the Kurrawang Wood Line. Starting from Kamballie at the southern end of the Golden Mile, the railway cut across to Kurrawang on the WAGR main line 13 kilometres west of Kalgoorlie. It then extended northwards from Kurrawang, shifting the line as the timber cut out. Finally, it swung south, again crossing the main line, this time at Calooli, 14 kilometres west of Coolgardie. From this point, the line stretched as far as 130 kilometres to the south and south-west.

It was a mobile establishment at the rail head. The main camp consisted of transportable buildings, crude by today's standards, as well as a number of dwellings permanently on railway wheels. When the main camp shifted to a new site, the location of all buildings relative to each other remained the same. The main camp did not shift very often, but the spur lines to the cutting areas were in a continual state of being taken up and relaid elsewhere.

Although the company had its own locomotives and rolling stock, at times WAGR vehicles travelled over the line. In order to assess royalty payments, the Railway Department would undertake periodical measurements of the lengths of the main and spur lines. This would be carried out using a pull-tricycle — colloquially known as an Armstrong — fitted with a revolution counter, the number of revolutions being converted into distance. In January 1932, I made one such measurement, at which time the longest spur had reached a point only a few kilometres west of Pioneer, a lonely siding on the Coolgardie–Esperance railway just 43 kilometres short of Norseman.

The most interesting part of the exercise was travelling on the locomotive of a loaded train en route to Kurrawang. Naturally, it was wood burning. At one stage, the fireman crammed into the firebox as much fuel as it would take; this was to raise a full head of steam in anticipation of a steep grade ahead. A siding had been provided to permit the halving of the load and taking it over the grade in two sections, but this was regarded as akin to defeatism, and the crews exerted every effort to surmount the grade in one piece.

This was also the first and only time that I have seen an engine driver oil the crank pin bearing on a locomotive using a large enamelled teapot as an oil can!

There were two intriguing items of equipment on the locomotive; a set of small seats outrigged from the side rails of the cab, and a coil of armoured hose coupled to a steam cock on the engine. The reason for the seats soon became apparent. The driver and fireman sat on them and literally rode outside of the cab. In this way they benefited from the breeze generated by the movement of the train, as well as avoiding direct heat from the firebox. However, the purpose of the hose remained a mystery for a little while longer until the firewood on the tender caught alight. Such an eventuality was inevitable, because the funnel did not emit sparks; rather did it belch forth lumps of burning wood.

Almost apathetically, the fireman uncoiled the hose, turned on the steam cock, sprayed the tender and extinguished the fire in a matter of moments. Throughout the whole episode, the driver, who seemed to be quite uninterested, did not once touch the regulator, and the beat of the locomotive continued steady and uninterrupted. It was not uncommon for the firewood being carried in the wagons on the trains to ignite and at Calooli, where the wood line crossed both the WAGR main line and the Goldfields water pipeline, the company had installed a row of standpipes from which water could be directed on to any vehicles whose contents might have caught fire en route.

Eventually, the depletion of the sources of wood and the increased use of coal and fuel oil on the mines forced the closure of the Kurrawang Wood Line. It was, however, an efficient little organisation when in operation.

When, in April 1942, I took up my third posting to Kalgoorlie as Assistant Engineer to E.W. Morris, urgent wartime rail activities resulted in a substantial increase in obligations and responsibilities. In addition, I was able to relieve him of some of the tasks rendered difficult to him after his return to work from his rail motor accident.

The task of modifying buildings and structures to permit the rail movement of over-sized military loads, and to direct the diversion of loading around those places where such adjustments could not be made, became the responsibility of the District Engineer. Indeed, over the two years during which I was stationed in the Kalgoorlie District, either Morris or I had to be on hand day and night to inspect and, where necessary, to determine the routing on the WAGR of military loading passing through Kalgoorlie from the eastern states.

The decision to station certain elements of the AIF's armoured division in Western Australia and, with it, the movement of General Grant tanks by rail on the narrow gauge system posed special problems. Not only did the tanks infringe standard clearances, but also was it necessary to strengthen the rail vehicles used for their transportation. This combination of excessive outline and weight meant that mishaps en route were to be expected.

On the night of Good Friday 1943, a westbound military train carrying the tanks was derailed between Nulla Nulla and Noongaar, some 260 kilometres and 35 kilometres west of Kalgoorlie and Southern Cross respectively. Approximately one kilometre of track was badly damaged and three General Grant tanks broke their lashings and finished on the permanent way, one upright and the other two on their sides.

After a rather disturbed night on the telephone, I left Kalgoorlie early next morning and, using both goods train and hitch-hiking, reached the scene shortly before midday, there to find the permanent way gangs hard at it effecting repairs. Learning that, on an eastbound military train held up at Merredin, 72 kilometres distant, was the Western Australian contingent of the railway construction unit of the AIF, I arranged for them to be worked forward to assist with the repairs. The unit, which included a number of my friends from construction days, had recently returned from the Middle East, and those on the train were travelling to the eastern states after home leave. The senior non-commissioned officer with the party was Sergeant Arthur Jackman, with whom I spent some time on construction and who, some eight years later, followed me to Port Augusta as Buildings Surveyor.

The men had been held up at Merredin for about eight hours and had occupied their time as soldiers are wont to do the world over. Consequently, when they arrived at the scene of the derailment their level of sobriety was minimal. Nevertheless, we set them to work.

With one man crouching on his hands and knees Middle East style and acting as cheer leader calling the shots, they proceeded to lay rails, bolt-up fishplates, bore sleepers and drive dogspikes virtually on top of each other. It was unnerving just to watch them, but for some incomprehensible reason, except perhaps for the guardian angel who seems to watch over the inebriated, there were no injuries.

This incident illustrated the ruggedness of the General Grant tank. The undamaged one pulled the other two on to their tracks. After some spilt battery acid had been wiped up, their power units were started and all three were driven to the Noongaar siding and reloaded on to railway flat wagons to complete their journey.

My association with the Kalgoorlie District Engineer's Office and with the Goldfields itself ended in June 1944, when I was transferred to Head Office in Perth to undertake preparatory work in connection with Sir Harold Clapp's enquiry into rail standardisation.

My three periods of service at Kalgoorlie were both happy and nostalgic. Not only did they provide me with the opportunity to absorb the Eastern Goldfields' romantic history, but they triggered memories of the fact that I had worked where my father had started his railway career 31 years earlier.

The Great Southern

In 1889 the Great Southern Railway Company — an English establishment — opened its private railway from Albany, on the south coast, to Beverley, 389 kilometres to the north, where it connected with the WAGR's line from Perth.

The line was built on the land grant system, whereby the company was granted a specified number of acres of land for every mile of line (251.5 hectares per kilometre) and, in this case, the land granted paralleled the railway on either side. The whole area became known as the Great Southern. The line was taken over by the State in 1896 and became part of Government Railway system.

Six stations on the GSR — Brookton, Narrogin, Wagin, Katanning, Tambellup and Elleker — were junctions for a total of 11 lines, six on the eastern side and five on the western; and, apart from branch lines serving agricultural activities, they constituted an integral part of a rail network with links to the Perth metropolitan area, the Eastern Goldfields Railway, the coalmining town of Collie and the port of Bunbury.

Of these lines, the Great Southern Division of the WAGR, which was administered from Narrogin, totalled 1526 route kilometres and extended from Beverley to Albany, Brookton to Corrigin, Narrogin to Merredin by two separate lines, Narrogin to Dwarda, Wagin to Hyden and Newdegate, Katanning to Pingrup, Tambellup to Ongerup, and from Elleker to Nornalup.

Apart from the Dwarda and Nornalup sections, all other lines leading westwards were under the control of either the District Engineer Perth or his counterpart at Bunbury.

The lines leading to Bunbury carried heavy loads of grain for export while, in the opposite

Hillman Reservoir, Western Australia, 1934, start of excavation (*Photo:* the author)

were suspended between two large iron wheels, looked something like Roman chariots, although their drivers walked alongside them.

Water was allowed into the reservoir immediately after the excavation was complete, although the roofing still awaited construction. It was the practice in Western Australia to roof railway reservoirs, as it saved as much as 2.5 metres of evaporation a year. The roof structure consisted of jarrah posts set on concrete blocks and supporting joists and purlins, and topped with asbestos-cement sheets, which at that time were not considered a health risk.

Because the reservoir was holding and continuing to receive water, we constructed a raft, using empty petrol drums for buoyancy and fitted with a timber jib. This enabled us to attach the posts to pre-cast concrete foundation blocks on dry land and, by means of the jib, to manoeuvre them into place even though the dam might be holding up to four metres of water.

Williams

Almost concurrent with the completion of the Hillman job, the decision was made to build another, though smaller, excavated reservoir at Williams, so off I went to Williams with Bob Henderson, Arthur Read and most of my gang.

Compared with Wurarga's and Hillman's lack of amusement and diversion, Williams provided an abundance of recreation; — sport, an itinerant moving picture show and an occasional swim in the Arthur River, 25 kilometres down the Albany Highway.

Not only did the transfer from Hillman bring me back to comparative civilisation, but it was at Williams that I met Doreen, and so set the shape of my life and saw the start of 60 glorious years of married bliss, preceded by two years of courtship by remote control. We had another reason too for the retention of fond memories of Williams. As a result of departmental exigencies, our daughter Rosalind happened to be born there in July 1942.

In 1940, I had been appointed to Narrogin, and it was there that Doreen became pregnant for the second time. However, after the outbreak in December 1941 of the war against Japan, — and particularly after the fall of Singapore, — there

was a dramatic increase in rail traffic between the Eastern States and Western Australia; and, at 48 hours' notice, I was transferred to Kalgoorlie to assist District Engineer Morris.

At that time, Doreen was six months into her pregnancy and to maintain contact with Dr Savage — her local medico who, in addition to practising at Narrogin, also consulted at Williams — it was decided that I should proceed to Kalgoorlie alone, and that Doreen and son Russell, then nearly four years old, should move to Williams and stay with her parents.

Rosalind, our pride and joy, was born at Williams on the morning of 2 July 1942; and, at age three weeks — accommodated in a makeshift baby capsule consisting of a cardboard cereal carton, adorned on the outside with decorative wallpaper and appropriately cushioned and blanketed inside — she accompanied her mother and elder brother by rail to join me at Kalgoorlie, where we spent the next two years while I completed my third term of duty on the Eastern Goldfields.

Before completing my Hillman and Williams story, I should relate the legend of W.E. Wood, to whom brief reference has been made in the Tin Pot Alley story. It was to him, the District Engineer Bunbury, to whom I reported while stationed on those two jobs.

'A very remarkable man and one upon whose head the span of 65 years rest [sic] very lightly.

'Small of stature but physically tireless, he is the embodiment of those characteristics which have been immortalised in Caesar, Napoleon, Disraeli and others. Indefatigably energetic, assiduously studious, relentlessly determined, he, like many great men, has erred only in that his personal standard is higher than that to which the average man can attain.'

Such a eulogy could only have been written about one of the giants of history — Churchill perhaps — and then by someone overcome with adulation.

But no; it was Wood writing his own valedictory. On the eve of his retirement in 1937, Clem Robinson, editor of the staff journal *The Railway and Tramway Magazine*, asked Wood for some biographical notes. In response, he submitted a 1500 word panegyric which, with tongue in cheek, the editor published verbatim, well knowing that the readers would quickly guess the identity of the writer.

My first close encounter with him was at the start of the Hillman job when Arthur Read, not aware that there was a telephone in the cabin at the siding, said: 'I suppose that they will put on a telephone for us.' Wood blustered: 'They? Who do you mean by "They"?'

Arthur replied: 'The telephone people', and this made Willie Wood furious. 'I'll have you understand that I'm the District Engineer and I'll do that. Don't you ever bloody-well talk "They" to me!'

Nevertheless, and apart from being the supreme egotist, Wood was a competent maintenance engineer, a good bushman and an excellent shot. It was somewhat unnerving to ride passenger with him on a rail motor section car and suddenly to find a double-barrelled shotgun traversing across the front of your face while he picked off a duck or a pigeon in full flight. However, I do not recall his bag ever having included a passenger.

Once, I was instructed to meet him at Bowelling, south of Hillman, ostensibly to assist him in an investigation, but my duties turned out to be more those of a retriever dog than of an engineer. The waterholes around Bowelling were the haunt of wild duck, and every time that Wood shot one — and he went nowhere without his gun — I had to strip and wade, or even swim, to recover the bird. Often, on returning to the bank, I would have to rid myself of a number of leeches. Usually, I was rewarded with the birds' giblets!

The stories about Wood were legendary among members of the Civil Engineering Branch, as were those he told about himself and his prowess. More-over, he seemed to believe them. No one else did.

At one stage he developed a mixture of bitumen and sawdust which when put into enlarged dogspike holes in sleepers, would, hopefully, restore their holding capacity. Known throughout the Branch as Wood's Great Peppermint Cure, the concoction, unlike its pharmaceutical namesake, did not work.

My departure from Narrogin in April 1942 ended my association with the Great Southern. Having to leave Narrogin and to be deprived of George Fruin's company and friendship was a sad disappointment.

Nevertheless, and in spite of the personal problems that it entailed, I feel that my accepting the transfer without protest was to my ultimate advantage. It resulted in a more meaningful participation in the railways' contribution to the war effort, and from a personal point of view I had the privilege of witnessing at first hand Ernie Morris' personal courage.

The South West

One Friday afternoon in August 1935, I received 48 hours' notice to transfer from Meekatharra in the Murchison to Allanson in the South West, five kilometres from Collie. It represented the ultimate in contrasts — from the mild Murchison winter to the cold, wet South West gloom where, in successive years, the rainfall amounted to 1320 and 1435 mm, and from sparse mulga scrub to massive jarrah and redgum trees.

The shift to Allanson, which preceded my Big Bell experiences, marked my introduction to railway construction after three years of digging reservoirs.

The Brunswick Junction–Collie railway, 41 kilometres long and opened in 1898, was, physically, one of the most difficult lines in the State; it was also most definitely the heaviest trafficked branch line. Its main purpose was to move coal from the

Staff quarters, Allanson; mess building in the foreground (*Photo:* the author)

Tracklaying, Allanson, 1936 (*Photo:* the author)

Newly laid track in cutting (*Photo:* the author)

Collie field to the Perth metropolitan area, but it also carried heavy loadings of grain and timber to Bunbury. In the reverse direction it handled large tonneages of superphosphate from the works at Picton Junction and as many as 24 trains worked over the line each day. The ruling grade in each direction was 1 in 40, and the line climbed 224 metres in only 24 kilometres from Brunswick Junction to the summit at Penrith before dropping 72 metres in the remaining 17 kilometres to Collie.

The curvature too was heavy; 134 curves in the 41 kilometres, some of them as sharp as 201m radius.

It was a line calling out for grade improvement and in 1934, Jack Shaw, an engineer with both a bent and an enthusiasm for railway location, set out to achieve this. After nine months of exacting work he surveyed a deviation 13 kilometres long which effectively reduced the ruling grade in the western, or heaviest trafficked, direction to 1 in 80. In this instance he also reversed the usual practice of increasing the length of line when effecting grade improvements, shortening the deviation by about 200 metres and at the same time eliminating eight curves. It was a fine piece of railway location.

Construction started in 1935 with Frank Carter as Resident Engineer. A New Zealander, Carter came to Australia in the early 1920s and, for a period, worked with the Commonwealth Railways at Port Augusta and then in the Northern Territory. When he came to Western Australia, joining the Railway Construction Branch of the Public Works Department, he worked on the surveys of the Leighton–Robbs Jetty and the Salmon Gums westwards railways. Later, he was posted to Meekatharra as Resident Engineer, succeeding Cedric Stewart, who was directed to other projects.

Our living conditions at Allanson, site of a former saw mill, were much better than those in my construction camps: a weatherboard cabin with 32 volt electric light supplied by a Delco portable power plant; a mess under the control of a cook; and amenities available at nearby Collie, a prosperous coal mining and railway town.

Bill Costello, our cook, had at one time worked in the kitchen of Melbourne's prestigious Menzies Hotel before graduating in reverse to railway construction camps. Bill was myopic and his habit of quietly and unobtrusively closing the mess door as soon as he had served the main course at lunch time made it as hard for the diners, with their normal sight, to determine the relative freshness of the cold meat as Bill, whose impaired vision failed at times to detect the ravages of the blowflies.

Farewell to the WAGR

On 22 May 1949, after 22 rewarding years, I left WAGR to join the Commonwealth Railways at Port Augusta, South Australia, as its Chief Civil Engineer. The move was not made without some reluctance, but there were a number of factors that influenced my acceptance of the position offered.

Following upon the blatant and persistent anti-railways prejudice shown by Minister

Hamilton River Bridge, three 50 foot (15 m) spans (*Photo:* the author)

Concrete arch culvert, Allanson, 1936 (*Photo:* the author)

Seward, as well as the grossly, unfair criticisms in the report of the Gibson–du Plessis Royal Commission, it became apparent that the Government seemed determined to import staff from elsewhere. At the time, it appeared to presage an impediment to my career path. I was pressed by Chief Civil Engineer Hood to submit an application for the position of Assistant Commissioner Engineering in the three-man Commission, but it was neither successful nor even acknowledged.

But perhaps the biggest incentive to the move was that of improved living conditions. Being transferred around the railway system by direction and not by choice resulted in my return to Perth, shortly before the end of World War II, at a time when there were rigid controls over new home construction. It was in that climate that, for five years, we were obliged to accept accommodation unbefitting a prospective senior officer; and this included a period of sharing a house with a stranger and under conditions of tension. Postwar, home building permits were virtually impossible to obtain, even though I offered the Housing Authority the right to allocate our existing house to any person of its choice, and to whom it would be both acceptable and within financial reach.

As a consequence, the prospect of a new modern house at Port Augusta was the deciding factor in the move.

It would be appropriate to observe that, after the disastrous decade that followed the creation of the three-man WAGR Commission, the administration reverted to that of a single Commissioner.

Bill Brodie and Tom Marsland acted as caretaker Commissioners until 1959 when Cyril Wayne, General Manager of the Tasmanian Railways, was appointed Commissioner of Railways for Western Australia. His arrival coincided with the system's upward climb to a position not excelled by any other railway in this country

The renaissance was brought about by Wayne's capable and sympathetic administration; the development of the Koolyanobbing iron ore deposit, thus providing a stimulus to the Perth–Kalgoorlie standard gauge project; the economic explosion that took place in Western Australia during the 1960s; and, most importantly, the enthusiasm and confidence displayed by the entire railway staff.

Even as an expatriate, it gave me a great deal of personal satisfaction to see the WAGR overcome the tragic aftermath of earlier unwarranted political antipathy and intervention.

Distances were measured in miles, chains, links and decimals of a link. In metric terms, one mile equalled 1.609 kilometres; one chain (66 feet) 20.117 metres; and one link (one-hundredth of a chain) 20.117 centimetres.

Levelling staffs were graduated in feet and hundredths of a foot, the latter approximating one-eighth of an inch or three millimetres. It was a good scale with which to work, and provided a satisfactory degree of accuracy.

The data obtained from the trial survey would be used to prepare a contour plan; and on it, the paper location, or the ultimate alignment, would be determined. Except in easy country where the ruling grade was not the predominant factor, the paper location always varied somewhat from the trial traverse, both in respect of the straights and of the insertion of appropriate curves. The essential characteristics of the paper location would then be transferred on to the ground in the form of the permanent survey.

In undertaking the paper location, it was necessary at times to try a number of possible alignments in an endeavour to minimise the earthworks. However, with the development of heavy mechanical equipment, the cost of earthworks has been reduced to such an extent that chasing the contours is now a thing of the past, and long gun-barrel straights are the norm. But it was not so prewar.

The permanent survey started with the establishment on the ground of those points where the paper location straights intersected, and, from the readings of the subtended angles, the essential characteristics of the curves were calculated and marked out on the ground. Then, starting from the zero point, the final alignment would be measured and levelled; and from this information the construction plan, known as the plan and section, was prepared in the drawing office — sometimes in a tent in the field. The plan showed, relative to true north, the bearings of the straights, the subtended angles at their intersections, and trigonometrical details of the curves; while the section indicated the profile of the country, the grading of the formation, the depths of cuttings and heights of banks, as well as the location of bridges and culverts.

The nature of material to be encountered in the cuttings was ascertained by bore holes sunk by hand auger, and was a muscle-wrenching operation. Where rivers or other defined watercourses were encountered, the sizes of the bridges and culverts were determined by a study of the stream beds and flood markings. For minor depressions, the catchment area was measured by a prismatic compass survey and paced distances, and the run-off factor assessed by an examination of the country. From this, the dimension of the culvert would be calculated.

The surveyor's bible was a volume of *Chambers' Mathematical Tables*, which, apart from a set of seven-figure logarithms, contained trigonometrical data necessary for calculation in the field of curve characteristics. These calculations were manual ones, undertaken without electronic or mechanical assistance. Indeed, the only mathematical aid at that time was a 10-inch (254 mm) slide rule, precise only to the third place and insufficiently accurate for survey calculations.

Survey instruments too were relatively primitive. My 1897 vintage Cooke Troughton and Sims theodolite lacked a moveable head, necessitating the plumbing of the instrument over a survey mark by no other means than the manipulation of its tripod legs. The length of accurate vision was also limited, a sight exceeding 20 chains (402.3 m) was virtually impossible; indeed, during the summer, the haze and shimmer was such that even shorter ones were difficult. On the Cue–Big Bell railway construction, I used to start surveying at about 5 am in an attempt to beat the shimmer. Accurate readings with a level were also restricted, generally to four chains (80.5 m), often even less.

Today, one sees tripod markers set over survey points, and a surveyor can sight them from long distances, but prewar, we had to resort to pickets. These were lengths of native timber up to six feet (1.8 m) long, cut from a growing tree and, using the chainman's razor-sharp axe, shaped to a long tapered point at its thinner end and to a shorter but more substantial one at the other. Using a small notch cut into it — or the stump if a branch had been removed — as the striking point, the picket was driven into the ground; and, using a plumb-bob on a long string, plumbed so that the

Driving a survey picket (*Photo:* the author)

Spinning a cross hair (*Photo:* the author)

tip of the finely tapered end was directly over the survey mark. It required a great deal of skill and a steady hand to do this, particularly when the tip of the picket might be more than four feet (1.2 m) above the peg, but both the surveyors and the chainmen became proficient in the operation. A small square paper, coloured half red and half white, affixed to the tip of the picket assisted the surveyor in his sighting of it.

Sometimes the cross hairs in the theodolite or level would break, generally as the result of moisture getting into the telescope. In the field, the remedial process involved the capture of a suitable spider.

First, a small forked twig — a miniature of that used in a shanghai — would be plucked from a tree. Next, a spider would be enticed to lodge on one of the prongs, and then the twig rotated so as to unseat the spider, which, in falling, would lay a thread across the fork. If more than one cross hair had been damaged, the twig would be rotated again and the spider encouraged to spin as many threads as might be required. Having done its job, the spider would be dispatched and, after having applied a touch of glue to the appropriate spots on the eyepiece, the thread would be carefully positioned and disconnected from the twig.

The chainmen's part in the survey should not be overlooked. Not only did they have to get the feel of the country, but they also had to understand the surveyor's procedures and, in the absence of walkie-talkies, interpret his signals from distances of 400 metres or even further. In time, a special rapport used to develop between them, and many a young engineer in his formative years — including me — was nurtured, indeed carried, by his chainmen.

Railway location was a slow and at times a frustrating operation, involving tent living — often in inclement weather — rudimentary facilities for the carrying out of calculations and plan drawing, and isolation in the bush for long periods. It was, however, an interesting and satisfying one.

Prior to the start of construction, the whole of the surveyed route would be walked by the engineer equipped with a proof copy of the plan and section. He would check the correctness of the alignment; the adequacy of the waterways proposed; the location of side drains to be constructed alongside the formation to protect it from run-off after rain; what road diversions and level crossings were necessary; where the line was to be fenced and the nature of any such fencing.

Work actually started with the clearing of the right of way. By today's standards, it was a laborious process. Such tools as chainsaws

Australian Railwayman

and bulldozers were not even thought of, and the cross-cut saw, axe and mattock were the only ones available. Consequently, in heavily timbered country, the task was akin to trying to crack a granite boulder with a rubber hammer. The disposal of the fallen timber and stumps could also be a problem. On one job, we utilised a 12-strong bullock team to drag them clear of the centre line, but in general it was necessary to drill holes in a log using a hand auger, then blast it apart with gelignite prior to burning.

In the light of today's powerful bulldozers, huge self-propelled scrapers and carryalls, the manner in which the earthworks were constructed prewar is barely comprehensible. Except for rock cuttings — where, in most cases, the holes to take the explosives were drilled either by jumper or hammer and tap — the only mechanical aids were the single furrow plough, dray, tumbling tommy and wheeled scoops, and wheelbarrow. The earth was broken up by a plough and, except where scoops were used, shovelled into drays by teams of four men and carted to a bank, or to a dump if surplus, and tipped.

The tumbling tommy scoop was a horse-drawn steel contraption, best described as being like a large grocer's scoop, holding about four cubic feet (0.11 cubic metres) and with two short wooden handles at the back. To fill it, the operator would grasp the handles and, with the horse pulling it along, would direct the front cutting edge into the earth. When full, the scoop would be dragged to the point of disposal and emptied by the driver again grasping the handles and overturning the scoop. The tumbling tommy had limited application, its use usually being confined to the excavation of shallow cuttings, or the construction of low banks from borrow pits alongside the line.

On rare occasions, a dragline might be available, but even those were prehistoric; indeed, at times they were steam-powered.

The earthworks gangers had a high degree of responsibility, giving lie to the belief that all navvies lacked intelligence. Each was issued with an earthworks book covering his section of the work, and in it were detailed the depth of cutting or height of bank at each chain (20.1 m); the alignment; gradient; batter (or angle of side slopes); the location of side drains and of bridges, culverts, cattle pits and other installations.

His first job was to transfer the centre line and level pegs clear of the proposed earthworks, keeping a record not only of the offset distances, but also any adjustment to the peg level due to any cross fall in the natural surface. He did this using a tape, straightedge and spirit level.

The ganger would then have to define the outer extremities of each cutting or bank, allowing for both the finished width of the formation and the side slopes, or batters. For example, a cutting five feet (1.5 m) deep, 16 feet (4.9 m) wide at the base, and with a 1 to 1 or 45 degrees batter, would be 26 feet (7.9 m) wide at the top, and the earthworks marked out to this dimension. On ground with no cross slope, this would represent 13 feet (3.9 m) on either side of the centre line; but, in most cases, there would be some side slope, and the ganger would have to adjust the setting out accordingly. This demanded a degree of accuracy on his part, particularly when it applied to a deep cutting on a sharp curve; but a good ganger was capable of completing the excavation with the centre line of the formation in the right place. To do this, he used a batter gauge, a right angled triangular wooden template with its adjacent sides of such lengths that, when the appropriate one was levelled with a spirit level, the hypotenuse lay at the right slope. Where a 1 to 1 batter applied, the adjacent sides were of the same length; while for

Tumbling tommy scoops on Trans Australian Railway construction, c. 1915 (*Photo:* Schiller Collection)

EARTHWORKS BOOK

MILES	CHS.	CUT	BANK	LINE	GRADE	BATTER	SIDE DRAIN	CULVERTS ETC.	GANGER'S NOTES
17	00	6'1"							Reg offset 16' left 1'9" down
	1	4'2"				1 TO 1			14' " 2'0" "
	2	3'0"							14' " 2'0" "
	3	2½"							12' " level
	4		3'9"	STR.	1				16' " level
	5		7'7¾"		IN		BOTH		22' " level
	6		9'3½"		80	1½ TO 1	SIDES	17M. 6c. 45L. 5' CONC. ARCH CULV'T.	25' " up 1'0"
	7		10'4½"						26' " up 2'6"
	8		9'6½"						25' " up 2'3"
	9		6'2"						18' " up 2'0"
	10	2¾"							12' " level
	11	2'11"							14' " level
	12	7'5½"		R. 25CHS	1	1 TO 1	LEFT		18' " level
	13	7'3"			IN				18' " level
	14	3'0"			89				14' " 9" down
	15		5'1¾"					17M. 15c 50L. 30" CONC. PIPE CULV'T	18' " level
	16		5'6½"						18' " level
	17		5'2"			1½ TO 1	BOTH		18' " level
	18		5'4¾"						18' " level
	19		6'1"						19' " level
	20		5'8¼"	STR.	1 IN				18' " level
	21		3'11"		80				16' " level
	22		3'8½"				LEFT		16' " level

RAIL AND SLEEPER BOOK

TANGENT POINT			LENGTH		LINE	RAILS					SLEEPERS				
						NUMBER		BENDING ORDINATE			JOINT	3'6"	3'6¼"	3'6⅜"	3'6½"
M.	C.	L.	C.	L.		40'	GREEN END 39'7"	NUMBER	MID POINT	¼ POINT	WHITE CROSS	WHITE SPOT	RED SPOT	GREEN SPOT	BLUE SPOT
17	06	84	6	84	STR.	22					22	154			
	18	08	11	24	R. 25c. RIGHT	34	4	4 34	STR 1½"	1⅛"	38	266			
	43	77	25	69	STR.	84					84	588			
	59	75	15	98	R. 30c. LEFT	50	4		STR.		54	378			
18	06	47	26	72	STR.	88					88	616			
	19	83	13	36	R. 20c. RIGHT	38	6	8 36	STR 1⅞"	1⅜"	44	46	262		
	46	71	26	88	STR.	88					88	616			
	57	38	10	67	R. 15c RIGHT	30	6	4 4 28	STR 1⅞" 2⅜"	1⅜" 1⅞"	36	46	32	174	
	65	85	8	47	STR.	28					28	196			
	78	67	12	82	R. 20c LEFT	37	5	8 34	STR 1⅞"	1⅜"	42	46	248		
19	21	09	22	42	STR.	74					74	518			
						573	25				598	3470	542	174	—

An early dragline (*Photo:* Schiller Collection)

a 1½ to 1 batter, the side set horizontally would be one and a half times that of the vertical. On curves, the formation was cambered to conform with the superelevation given to the track and here, too, the earthworks ganger had to set out the work to provide for this, still using the same rudimentary tools.

Between chainage points, levels were set with the help of boning rods, virtually three wooden T-squares of precisely the same length. Setting two of the boning rods on consecutive points of known level, the ganger would fix intermediate ones by squinting from the top of one rod to the other and adjusting the height of the intermediate one so that the tops of all three were in alignment

I witnessed examples of the remarkably accurate excavation of deep cuttings on sharp curves, quite an achievement by men armed with only the most basic of tools.

The tracklaying itself was preceded by two operations; a re-survey of the centre line and preparatory work by the yard gang in the depot. However, when re-centring, had the pegs been driven on the centre line, not only would they have been damaged — or even destroyed — when the sleepers were laid out on the formation, but any surviving ones would have been buried under the ballast. Therefore, the pegs were offset six feet (1.8 m) to the left. The left-hand side was adopted because the horse hauling the platelaying trollies walked on the right-hand side of the formation. The re-centring was not done to a face, but as each section of the earthworks was completed. When one particular piece might be finished only just ahead of the platelaying, the surveyor would

Using a batter gauge (*Photo:* the author)

Levelling with boning rods (*Photo:* the author)

be jammed between a team of horses on one side and an active and extremely vocal platelaying gang on the other. This happened to me on two separate jobs, the nearest that the rails got to me and my theodolite being two pairs of rails, or 24 metres!

Platelaying was not just an exercise in brawn; it was a complex undertaking. In the days before long welded rails and when single ones up to 40 feet (12.2 m) were used, those to be laid in sharp curves were given some curvature before laying, so as to eliminate any tendency towards angled joints. This was done by the yard gang, using a hand-operated machine called a rail press. Essentially, it consisted of two stops set about two metres apart, against which the rail to be curved was stood upright. Midway between was a die which matched the rail's profile and fitted against it. A worm gear connected the die with a large one-man-operated wheel, the inertia of which, when rotated, applied horizontal pressure to the rail. By applying this pressure at various points along the rail, the yard ganger, using only a thin cord, a two-foot (61 cm) rule and a trained eye, would give the rail sufficient curvature so that it could be laid in the track without elbows at the joints. However, care had to be taken not to over-bend the rail, a circumstance that would have been worse than not bending it at all.

Then, on curves, the inner rail tended to creep ahead of the outer one and so throw the rail joints out of square. To counteract this, a number of rails were shortened by one fishplate hole, or five inches (127 mm), and were laid in the inner leg whenever a pair of joints became two and a half inches out of square. To distinguish the shorter rails from the others, their ends were painted green and they were known as green ends.

The handling of the sleepers was not necessarily straightforward either. On the narrow gauge, a certain amount of slack, or wide gauge, was allowed on curves under 25 chains (502.9 m) radius, the amount varying with the degree of curvature and ranging from ¼ inch to ½ inch (6.4–12.7 mm). The rail seats on the sleepers were adzed by machine and, except for the joint sleepers, the dog spike holes were drilled by the same machine — either to neat gauge or allowing for the required slack. For identification, each category of sleeper was distinctively marked.

The yard ganger had another important responsibility; to load the work train with each day's allotment of rails and sleepers in precisely the order in which they were to be laid in the track, together with the required number of fishplates, fishbolts and dogspikes. To enable him to do this, both he and the platelaying ganger were provided with a rail and sleeper book for each construction job. In it were recorded such details as the number of rails required for each individual straight and curve — including green ends on curves — the bending ordinates for the curved rails, and the number and classification of sleepers for each straight or curve.

Adzing and boring gang, Cue–Big Bell railway, 1936 (*Photo:* the author)

Each day's quota was three-quarters of a mile (1.2 km) and consisted of 99 pairs of 40-foot (12.2 m) rails, 1584 sleepers, 198 pairs of fishplates, 792 fish bolts and washers, and 6336 dogspikes. In loading this material on to the work train, the yard ganger had to keep a running record of the mileage at which each day's quota ended, so that, on the next day, he could continue the sequence without error.

Rails and sleepers recovered from the Western Australian Manganese Company's line and stacked at Meekatharra were used on the Cue–Big Bell railway, and each day's allotment of material was railed 116 kilometres to Cue the night before. The remoteness of the yard gang from the actual tracklaying meant that the yard ganger had to be especially careful in the loading of the work train because, to all intents and purposes, communication with the platelaying ganger did not exist. On one occasion I went to Meekatharra to find the ganger alcoholically *hors de combat*, and the members of the gang had taken it upon themselves to load the work train without the assistance of the rail and sleeper book. Fortunately, at that time, we were in the process of laying a long straight, without the complication of curved rails, green ends or slack gauge. A new yard ganger took over the next day.

When the work train reached the head of the road, the material was offloaded on to sleeper cribs alongside the track. After the empty train had been drawn back clear it was reloaded on to plate laying trolleys, again in precisely the same order in which it was required in the track. Each trolley held six rails and 48 sleepers, the latter resting crosswise on two of their number placed on edge longitudinally to keep the others clear of the rails. In turn, each loaded trolley would be horse-drawn to the railhead. Then, after the required number of sleepers had been deposited on the formation — and, in doing this, it was essential that they were laid heartwood down — a pair of rails would be 'galloped out' by the linkers-in, a team of eight men, four to each rail, who, with their bare hands and without any thought of either gloves or tongs, pulled them off the trolley. At the moment before the trailing ends of the rails were clear, the leading hand, designated the squinter, would call out 'Go', and the linkers-in would release their hold, jump clear and allow the rails to fall freely on to the sleepers. They would then be placed on their feet and pulled into something resembling the gauge, thus allowing the trolley to be pushed forward over them.

The procedure would be repeated until the trolley was emptied of material. It would then be removed from the track and a loaded one brought forward in its place. The operation would then continue until all trolleys were cleared of material.

Cue–Bell railway construction, 1936 (*Photos:* the author)

Tracklaying, Western Australia, 1930s (*Photo:* Westrail)

The linkers-in were followed by other members of the gang fulfilling a number of functions. Some fitted the fishplates to the joints and, sitting astride the rail with dextrous wrist movements, they tightened the fish bolts to the limit with a small fishing spanner. The back bolters followed and, with long-handled spanners, would tighten the fish bolts to such a degree that the split ring washers on them would be flattened. Tension wrenches were unheard of in those days.

Successively, other members would adjust the spacing and squaring of the sleepers that had been dropped more or less haphazardly on to the formation. Others — known as enterers — would insert the dogspikes into the pre-bored sleepers and drive them partly down. Then the bedders — the aristocrats of the gang — would use long-handled spiking hammers to bed the partly driven dogspikes against the foot of the rail. Finally, the joint sleepers would be hand bored and spiked meticulously to gauge.

The noise emanating from the men, who seemed to enjoy shouting in unison, was deafening. In reality, however, the gang consisted of a finely tuned group, working at high pressure and out to complete the day's quota as early as possible. It was truly disciplined pandemonium. The men also accomplished by brute force an amount of work that does not suffer very much by comparison with that achieved in recent years using sophisticated mechanical plant.

There was quite a measure of danger associated with plate laying, because the men had to scamper over the bare sleepers that had been laid out previously. Indeed, broken legs and the loss of fingers and toes seemed to be the accepted occupational hazards of the tracklayer. One afternoon at Allanson, a loaded trolley derailed on newly laid track, spilling six rails and 48 sleepers. All but one man scrambled clear, the exception finishing face down on the formation with both legs under a pile of rails. It seemed inevitable that the two and a half tons of steel would have broken his legs, perhaps even severing them. Fortunately, however, he had fallen between two adjacent sleepers, and these had taken the brunt of the load, leaving the man with nothing more than serious bruising.

The plate laying gang shifted camp about every ten days, moving as the head of the line crept forward. Consequently, their living conditions were extremely primitive, their camps little more than bivouacs.

The final activity was the ballasting of the newly laid track. The ballast material was run out from bottom-dump rail hopper wagons, and spread evenly by a ballast plough — a railway vehicle fitted with blades similar to those on a road grader — either hauled or pushed by a locomotive. Where

Driving dogspikes on new construction, Western Australia, 1930s (*Photo:* Westrail)

Trans Australian Railway construction, 1912–17. Sleepers being transported to rail head by camel team (*Photo:* Australian National)

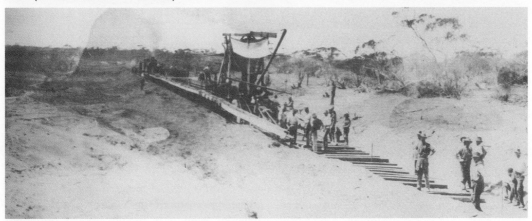
Tracklayers in operation, Trans Australian Railway, c. 1916 (*Photo:* Schiller Collection)

Tracklaying Stirling North–Marree standard gauge railway. Procedure, using front loader to handle the long welded rails, developed by Assistant Chief Engineers Milton Moore and Senior Roadmaster Jack Gillies (*Photo:* J.H. Sykes)

Launching prefabricated bridge spans, Stirling North–Marree railway. Launching device designed and constructed by Milton Moore (*Photo:* J.H. Sykes)

crushed granite, diorite or quartzite was used as ballast, it was loaded into the hoppers direct from the storage bin at the quarry. But on most of the early lines in Western Australia, sandy laterite gravel was obtained from pits alongside or near the railway and loaded into the wagons either by hand or by two-horse wheel scoops. Where the first method was used, two men were expected to fill eight 9 cubic yard (6.9 cubic metre) wagons in an eight hour shift.

After the ballast had been run out and spread, the skeleton track was lifted through it by a team of men pulling on a long wooden lever, and the ballast packed under the sleepers, either by round-mouthed shovels or, where crushed metal ballast was used, by beaters — pick-like tools with a hammer-head. Profile pegs — set at every four chains and at changes of grades on straights, and at every chain on curves — together with the off-setted centre line pegs, enabled the lifting ganger to lift and line the track to a degree of accuracy that was a tribute to his eyesight. Indeed, the final result was better than that produced by today's mechanised lifting and lining machines, wherein there is a certain amount of inbuilt averaging in both operations.

Tracklaying, Oodnadatta–Alice Springs railway, 1929 (*Photo:* Northern Territory Archives)

Matisa tie tamper; first introduced into Australia, 1949 (*Photo:* Commonwealth Railways)

Tracklaying, Tarcoola–Alice Springs railway, 1979 (*Photo:* Australian National)

Mannix undercutter, South Australian Railways, 1970. Machine lifted up the track, removed old ballast, knocked off sleepers needing replacement, and then lowered the track back on to a level formation (*Photo:* Martin Kitchener)

Except for the tracklaying machines hired from North America and used on the construction of the Trans Australian Railway, it was not until the early 1950s — when some primitive mechanical aids were used on the Stirling North–Marree standard gauge railway — that railway construction in this country relied on anything but Clydesdale and man power, and mostly the latter.

The transition to mechanical tracklaying and maintenance that has taken place since the 1950s has been dramatic. Indeed, the Matisa track-tamping machines first used on the Australian railways in 1949 and the primitive Nordberg dogspike drivers and lifting jacks acquired a few years later would be unrecognisable alongside today's sophisticated equipment. Fifty years ago, any prediction that the work would be taken over by the mechanical monsters that one sees in current use would have been dismissed as hallucinatory. Yet it has happened and, if there were to be a requiem for the former days, it should be for the passing of a group of men who spent their entire working lives toiling, sweating, and living at times under the most inhospitable conditions

imaginable, in dirt-floored tents pitched over rough poles cut from the bush and with the headroom so restricted that one could barely stand upright. But these men were indestructible, and I am proud to have lived and worked with them.

Except for those rare occasions when a contractor conducted a ranch — or bush boarding house—the men cooked for themselves in the open and their diet was predictable and rugged; steak, chops, stew, or eggs, with boiled potatoes and onions, followed by bread and jam. Butter was a luxury enjoyed only during the cooler months. Strong black billy tea — indeed strong enough to tan a hide — attested to the indestructibility of those men.

The single men on the staff — the engineers and timekeepers — were housed in the same way, but their tents were set on sawn timber frames with adequate head room, and were timber floored, generally with old sleepers. In some cases too they had the advantage of eating in a mess supervised by a cook.

The married staff members lived in relative comfort in demountable three-roomed hessian-clad houses that they took with them from job to job.

The most outstanding of those construction men with whom I worked was Bob Henderson, the finest earthworker that I have ever seen. We started our association when I was put in charge of my first job. There was I, the engineer, 22 years old, less than one year out of the university and a raw novice, teaming up with Bob, my foreman, 60 years of age and a past master at his work. The situation was indeed ludicrous and it was a strange alliance; but, thanks to Bob's understanding and tolerance, we worked harmoniously together for three years and through three separate jobs.

Bob Henderson was a remarkable character. Tall, but with that slight stoop so characteristic of men who have spent a lifetime on manual work; raw-boned and strong; and, with his droopy moustache and sharp features, in profile he bore a striking resemblance to Henry Lawson.

Like Lawson too, he was deaf, in his case the result of putting his head too close to an explosion. Nevertheless, he was an amazing workman. Not only could he do two men's work on his own, but he was also an excellent organiser and supervisor. Between us, we devised an effective system of communication to overcome his deafness. For example, if I wished to convey the dimension 7 feel 4 inches to him, I would hold up seven fingers, touch my boot and then hold up four fingers, a procedure that, incidentally, would be difficult today with metric measurements. Then, to attract his attention when he was facing away from me, I would throw a stone, aimed just to miss him. By the end of our three years together, I had scored the possible; not once did I hit him by mistake.

But it was in the matter of complaints that we contrived our best ploy. By mutual arrangement, Bob became the unofficial complaints officer. Anyone who has suffered the frustration of shouting into an unresponsive ear will understand.

Shortly after we parted company, Bob was fatally injured at Yarloop on the Perth–Bunbury railway when, in the course of crossing the line, he was struck by a passing locomotive.

A close second to Bob Henderson would have been Bob Airey, also an excellent earthworks ganger, but he had a weakness.

After a ten days' spell in Perth over the Christmas break, Bob returned to the camp at Allanson cold sober, and determined to create, at least for him, a record for total abstinence. He held out until Easter, even though those three months must have been agony for him; but, bravely, he stuck it out. He even survived the Easter weekend in Perth before the inevitable happened.

Bob arrived back in the camp shortly after midday on Easter Monday and went into the nearby town of Collie for a meal — and it proved too much for him. No doubt the satisfaction of having teetotalled for so long seemed to have warranted just one small drink … But Bob Airey did not start work on the following or any other morning, at least insofar as that particular job was concerned. It was a sad ending to three months of admirable, yet futile, self-discipline.

A more recuperative trio were the McCarthy brothers, Jack, Jim and Paddy. All three were competent earthworkers and skilled platelayers, possessing not only unerring eyes for lifting and lining the track, but also the capacity for coming up for work of a morning irrespective of how they had spent the preceding 12 hours.

On the other hand, there was Jack Gill, an experienced and thoroughly capable general foreman. Not only did he possess a remarkable eye for aligning the track, but he also had the capacity for fluent profanity that was spellbinding. It was said that once, when he was in charge of a ballast train and it went without him, Jack's comments turned the rails a deep shade of cherry red!

When I knew him, Jack was a rabid and obsessed teetotaller, but he had not always been so. A few years earlier, he had gone to the Perth railway station at a time when a batch of men were being given warrants to travel the 966 kilometres to Meekatharra to work on the construction of the railway to Wiluna. One of the men engaged for the job did not turn up, so the Transport Officer, Ned Kinsella, gave the warrant to Jack. He arrived at Meekatharra in anything but a fit condition for work. Knowing Jack's worth when sober, the Resident Engineer, Cedric Stewart, gave him a chance and deposited him at Paroo — a desolate siding 100 kilometres east of Meekatharra and 68 kilometres west of Wiluna — with an 18 litre tin of drinking water and left him there for a week to dry out. Jack Gill signed the pledge, in spirit if not in writing. Ordinarily, a week at Paroo would drive a sober man to drink; in Jack's case, it did the reverse.

Still, it would be wrong for the reader to presume that railway construction workers were a mob of inebriates, far from it! Rather, these reminiscences should indicate their toughness under harsh living and working conditions. Without men of this calibre, our railways would never have been built.

As an epilogue to this story I must confess that, although a lifelong teetotaller, on one occasion I did in fact suffer a hangover.

It was while stationed at Allanson that, one Friday evening, we were celebrating Resident Engineer Frank Carter's birthday. When we came to drink his health, I had only two choices; water or milk. I chose the latter, but at the same time could not resist the pickled onions also on offer. I can vouch for the fact that pickled onions and milk are not compatible. I woke up next morning with a massive hangover!

8 Commonwealth Railways, 1949–54

Where else but in Australia would the Chief Civil Engineer of major railway be obliged to spend almost 50 percent of his time virtually on the wallaby, and to travel more than 20,000 kilometres a year by gang section or rail motor car, inspecting the track? Or having to unroll his swag and sleep rough, possibly on the concrete floor of shearers' quarters or, indeed, under the stars? Or to set the pace for a gang of men repairing the track after a washaway? Or to take personal charge of a breakdown gang at the site of a derailment? Only on the Commonwealth Railways in the 1940s and '50s could this have happened. Actually, in attire as in living and working conditions, there was little to distinguish him from his subordinates.

My appointment as its Chief Civil Engineer was also somewhat unique. Towards the end of 1948 and coinciding with P.J. Hannaberry's elevation to Commonwealth Railways Commissioner, applications for his former position of Chief Civil Engineer were invited nationwide and I was one of the unsuccessful applicants, G.G.Bennett of the Victorian Railways being appointed with J.B.Horrigan — a senior colleague of mine in the WAGR — runner-up. However, after approximately three months in the position, Bennett relinquished it to return to Victoria and, although offered the vacancy, Horrigan declined it.

At that time, I was in Melbourne attending an Australian and New Zealand Railways subcommittee meeting on bridge design, and Hannaberry contacted me at my hotel and offered me the position. In doing so, he suggested that, on my way back to Perth, I stop off at Port Augusta and see for myself what the town and the job had to offer.

This I did, and — having ascertained that the Chief Civil Engineer's job was essentially a hands-on and not an administrative one — I wandered around the town on my own in an attempt to get the feel of the place. Despite its arid environment, I came to the conclusion that it was a town in which one could live. So I accepted Hannaberry's offer, and on the weekend of 28–29 May 1949, we arrived at Port Augusta — I by motor inspection car all the way from Kalgoorlie, and Doreen and family by the Trans Australian.

The establishment of the Commonwealth Railways as an autonomous authority might never have eventuated but for two things: a belated reluctance by South Australia to continued participation in the Trans Australian Railway project, and its desire to surrender sovereignty over its northern territory and so relieve the impoverished state of the financial burden associated with its administration.

The genesis of the Trans Australian Railway goes back long before Federation. During the 1880s and with the blessing of the Western Australian Premier, Sir John Forrest, a London syndicate proposed a railway from York, at that time the eastern extremity of the Western Australian system, to Eucla on the Great Australian Bight near the South Australia border, and on to Port Augusta. The basis for the construction was a land grant of 12,000 acres per mile (3018 ha/km). Little did the proponents know that, had the land grant followed the usual chequerboard pattern throughout the length of the line, only about 10 percent would have been arable, and even that subject to the doubtful prospect of finding adequate underground water supplies.

Such was the enthusiasm at that time that an Anglo-French consortium proposed another west–east railway from Roebuck Bay, on WA's north-west coast, to Oodnadatta, then the terminus of the Great Northern Railway. As this proposal would have implied a deviation from the Adelaide–Darwin railway, the South Australian Premier rejected it. In fact a more futile undertaking would have been hard to imagine. Roebuck Bay was the jumping-off place to nowhere, and the country between it and Oodnadatta consisted of either the Great Sandy Desert or near desert.

Preliminary reconnaissances of a route between Port Augusta and Kalgoorlie were carried out by the colonies of South Australia and Western Australia at about the turn of the twentieth century; but after Federation the South Australian Premier, Charles Kingston, reversed his earlier advocacy and opposed its construction on three grounds. First, if built to the 1435 mm standard gauge, it would mean the introduction of a third gauge into his state; second, it would prejudice the prospects of the ultimate completion of the north–south railway; and third, he could not see that its construction would bestow any benefits on South Australia. He argued therefore that the east–west transcontinental railway should be the responsibility of the Commonwealth. Had he not adopted this stance, it is reasonable to assume that the two states would have owned and operated the railway, and that, as a corollary, the Commonwealth Railways Department would not have been created. The line was in fact built by the Construction Branch of the Department of Home Affairs, and the Commonwealth Railways did not come into being until the passage of the Commonwealth Railways Act in 1917. Significantly, it remained under the Department of Home Affairs, or its successor the Department of the Interior, until 1950.

Somewhat similar circumstances surrounded the establishment of the Australian National Railways in the 1970s. The new organisation would not have been created but for the centralist policies

PRINCIPAL PLACES MENTIONED IN NARRATIVE

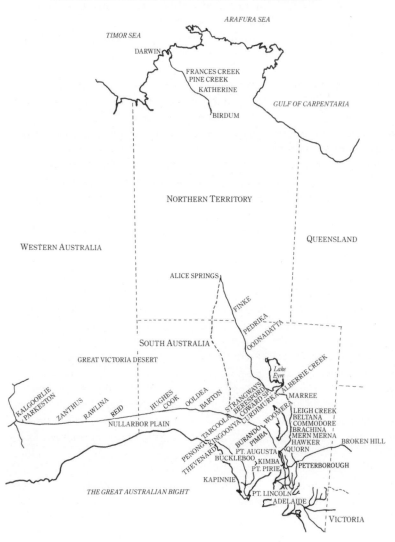

of the Whitlam Government; a power hungry Commonwealth bureaucracy; a Federal Minister of Transport who was prepared to agree to any number of concessions in order to swallow up the state railway systems; and the gutlessness of the South Australian and Tasmanian Labor Governments which, unwilling to face up to the long overdue pruning of their railway networks in line with the changing transport pattern, saw the takeover offer as a golden opportunity to free themselves for all time of their responsibilities.

To return to the Trans Australian survey, despite strong opposition from some senators, the Bill authorising the work was passed in 1907 and the survey completed by 1909. Alternative routes were considered: one from Port Augusta through Tarcoola to Kalgoorlie; and the other through the Gawler Ranges and Fowlers Bay and passing a few kilometres north of Eucla. The Bill for the construction of the railway was introduced into the Federal Parliament on 20 September 1911 by King O'Malley, Minister of Home Affairs, and received Vice Regal assent on 12 December. Construction started from both ends in 1912 and the rails met at a point near Ooldea and 628 kilometres west of Port Augusta on 17 October 1917.

Incidentally, in 1903, in an Act passed by the Western Australian Parliament authorising the Commonwealth to make laws for a railway between Kalgoorlie and the state border, provision was also made for the State to build concurrently a railway from Kalgoorlie to Fremantle to the gauge adopted for the Trans Australian Railway. It took more than 65 years for this to be accomplished.

The Central Australia and the North Australia Railways were entirely different propositions, and were inevitably linked with South Australia and the South Australian Railways. Together with the Overland Telegraph, they represent possibly the most courageous projects in the nation's history.

Even before the Overland Telegraph had been completed, the idea of a north–south transcontinental railway was born, and in 1872 a Bill for the Port Augusta to Palmerston Railway, to be constructed under the land grant principle, was only narrowly defeated. Work eventually started at the southern end in January 1878, and the railway crept gradually northwards, finally reaching Oodnadatta in 1891. Known as the Great Northern Railway, it extended some 769 kilometres north of Port Augusta and 1107 kilometres from Adelaide.

At the northern end, construction of the Palmerston (Darwin) to Pine Creek railway was authorised in 1883 and work commenced in 1887, the contractors, C. and E. Millar, employing up to 3000 Chinese labourers. The line was opened in 1889.

Although these two phases represented the end of actual construction under state auspices, hopes were always held for the ultimate completion of this north–south transcontinental rail link. In 1896, a number of syndicates made offers to the South Australian Government to provide the connection between Oodnadatta and Pine Creek, again on the basis of land grants, but the State declined to accept any of the proposals. However, in 1902 the Transcontinental Railway Act was passed by the South Australian Parliament and tenders called for the completion of the 1710 kilometre link. Provision was made for land grants totalling 32,225,000 hectares, as well as the successful tenderer being given the right to operate train services. Negotiations with the contractor proceeded almost to the point of signature before breaking down because of the Commonwealth Government's ban on the employment of Asiatic labour on the project. Had this hitch not occurred, the Northern Territory might well have developed in an entirely different way and at a vastly different speed.

It is significant that, in the matters of concept, negotiations and to some extent actual construction, the north–south transcontinental railway preceded the east–west. This might well be attributed to the fact that the former was an entirely intrastate undertaking, unimpeded by interstate jealousy or parochialism. It is significant too that, although taken over by the Commonwealth, the South Australian Railways continued to operate the Port Augusta–Oodnadatta section on the Commonwealth's behalf until 1926.

Under the provisions of the Northern Territory Acceptance Act of 1910, as well as those of the Railway Standardisation Agreement Acts of 1946 and 1949, the Commonwealth promised to complete the north–south rail link; but, apart from the extensions to Alice Springs and Birdum in 1929, no Commonwealth Government of any political persuasion has moved to honour those promises. It fell to private enterprise to do so, and this 94 years after the passing of the Northern Territory Acceptance Act.

When the extension from Oodnadatta to Alice Springs was contemplated, consideration was given to the alternative of a standard gauge line from Kingoonya on the Trans Australian Railway direct to Alice Springs, but this was rejected in favour of the narrow gauge from Oodnadatta. It took innumerable washaways and interminable delays to traffic to correct this, the Tarcoola–Alice Springs standard gauge railway becoming a reality over 50 years later, and an integral part of the finally achieved Adelaide–Darwin rail link.

The enthusiasm for railway construction in South Australia's far north did not wane with the completion of the Port Augusta–Oodnadatta railway in 1891, and surveys or reconnaissances were undertaken for lines along both the Birdsville and Strzelecki tracks, while trial surveys were carried out in the 1920s for three major railways in the Northern Territory. Radiating out from Anthony's Lagoon, they were directed westwards towards Newcastle Waters, southwards through Brunette Downs, and northwards to the mouth of the McArthur River on the Gulf of Carpentaria.

The Australian Capital Territory Railway was yet another example of either interstate jealousy or a manifestation of Federal power hunger, something seemingly endemic to Canberra. When the area now constituting the ACT was excised from the State of New South

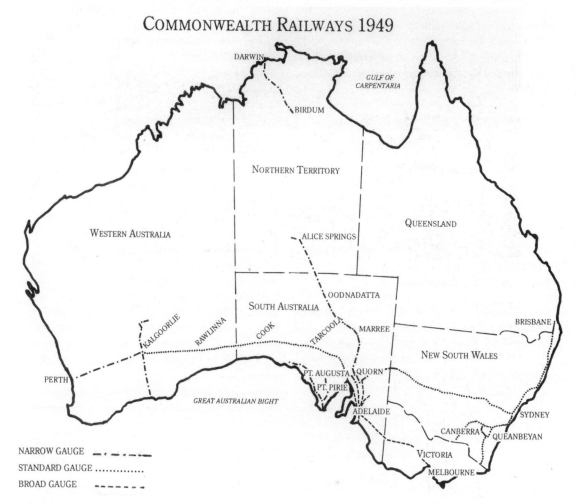

COMMONWEALTH RAILWAYS 1949

NARROW GAUGE
STANDARD GAUGE
BROAD GAUGE

Australian Railwayman

Wales, either the other states or the newly established Federal administration would not countenance the meagre eight kilometres of line connecting Canberra with the New South Wales Government Railways being part of the latter system. Consequently, we had a tiny branch line, with one station but not any locomotives or rollingstock of its own. Such was the specious prestige bestowed on this insignificant spur line that, when the Duke of Gloucester was appointed Governor-General of Australia, Ned Herbert, one of the Commonwealth Railways' senior officers, was taken away from his worthwhile duties and transferred to Canberra as stationmaster so that the dignity of the position could be maintained. Perhaps it was thought that the gold crown on the Commonwealth Railways stationmaster's cap looked more imposing than did the simple gold braid on that of his New South Wales counterpart.

Until 1978, when it took over the non-urban lines of the SAR and the Tasmanian Government Railways to become the Australian National Railways, the Commonwealth Railways remained a relatively small system with uncomplicated working. It was essentially a long haul railroad, devoid of the complexities of commuter, seasonal and branch line operations, or of the multitude of minor traffics that plagued other railways. There were no large stations, goods depots or marshalling yards; and apart from Leigh Creek coal, wool, livestock and, for a short period, Frances Creek iron ore, it did not generate any other traffic of its own. However, the completion of the Port Augusta–Whyalla railway, together with a substantial surge in intersystem traffic, has altered this.

Despite the relative modesty of its activities, the Commonwealth Railways received far more than its rightful share of the Australian railways' financial cake. When related to its comparative level of activity, its allocation for capital works, received direct from the Commonwealth Government, was approximately three times greater than that granted to the other systems through their funds-starved state treasuries. Nor, at that time, were those funds for capital works subject to interest charges.

On the other hand, the system had problems

Ellen Street station, Port Pirie, used when trains ran down the main street (*Photo:* the author)

peculiarly its own. When World War II came closer to home, there was a sudden and dramatic change in its work load. Traffic on all sections, from Darwin to Port Pirie and Kalgoorlie, increased beyond comprehension and threw a fantastic burden on its slender resources. A number of improvements were effected as part of the defence budget, including new locomotive depots, extensions to the Port Augusta workshops, and the provision of additional locomotive water supplies. But critical deficiencies remained in the areas of locomotive power, rollingstock and personnel.

Perhaps the most unconventional step taken to overcome the rollingstock shortage was the adaptation of cattle vans to carry troops between Port Pirie and Kalgoorlie. The wagons, which had open planked sides, were lined and fitted with toilets, and in these improvised vehicles the troops stretched out on the floor and endured up to three days' inconvenience on the 1782 kilometre journey.

In an attempt to alleviate some of the shortages, help was sought from other railways. On the narrow gauge, T class locomotives were hired from the SAR, which also helped out with the maintenance of Commonwealth Railways' locomotives and rollingstock. Some second-hand standard gauge 4-6-0 type locomotives of almost Stephensonian vintage were obtained from Canada. With large driving wheels and only modest tractive effort, they could barely pull the proverbial hat from one's head. The manpower shortage was relieved in part by calling for volunteers from other railway systems, and the response was good.

Trans Australian freight train at Yorkey□s Crossing at the head of Spencer Gulf, South Australia (*Photo:* Australian National)

Tent Hill, formerly the 17 Mile, then the 73 Mile camp, Trans Australian Railway; site of the quarantine camp during the pneumonic influenza epidemic in 1919 (*Photo:* the author)

Windmill, Kultanaby, Trans Australian Railway (*Photo:* Schiller Collection)

Prisoners of war and civilian internees were seconded to the system, and were stationed on the Nullarbor Plain to be employed on resleepering work. In the interests of security, the Commonwealth Railways mounted a machine-gun on the canopy of a motor inspection car to patrol the line and to prevent the escape of prisoners or internees. However, the country was so forbidding that any thought of escape would have been unwise. In the few cases where it was attempted, the escapees welcomed recapture.

Oddly, some internees succumbed to the fascination of the Nullarbor, or perhaps they were happy to remain more or less incommunicado, and stayed there after the war's end. One such man, Johnny Zanardo, rose to the position of ganger at the 757 mile camp, and imposed a standard of discipline on those under him that made the wartime one benevolent by comparison.

As a result of this resleepering, the Trans Australian Railway was, in 1949, in reasonably good condition, although very little relaying had been done, and, for the greater part, the original rails, laid before 1917, were still in the track.

The strategic importance of Darwin meant that the Central Australia Railway (CAR) and the North Australia Railway (NAR) were called upon to bear the heaviest loads. Both were pioneer

The long straight Nullarbor Plain, Trans Australian Railway (*Photo:* Australian National)

The main — and only — street of Cook, self-proclaimed 'Queen City of the Nullarbor' (*Photo:* the author)

lines, unballasted and of light construction, and in 1942, after 50 years of neglect, were ill-equipped to stand up to the demands of a world war. But stand up to them they did, even though the legacies of old, light and crippled rails, together with poor sleepers, made their continued maintenance a herculean task. Indeed, the karri sleepers in the track north of Oodnadatta had so broomed out at the ends that, when I first saw them, they resembled, more than anything else, double ended shaving brushes! Moreover, the feet of the rails had cut into the sleepers by as much as two and a half centimetres, leaving them free to move up and down by this amount.

It was both fascinating and frightening to stand alongside the track and watch the rails move vertically in a rhythmical curve in front of the locomotive of an approaching train. On the NAR between Darwin and Birdum, the sleepers were either termite-resistant ironwood or steel, but the light rails were on the verge of breakdown.

In general, that was the position when I joined the Commonwealth Railways in 1949.

A Somewhat Unique Railway

The remoteness of its territory, the absence of any worthwhile settlements between its terminals, the almost entire lack of water, either potable or

First westbound Trans Australian at Immarna, South Australia, 23 October 1917 (*Photo:* B.H. Gillman)

Kalgoorlie, Western Australia, departure of the first eastbound Trans Australian, 25 October 1917 (*Photo:* Westrail)

suitable for steam locomotives, and the logistic problems associated with the supply of materials and stores resulted in the operations of the Commonwealth Railways being different from those of other railways, at least in this country. During my association with it, we worked to four time zones: to South Australian standard time from Port Pirie to Tarcoola and Alice Springs; to Western Australian standard time between Parkeston and Rawlinna; and to our own central time, midway between the two, for the length of track between Tarcoola and Rawlinna; while the Commissioner's office in Melbourne worked to eastern standard time. On the NAR, while the official time coincided with that for South Australia, the fickleness of the train running was such that a calendar rather than a clock might have been more appropriate.

Trainload of 876 bales of wool loaded at Hesso, Trans Australian Railway (*Photo:* Schiller Collection)

The train controller at Port Augusta faced three clocks, one for each of the time zones between Port Pirie and Parkeston. Working to them was not confusing, and indeed gives the lie to those who clamour for one standard time for the whole of the eastern half of the continent. There might be some reasons justifying it, but confusion is not one of them.

Until the late 1930s, only about one half of the Trans line had been ballasted, and a top speed of 72 km/h applied throughout. Therefore, until 1937 — that is before the standard gauge was extended from Port Augusta to Port Pirie and the South Australian Railways' broad gauge from Redhill to Port Pirie — the Perth–Adelaide train journey occupied nearly 72 hours and necessitated three changes of trains. One night was spent on the narrow gauge between Perth and Kalgoorlie; two nights and one and a half days on the Trans train to Port Augusta; several hours on the antediluvian though somewhat quaint narrow gauge through the Pichi Richi Pass to Quorn and on to Terowie; and, finally, the SAR broad gauge between Terowie and Adelaide. In 1937, when the Port Pirie and Redhill route was opened, the journey was shortened by about eight hours and one break of gauge eliminated.

The completion of the ballasting of the line and the acquisition of large steam locomotive power shortly before World War II permitted running at 97 km/h, and only one night was spent on the Trans Australian section. However, this did not last for long, wartime exigencies necessitating a reversion to the slower time table. This situation

Port Augusta, South Australia, c. 1890 (*Photo:* South Australian Archives)

Port Augusta, c. 1949 (*Photo:* City of Port Augusta)

The wharf, Port Augusta (*Photo:* the author)

The original Port Augusta railway station serving the Port Augusta–Government Gums railway (*Photo:* the author)

Present Port Augusta railway station (*Photo:* the author)

persisted until 1952, when diesel electric motive power became available for all passenger trains.

On the CAR there was a nominal speed limit of 48 km/h. But, due to the condition of the track, as well as to the frequency and extent of flood damage, this speed was rarely maintained and restrictions as low as 24 km/h were often imposed for lengthy periods and over long sections of the line.

Locomotive coal had to be shipped from New South Wales to Port Augusta, where it was unloaded and then railed as far afield as Parkeston and Alice Springs. This of itself was bad enough, but when the quality of the coal deteriorated in the immediate postwar years, the difficulties were compounded.

Water was an even bigger problem. On the Trans line there were surface reservoirs at ten locations, but rarely did they hold water. When the occasional and unpredictable downpour did occur, it did more than fill the reservoirs; it washed out the track at the same time. Bores or wells existed at five locations, and these were the standard source of locomotive water, but the quality was so bad that, even after chemical treatment, it would have been rejected but for the absence of a better alternative. The magnitude of the problem becomes apparent when it is realised that no permanent water supply existed between Kingoonya and Reid, a distance of 681 kilometres. Water trains were regular features of the operations, while almost all drinking water had to be railed from either Port Augusta or Parkeston. Before the introduction of diesel electric motive power in 1951, the water supply situation was our biggest day-to-day worry

on the Trans line. The pumpers were not the most reliable of employees; neither were their pumps free from caprice when worked to death and in unskilled hands. Equipment was forever breaking down and George Pauley, the Water Supply Engineer, had an unenviable job. Once, at about 1 am, he even retimed an engine by remote control.

The trouble was at Zanthus, and George was at Port Augusta, nearly 1500 kilometres away. The pumper could not start the engine, so he telephoned for help. George instructed him to retime it, explaining each procedure step by step. When the process was completed, the engine started at first attempt.

On the CAR, the water supply position was not so critical. The surface reservoirs were more reliable, while supplementary supplies were available from wells and bores. From Marree to some distance north of Oodnadatta the bores were artesian and the water needed chemical treatment before use in the steam locomotives. The artesian bores flowed continuously and the water flowing from them was hot. It was not uncommon during the war years for troops on military trains to take a quick plunge into what they assumed to be a cool refreshing stream. Their consternation on discovering it to be the reverse was generally expressed in true Australian vernacular.

Once flowing, artesian bores should not be turned off. When, at Beresford — 153 kilometres north of Marree — an attempt was made to do so, the internal pressure perforated the bore casing. The artesian water broke through the ground to the surface at a number of points, jeopardising the fresh water in the nearby surface reservoir. We tried everything to stop the flow, even to dropping

Depot Creek dam in the Flinders Ranges; Port Augusta's water supply until the completion of the Morgan–Whyalla pipeline in 1944 (*Photo:* The Rose Stereograph Company)

bags of cement, with heavy chains attached, down the bore, but were not successful. Thereafter, the Beresford station yard became waterlogged and almost overgrown with bullrushes.

With those problems of coal and water, it was no wonder that the Commonwealth Railways provided a copybook exercise in the application of diesel motive power. It was first introduced on the Trans Australian route, the naming of the first diesel electric locomotive, the Robert Gordon Menzies, taking place at Port Pirie in October 1951. The dieselisation of the CAR and NAR followed soon after, and the overall economic benefits were startling.

Concurrent with the placing of orders for diesel electric locomotives, Hannaberry purchased three Budd diesel hydraulic rail cars from the US. They were intended for use on short haul passenger services, working as far afield as

Woomera and Tarcoola, but primarily between Port Pirie and Port Augusta, where they replaced the old-fashioned mixed trains known locally as the Snake Gullies. The Budd cars, which arrived in March 1951, were at that time the finest of their type in Australia but were subsequently equalled, if not surpassed, by Australian designed and manufactured rail cars.

The Budd Company sent out Joe Grosset to train local railwaymen in the operation and Joe, a very likeable chap, expressed the desire to see how they would behave when 'rolling along at 100 miles [163 km] an hour'. To oblige him, over a weekend in April 1951 a test run was made to Kalgoorlie and return. The Hughes length, on the 'straight' some 90 kilometres west of Cook, had at that time a stretch of track that that would have borne comparison with the best in the world; so Joe Grosset was given his head. The rail car reached 93½ mph (150.5 km/h), not quite as fast as Joe would have liked, but as much as it could do. We took a track recording of the run and it was a credit to a highly pleased Bill Glasson, the ganger at Hughes.

Living conditions had always been rigorous on the Commonwealth Railways. During the construction of the Trans Australian Railway, standard accomodation for married men consisted of two tents, face-to-face on sawn timber frames, and with a tent fly canopy in between. Eventually, the tent frames were sheathed with weatherboard, lined and ceiled with three ply,

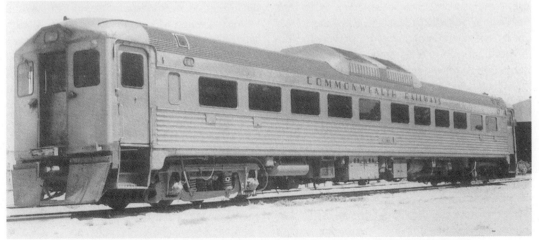

Budd diesel hydraulic rail car, Commonwealth Railways, 1951 (*Photo:* Australian National)

given a galvanised-iron roof, and designated tent houses. These tent houses became the standard accommodation for the majority of maintenance and operating staffs. After World War II, and thanks to Hannaberry's efforts, the tent houses were replaced by modern timber framed and iron roofed bungalows meaning that, in my time, the standard of accommodation on the TAR was very good.

Apart from that provided for stationmasters — and, including Quorn and Alice Springs, there were only eight on the whole line — most of the housing on the CAR consisted of barracks-like stone structures which had been there since the 1880s. In some instances, they housed a number of married families living semi-detached; in others, they constituted a single men's mess.

On the North Australia Railway, the condition of the housing at that time was indescribable. The only parts that had not succumbed to the ravages of termites were made of either concrete or iron. Indeed, I saw young children running from room to room in the ganger's house at Katherine, not through the doors but through what remained of the masonite walls after the white ants' appetites had been satiated.

Before the advent of diesel electric locomotives on the Trans line, there had been fairly large establishments at Tarcoola, Cook and Rawlinna, as well as at Port Pirie, Port Augusta and Parkeston. Train crews changed at Port Pirie, Port Augusta, Pimba, Tarcoola, Barton, Cook, Reid, Rawlinna, Zanthus and Parkeston, while the steam locomotives were given hour-long services at Tarcoola, Cook and Rawlinna. After dieselisation, trip lengths were doubled and the home stations for train crews limited to Port Pirie, Port Augusta and Parkeston. Crews worked between Port Pirie and Port Augusta, Port Augusta and Cook, and between Parkeston and Cook. Those working to Cook from either end of the line had intermediate lay-offs at Tarcoola and Rawlinna while those formerly living at Tarcoola, Cook and Rawlinna were transferred to the more congenial environments of Port Augusta and Parkeston

At that time too, the entire train working staff on the CAR was stationed at Quorn and, except for the Leigh Creek coal trains, what was known

as relay working applied right through to Alice Springs. Each train was manned by two crews, one working a seven-hour shift and the other resting—if seven hours in a non air-conditioned relay van, bouncing over a rough track in intense heat could be described as a rest!

All functions associated with the maintenance and construction of track and structures were controlled from the Chief Civil Engineer's office in Port Augusta, with lines of communication stretching nearly 1700 kilometres to Parkeston and over 1200 to Alice Springs. In respect of the NAR, however, the Chief Civil Engineer's role was an advisory one. The engineering staff was small and the only officers of the branch permanently in the field were two senior roadmasters and roadmasters at Port Augusta, Tarcoola, Cook, Rawlinna, Parkeston, Quorn, Marree and Alice Springs. Consequently, a great deal of field work fell to the Chief Civil Engineer, and as a result I came to know and to greet every one of my 92 gangers, as well as a number of fettlers, by their first names.

As both the TAR and CAR were long, single track railways, a mishap on any one section tied up the entire traffic operations until repairs had been made. Moreover, the remoteness of the territory meant that the delays arising from such accidents were inordinately long.

Contrary to popular belief, the Trans line was not just one long straight and devoid of any steep grades. The 1783 kilometres from Port Pirie to Kalgoorlie contained 443 curves including 69 in the 138 kilometres between Mount Christie and Ooldea, through what were known as the Barton sandhills and where the predominant grade was 1 in 100 without compensation for curvature.

Speeds on the CAR were only one half of those on the Trans line, but the track lacked ballast throughout its entire length. There were also some sections with very light rails weighing only 41 pounds per yard (20.34 kg/m) and which resembled, more than anything else, two parallel strands of heavy gauge fencing wire; and rails of this fragility had to support large tonnages of Leigh Creek coal. Between Telford (Leigh Creek) and Oodnadatta the line consisted of short and crippled rails weighing 50 pounds per yard (24.80 kg/m), of antique origin and subject to frequent

(*Above and left*) Washaway, Brachina, Central Australia Railway, February 1950 (*Photos:* the author)

fracture. During one of his inspections of this length, Bill Stephens, the Senior Roadmaster, found 14 broken rails, a circumstance critical enough to warrant a gang patrol ahead of each northbound and southbound Ghan.

North of Oodnadatta, the rails were relatively new, but the condition of the sleepers was beyond belief. And to say that the CAR was prone to flood damage to a degree unique in the world would not be an exaggeration. However, the Tarcoola–Alice Springs standard gauge railway, built on a route skirting, wherever possible, the headwaters of the many streams that were normally dry but torrents after thunderstorms, went a long way towards minimising the hazard.

South of Oodnadatta, the numerous bridges, although suffering from flood damage, generally remained intact. However, in February 1950 heavy rains caused one arm of the Brachina Creek, 132 kilometres north of Quorn, to leave its course, cut a new channel and render 37

metres of bridging redundant, as well as about 60 metres of track swinging in the air. There was no way by which the stream could be restored to its original bed; so, with the early construction of the standard gauge line to Leigh Creek in mind, we dropped the track into the stream bed and anchored it there. It lasted in that position for six years until superseded by the new line.

North of Oodnadatta, the circumstances were entirely different. During construction of the line, all streams were bridged, but the unpredictability of the river flows resulted in almost every bridge being washed out in the first few years. The track was lowered into the stream bed, as was done at Brachina, anchored with old rails and stone paved. This resulted in a stable roadbed over which the trains could pass, even though water might be flowing over the line. In most cases, the stream flow was not very deep, but the Finke was an exception. Here, the flooding might exceed two metres after heavy rain in the back country.

In the days of steam, drivers would take their trains through the Finke if the depth of water over the rails did not exceed 21 inches (533 mm). It was quite an experience watching this happen because, apart from the impressive bow wave in front of the locomotive, there were the additional hazards of it stalling in mid-stream, as well as the heavy grade on the north side of the river which had to be surmounted with wet wheels. Diesel locomotives were unable to negotiate anything

Washaway, Commodore Swamp, February 1950 (*Photo:* the author)

Washaway, Willochra Plain, Central Australia Railway, c. 1912 (*Photo:* Port Dock Station Railway Museum)

but minimal flows of water over the rails, and perhaps this was the reason why there were more delays during the latter days of the old narrow gauge line.

It would now be safe to reveal a little piece of deception that we practised at the Finke crossing. To indicate the depth of flow, marker posts were set in the ground alongside the track approaching the stream bed, but by exercising some licence in respect of the actual depth of water compared with that shown on the marker posts, the enginemen were misled to the extent of six inches (152 mm). The trickery was worthwhile. I do not recall it ever having resulted in a train stalling in mid-stream. On the other hand, it did minimise delays to traffic.

Of all the inconveniences caused by flooding on the Central Australia Railway, the most frustrating delay would have occurred during the 1950 washaways. We were camped at Brachina, but as there were reports of damage further north, I set out with my driver, Frank Pierce, on a gang section car to find out the facts. The ride was not without its moments of excitement. We encountered a great deal of water along the way, but the real thrill was when we had to ride the section car over washouts up to eight feet (2.4 m) deep by 60 feet (19.3 m) long, trusting that the sleepers were sound enough to hold the rails to gauge. In some instances, the swinging track was not level, and we had to lean out, yachting fashion, to maintain the section car in equilibrium. At Marree, we encountered a couple sitting on a wooden garden seat under the hotel verandah. The man introduced himself as the Shire Clerk from Birdsville, 450 kilometres away to the north. Three days earlier, they had driven to Marree, intending to take the train to Adelaide for their three weeks' annual leave. They had missed the train by about 20 minutes, but were not worried, thinking that they would catch the southbound Ghan two days later. To the best of my knowledge, they spent their entire annual leave at Marree.

Another problem encountered on the Central line and not met elsewhere, in Australia at least, was sand drift. In this country, some drift was inevitable, but here it had been aggravated by the flagrant overstocking of the land by the early pastoralists, and remains a monument to their greed and bad husbandry. At certain locations, the Commonwealth Railways had constructed wind chutes alongside the line. These consisted of galvanised-iron fences about four metres high, but with the bottom one and a half metres open, and with the whole structure tilted away from the track. The tunnel effect induced an increase in the wind speed, and this, it was hoped, would carry the sand over the rails and clear of the line. In other places, men were employed with horse-drawn scoop teams clearing the permanent way of the drifting sand.

Apart from the matters of old rails, bad sleepers, washaways and locomotive water, the main problems facing the Chief Civil Engineer during my term with the Commonwealth Railways, were not technical ones. They were the remoteness of the territory, manpower and material shortages, and staff welfare. Where else in the world would the Head of Branch be obliged to travel further than from London to Rome to attend a derailment or a washaway, and the same distance back again after the damage had been repaired? But this was accepted as a fact of life by those associated with the Commonwealth system.

If anything, the manpower position became even more critical after the war, when the prisoners of war and most of the alien internees had gone. A few self-sponsored Dutch migrants joined us for a short time. They were excellent workers, but the harshness of the terrain, the rigorous climate and the absence of social contacts mitigated against their staying. Once, when I asked one of them stationed at Mern Merna — a camp of five families living in semi-detached stone cottages, built in the 1880s and located in the loneliness of the Flinders Ranges far from any town or village — how he liked it there, he answered simply: 'We came from Rotterdam.' It must have been a shattering experience.

At times we were forced to go to extreme lengths to cope with both labour deficiencies and lingual problems, the latter occasioned by the mixture of Australian, Greek, Italian, German, Dutch, Yugoslav and other nationalities. Because so few men could either converse in or indeed understand English, we had to resort to relayed instructions. At Anna Creek, between Marree and Oodnadatta, we had an excellent Yugoslav ganger, Frank Sujkle, who could speak English as well as one or two European languages. The roadmaster would give Frank the necessary instructions and he would relay them over the telephone in the appropriate tongue. However, the ultimate action in respect of the manpower shortage involved the appointment of a man to the position of ganger even before he had begun work with us, and irrespective of whether he possessed any permanent way experience. One weekend there had been an alcohol-induced disturbance at Alberrie Creek, 52 kilometres north of Marree, and Bill Stephens, the Senior Roadmaster, had gone there to sort things out. Looking over the men on the Sunday afternoon, he noticed one who appeared to have been drinking less than the others, so Bill said to him: 'How long have you been here?'

The answer came: 'Since last Friday's train.'

He was told: 'All right. Tomorrow you will be in charge of the gang.'

When I joined the Commonwealth Railways, apart from the acute shortages of manpower and materials, three things were apparent: the aftermath of the extraordinary heavy wartime load; the prospects of increased rail movements of coal from Leigh Creek; and a determination by Pat Hannaberry not only to hold the current level of traffic but to increase it.

Prior to World War II, there had been virtually no freight traffic on the Trans Australian Railway, the weekly service amounting to three passenger trains and one goods train in each direction. On the Central Australia Railway too, traffic had been light. Apart from a seasonal but relatively heavy movement in cattle, only The Ghan, the Marree Mixed and perhaps two through freight trains operated each week. However, in the mid-1940s large tonnages of low grade coal had been railed from Telford (Leigh Creek) to Quorn and on to Adelaide. This traffic would not have continued had not the South Australian Government decided to eliminate for all time the State's dependence on supplies of New South Wales coal for electric power generation and establish a large power station complex at Curlew Point near Port Augusta, to be fuelled entirely with Leigh Creek coal. The prospect of this traffic put the lower end of the CAR in a completely new light.

Safari—Chief Civil Engineer Style

I joined the Commonwealth Railways, not at its operational headquarters at Port Augusta but at Kalgoorlie, its western extremity, and travelled over the Trans line by motor inspection car. It meant therefore that I started my five years on the wallaby from the very first day. My introduction to the job also came with another shock.

I was greeted with 'Mr Fitch, this is your swag,' when met there by Maintenance Engineer Vic Noble, Water Supply Engineer George Pauley, Roadmaster Lindsay Martlow and Driver Norm Cottel. It had been arranged that we travel to Port Augusta by this means, taking eight days for the journey. Having been across the Trans line as a passenger on a number of occasions, I was conscious of its isolation, but I was unprepared for the fact that, as Chief Civil Engineer, I would have to carry my swag.

In time, I became so attached to my swag that, for the years from 1949 to 1954, I did not venture away from Port Augusta without it. For the greater part of that time, neither my activities, my attire nor my living conditions were much different from those of my subordinates, be they engineers or labourers. My swag, too, was just an ordinary bluey, no different front any other. Rolled inside a second-hand khaki-coloured canvas ground sheet were two bed sheets, pillowcase, blankets, towel, cake of soap and toilet roll, all secured by two leather straps.

The ground sheet did not necessarily mean that the swag was designed specifically for sleeping under the stars; its prime purpose was that of a carry-all. But, because of the frequency with which emergencies arose, I often did in fact bed down in this manner. Nevertheless, it must be said that the silent crystal clear desert nights, especially on the Nullarbor, have a spell all of their own; but so too have the flies the unfailing habit of crawling all over one's face at the first glint of daylight.

As Chief Civil Engineer, I had to carry out a great deal of track inspection; in some years as much as 50 percent of my time. Both the Trans Australian and the Central Australia Railways were covered in their entireties at least twice a year, and the important sections more often. However, it was the washaways and derailments, when one left Port Augusta not knowing precisely when one would return, that occasioned the greatest use of the swag. Track inspections were in effect safaris, and were made by motor inspection car. That used on the Trans line, a Chevrolet, was the same vehicle that had earlier patrolled the Nullarbor Plain to guard against the escape of prisoners of war or alien internees. A Ford station sedan, modified to travel on the narrow gauge railway, was used on the CAR while a small Morris used to bounce its way between Darwin and Birdum.

I would be accompanied by the Water Supply Engineer, the Senior Roadmaster, the Roadmaster over whose district we were travelling at the time, and a driver. We would set out from Port Augusta and inspect to either Alice Springs or Kalgoorlie, and be on the track for seven or eight days. The swags would be unloaded from the motor inspection car at each night's stopover and laid out on wire stretchers in rest houses along the line. The rest houses were simple one- or two-roomed weatherboard cabins, without air-conditioning, cooling fans, electric light or refrigeration. One room held four beds while the other — and this only on the Trans line — was the kitchen. Lighting was by kerosene pressure lamp.

Water for drinking, cooking and washing was obtained from a galvanised-iron rainwater tank. Some distance away, lonely and forlorn on the prairie, stood the toilet. It consisted of a deep hole in the ground — deep enough it was thought to deter the blowflies — and surmounted by a small cubicle housing a toilet seat. Because of its propensity to capsize in strong winds, the little hut was strutted on the outside with old sleepers and anchored with fencing wire.

On the Central line, where most of the gangs consisted of single men living in a communal mess, the routine was somewhat similar, except that we shared their accommodation at the nightly stopovers and had our meals with them

The Chief Civil Engineer did not receive any preferential treatment. He manhandled his swag just like other members of the party, unloading it from the motor inspection car, making up his own bed, rolling it up in the morning and reloading it on to the car.

Climatically, the region in which I worked was similar to that of Western Australia's Murchison and Eastern Goldfields. It was just as hot and just as dry; it was also just as prone to unpredictable yet devastating thunderstorms. The average maximum summer temperatures at such places as Cook, Tarcoola, Marree, Oodnadatta and Alice Springs hovered around the Fahrenheit century. Port Augusta too could be grouped with them, but it did have the benefit of being located at the head of the narrow and tapering Spencer Gulf. Nevertheless, over the four months from December 1950 to March 1951 the town recorded 36 centuries; that is, almost one day in every three.

Track maintenance programmes were based on the Hallade recorder. A French invention, the Hallade consisted essentially of three pendulums acting on different axes. When set up over the trailing bogie of a railway car, it recorded on a continuous paper roll the longitudinal, vertical and transverse oscillations of the vehicle. While the instrument recorded the movement of the car rather than the track condition, by using the same car for every test run, its innate characteristics soon became apparent, and any abnormal movement of the pendulums indicated a track irregularity.

The recorder was run over the lines every two months, after which the maintenance programme for the ensuing period was determined. Indeed, except in the case of an emergency, a ganger was not permitted to work at any spot on his length other than that indicated on his Hallade roll and to priorities laid down by his roadmaster.

Seated in a motor inspection car or on a gang section car, the Chief Civil Engineer would have on his knees a wooden box fitted with two hand-operated spools holding the roll from the latest test run. By winding the roll from spool to spool he could keep in front of him a recording of the section of the track over which he was then travelling.

Frequently, a stop would be made to check the standard of the ganger's work, not only by means of a rail gauge but also by kneeling down on the ballast with one's eyes at rail level and squinting along the running top.

On track inspections, the driver would double as cook, his food supplies on the Trans Line being obtained from the departmental stores at Port Augusta, Tarcoola, Cook and Rawlinna, as well as from the passing Tea and Sugar train, known colloquially as the Sugar. Bread was purchased from the railway bakeries at Port Augusta, Tarcoola and Rawlinna.

A normal inspection of this line would involve overnight stops at Wirrappa, Wynbring, Watson, Hughes, Loongana, Naretha and Karonie. There was a certain degree of uniformity about the places; at all but one they consisted of nothing more than a siding, station name board, telephone cabin, gang tool shed and six fettlers' cottages. The exception was Loongana, which in my time boasted a stationmaster and, as a result, the establishment rose from six to seven cottages. When Kalgoorlie was reached on the eighth day the motor inspection car would then be loaded on to a railway flat wagon and the party return to Port Augusta by train.

Despite the long distances and the loneliness, inspection trips were not boring. Contrary to popular belief, it was not all Nullarbor Plain; nor was it without its historical and geographical points of interest.

For the first 514 kilometres to Wynbring, the line passed through pastoral country, with myall, mallee, mulga and salt bush the predominant vegetation. The terrain too was varied: flat-topped mesas; treeless gibber plains, on one of which was located the Woomera rocket range; and a number of salt pans.

The first siding out of Port Augusta — originally called the 17 Mile, then the 73 Mile after the extension of the line to Port Pirie, and latterly Tent Hill — was, during the pneumonic influenza epidemic of 1919, the site of a camp where westbound passengers were quarantined, at their own expense, for ten days, in an optimistic but futile endeavour to prevent the spread of the disease to Western Australia. My mother and my sister Jean spent the statutory period in the camp in April 1919 when they were returning to Western Australia from a holiday in Victoria. (There was another camp at Karonie, 111 kilometres east of Kalgoorlie, in which east-bound passengers were incarcerated for the same period.)

Wynbring, a gang camp situated at the foot of a granite outcrop and surrounded by mulga scrub, had some claims to history. It was here that the explorer Ernest Giles camped in 1875 when travelling from Fowlers Bay to Beltana and again in 1876 on his transcontinental trip to Western Australia. Here too Mrs Daisy Bates spent the years 1941–45 before deteriorating health forced her return to civilisation.

On the third day, after leaving Wynbring, we would enter the mallee and desert oak covered sandhills, which extended for the next 170 kilometres to the eastern edge of the Nullarbor Plain, and where the line, which consisted almost entirely of sharp curves, climbed steadily through Barton and Immarna before descending over the final 32 kilometres and debouching on to the

Plain at Ooldea. It was a lonely section. At the 397 and 416 Mile camps, single maintenance men batched in tiny weatherboard cabins. Latterly, these places were endowed with the august titles of Mount Christie and Mungala, but in no way did that lessen their isolation.

Ooldea was one of the better known places on the Trans Australian Railway. The Ooldea soak, some distance from the siding, had for centuries been the home of a large Aboriginal community; Daisy Bates also lived there for 22 years. The arrival of a passenger train at the siding used to arouse a great deal of activity among the indigenous residents, eager to display their boomerangs and model goannas, which were hastily fashioned out of immature wood and made especially for sale to unsuspecting passengers. The Ooldea Aboriginal community was eventually resettled at Yalata, 100 kilometres to the south and adjacent to the Eyre Highway.

Between Ooldea and Watson, the railway traversed two almost indistinguishable curves before entering the world record 470 kilometre straight. Watson, which was the railhead for the then embryonic Maralinga testing range 50 kilometres north, was also the site of an abandoned limestone quarry, from which thousands of tonnes of ballast were obtained for the railway. Once, in the Immarna sandhills nearby, when on my hands and knees squinting the track, my eyes alighted on a piece of ballast in the form of a perfectly shaped scallop shell fossilised into the limestone, a relic of the time when this land was under the sea.

The inspection of the Nullarbor took three and a half days, including two and a half on the straight itself. The horizon was limitless, and one would travel for eight hours each day with no vista other than a pair of rails, paralleled by a telephone line stretching out to infinity across a flat, treeless limestone plain. From departure in the morning to arrival in the evening, the picture was the same.

The straight would be left at Nurina, but that did not herald the end of long straights. Except for an occasional curve, inserted no doubt for no other reason than to correct a survey error, the line continued gun-barrel fashion for another 246 kilometres.

The narrow gauge railway through the Pichi Richi Pass between Port Augusta and Quorn (*Photo:* the author)

Quorn railway station, old Central Australia Railway; currently headquarters for the Pichi Richi Railway Preservation Society (*Photo:* the author)

Ruins of Kanyaka sheep station north of Quorn, which once ran 40,000 sheep and supported 70 families (*Photo:* the author)

Stunted vegetation would reappear near Naretha, while at Kitchener — 60 kilometres further west and 726 kilometres from Ooldea — the mallee and salmon gums of Western Australia's goldfield's plateau would come into view, and would continue to Kalgoorlie, 1691 kilometres from our starting point at Port Augusta.

Finally, eight days after setting out, we would pass through Golden Ridge, scene of some early mining activity, skirt the Golden Mile and arrive at Kalgoorlie.

The sidings along the way perpetuated the names of former politicians — Barton, Watson, Fisher, Cook, Hughes, Deakin, Reid and Forrest — as well as two World War I leaders — Haig and Kitchener. Since my time there, eight other names have been added, five of them — McLeay, Lyons, O'Malley, Chifley and Curtin — politicians; two — Ferguson and Denman — Governors-General; and one, Blamey, a soldier.

No doubt the deceased gentlemen would have been gratified at the thought of their names having been immortalised, but their pleasure would surely have been dimmed were they to realise the insignificance of the places upon which their names had been bestowed. Indeed, one wonders just how much sycophancy entered into the selection of the names.

Inspections to Alice Springs, although basically the same, were more interesting, even if the condition of the track gave cause for continued

A close-up of the gang camp built in the 1880s at Curdimurka, Central Australia Railway (*Photo:* Simon Coxon)

Ruins of the railway cottages, Mern Merna (*Photo:* the author)

Curdimurka, 101 kilometres north of Marree (*Photo:* Simon Coxon)

Curdimurka, Central Australia Railway. The remains of the Kennicott water treatment plant and overhead tank (*Photo:* Simon Coxon)

railway cross the Flinders Ranges three times — between Port Augusta and Quorn; Hawker and Hookina; and between Beltana and Copley — but it also ran parallel with them for most of the way. In some places, the line sat precariously on a ledge cut out of the mountain, with a precipitous face on one side and, a dry stone retaining wall on the other.

At Quorn, the railway turned north across the Willochra Plain, its desolation a monument to the nineteenth-century idiocy of destroying the native vegetation in a misguided attempt to grow wheat there. Unfortunately, an occasional freak season led the early settlers to believe that they could trifle with nature.

On the way, we would pass the ruins of the Kanyaka station homestead, where 40,000 sheep had once supported 70 families, and Beltana, site of Sir Thomas Elder's early camel station, the

Smith of Dunesk Mission and John Flynn's first inland base. It was from Beltana too that Ernest Giles commenced his east–west crossing of the continent. Telford, 40 kilometres further north, was the railway station for the Leigh Creek coalfield, while Lyndhurst was the railhead for the Strzelecki Track to Innaminka, and latterly for the Moomba gas fields. Just north of Lyndhurst was Farina — formerly called Government Gums, and terminus of the first section of the north–south railway — its name yet another reminder of man's folly in trying to push nature too far.

The next phase, the Lake Eyre country which extended for 500 kilometres to beyond William Creek, was forbidding. Almost entirely devoid of vegetation, subject to sand drift — not a little of which could be attributed to overstocking — and with a thin alkaline surface crust, it possessed a number of places of some interest.

Marree — originally called Hergott Springs but renamed during the World War I anti-German hysteria — was the centre of South Australia's Islamic community, and also jumping-off place for the famous Birdsville Track.

Near Curdimurka, 100 kilometres beyond Marree, the railway skirted Lake Eyre South and here, according to the plans, the line was about

Opening of the Darwin–Pine Creek Railway, 1 October 1889 (*Photo:* South Australian Archives)

Darwin Railway yards, Northern Territory, c. 1932 (*Photo:* Darwin City Council Collection, Department of Chief Minister, Northern Territory)

Adelaide River railway station, North Australia Railway (*Photo:* Northern Territory Administration)

unlawfully from former army fuel dumps and that the authorities and the purloiner — whose name was bandied freely around the town — were both playing wait-and-see.

The Katherine story had a similar ring to it. It seemed that, one night, someone had pushed an ex-army four-wheeled-drive Waukesha truck over to the tree, attached a block and tackle to a limb and removed the engine from the chassis. Unfortun-ately for the miscreants, daylight intervened before the operation could be completed; so the engine remained suspended while all Katherine watched and waited. It had been so elevated for some months when I saw it.

Gold mining — which had prompted the first real development in the Territory — had virtually disappeared; the Rum Jungle and the Frances Creek projects had not even been contemplated; and the explosion in tourism was not even a dream. Indeed, the only activity of note was the abortive attempt by the Bovril Company to establish processing works at Katherine.

At the few settlements along the line, Territorians from way back, as well as newcomers who had fallen under the spell of the Top End, lived happily under the trying conditions. In between, it was deserted, with only the maintenance gangs, an occasional prospector and some picturesque individuals who had 'gone troppo' and who camped in the bush, unkempt, sometimes bare-footed, and living off what they could catch or shoot. Some of these characters worked spasmodically on the railway, but their contributions did not add to its efficiency.

In those years, the labour shortage in the Northern Territory was such that work on the railway held few attractions. Consequently, while the gangers were generally dedicated men who, with their wives, were content to live and work on this truly pioneer railway, most of the men under them did not constitute the flower of the Territory's manhood. Indeed, many of them had left Darwin for their own good.

On my first inspection of the line, Roadmaster Jack Wood — whom I first knew in Western Australia — told me with some satisfaction that he had succeeded in engaging three men, and had re-established a gang at a siding about 200 kilometres down the line. When we arrived there, I was not overly impressed with the new employees. Inside the ramshackle hut I found three dirty hessian bunks — each with an equally

Locomotive taking water, Darwin River, North Australia Railway, c. 1900 (*Photo:* Northern Territory Administration)

Arrival in Darwin of the first Ghan from Adelaide, 3 February 2004 (*Photo:* Yvonne Lamotte)

Darwin standard gauge rail terminal (*Photo:* Yvonne Lamotte)

dirty blanket — a couple of loaves of bread and three tins of meat, their only food supply until the next train, due in three days' time. I could not envisage our getting our money's worth out of the new gang.

Perhaps the best story indicative of the nature of this railway in the postwar years was related to me by Fred McAuley, Chief Mechanical Engineer for the Commonwealth Railways in 1949 and 1950.

It had been decided to convert the steam locomotives from coal to furnace oil burning, and Fred had gone from Port Augusta to Darwin to supervise the installation of the equipment. Having completed the conversion of the first locomotive, he decided to travel on the footplate with the crew on its run to Larrimah.

About 60 kilometres out, there was a sharp curve at the start of a steep grade leading to a bridge over the Darwin River. After having checked his speed on the curve, the engineman opened the regulator to gain momentum to take the train up the grade on the other side of the river. Some distance up that grade, the locomotive literally jumped a washout. Miraculously, and thanks to the ironwood sleepers, the gauge held long enough for the engine to negotiate the gap; but then the track collapsed, pitching several goods vehicles into the hole.

While McAuley and the train crew were contemplating the wreckage, and at the same time thanking Providence and the ironwood sleepers for their good luck, the gang whose camp was further down the line arrived on their section car. The ganger, seemingly oblivious to the accident, dismounted, walked up to the guard and asked:

'Where's our bread?'

After the bread had been retrieved from the guard's van, put down on the ground where it became waterlogged, and then on to the side of the locomotive to dry out — and where it became black with grime — McAuley said to the ganger:

'Did you have any rain last night?'

'Yes, about eight inches,' came the reply.

'Did you patrol your length this morning?'

'Yes.'

'Which way did you go?'

'To the other end of the length.'

'Do you usually get washaways that end?'

'No.'

'Then why did you go that way?'

'We knew the train was coming, so we went the other so that we wouldn't run into it.'

The exchange ended with the Chief Mechanical Engineer saying: 'You're suspended.'

One Thursday afternoon, shortly after the weekly southbound train had gone through, I called in at the 22 Mile camp south of Darwin, where a handsome ebony-black Aborigine, dressed in clean khaki shorts and boots but nothing else, was in charge of a gang of not too prepossessing white fettlers. Inside his cottage — a concrete-floored galvanised-iron former army building — were two small naked children, a couple of pigs and several Aboriginal women. The women were members of his wife's family, and had come to the camp to collect their share of the stores that had come out from Darwin on the train. The ganger, whose surname of McClelland suggested some Scottish dalliance along the way, was said to have been the provider for such an extended family that his fortnightly account with the departmental provision store generally absorbed his entire wages packet.

My five years as Chief Civil Engineer for the Commonwealth Railways had their moments. For the most part they were associated with emergencies thrust upon the branch by four things — the remoteness of the territory; the fragility of the Central line and its legacy from the almost impossible wartime traffic task that it had to bear; supply problems in respect of fuel, water and sleepers; and, most of all, the frequency of derailments and washaways. To these should be added the strain placed on our domesticity by my frequent and often unpredictable absences from home.

Derailments were the biggest bogey. Unfortunately, both engines and the vehicles behind them had the pernicious habit of leaving the rails, and then —possibly from some cussedness on the part of nature — generally at night. I have forgotten the number of times that I have been roused from my bed. Instinctively, I knew why. In the author's experience, the CAR would vie with SAR's Eyre Peninsula in respect of their frequency.

my hands, grazing the insides of my thighs and tearing my trousers, but not in restoring the telephone circuit.

Damage extended as far north as the Finke. Apart from a number of small washaways, several streams flowed over the line. The bridge at The Peake, south of Oodnadatta, was 1.4 metres under water but undamaged, but, to the north, the Finke flowed 1.7 metres over the rails, while at the Alberga, Hamilton, Ross and Stephenson Rivers the flood levels reached one metre.

On the trip to Finke and back, on which I was accompanied by Acting Roadmaster Bill Glasson, we had to push the quad through those rivers where the track had been lowered into the stream bed, and after each crossing we had to dry out the ignition.

In addition to the regular gangs, we shanghaied every able-bodied man that we could find and set them to work, not only to build a deviation around the Stoney Creek bridge but also to effect permanent repairs elsewhere. They worked extremely long hours, but when the paymaster arrived they declared a 24 hours' stop-work and adjourned to the Oodnadatta Hotel.

Railwaymen are magnificent under such circumstances. Ordinarily, they might grumble and work only as hard as they are obliged to do, but come a derailment or a washaway and they will toil around the clock without complaint, indeed with good humour. Perhaps the fact that, as was my case with the Commonwealth Railways, the boss was one of them, sharing the long hours, the water, the mud and the discomfort, helped in this regard.

I did learn one lesson from these washaways. Always take not one but two bulldozers or front-end loaders with you. If you do not, the one that you do take will inevitably become bogged and, without a second one to extricate it, you will be left bereft of any mechanical assistance whatsoever.

The Central Australia Railway's propensity to washaways must have been a dominant factor in the decision to replace it with the standard gauge line from Tarcoola to Alice Springs. Opened in 1980, the new line skirts, wherever possible, the headwaters of the streams that flow eastwards to Lake Eyre. As I have already noted, had it not been for South Australia's insistence that the narrow gauge route be retained, the standard gauge line would have been an accomplished fact over 50 years earlier.

The Stirling North–Marree Standard Gauge Railway

When, in June 1956, coal started to move over the new standard gauge railway from Telford to Stirling North near Port Augusta, the event was not just the culmination of a straightforward railway project. The circumstances leading up to it included protracted Commonwealth–State argument, a Royal Commission lasting 12 months, and a degree of bitterness and ill feeling between certain of the principals which, in the long term, prejudiced their professional standing, their careers and their health.

Coal of low calorific value and high ash content had been found near Leigh Creek, 610 kilometres north of Adelaide, as far back as 1888, but no significant development of the field had been undertaken. The coal had been tested in a locomotive in 1897 and the most noteworthy result had been the destruction by fire of a number of wagons on the train, caused, it was thought, by the excessive discharge of sparks from the locomotive's funnel.

Major exploitation of the coal deposits did not occur until World War II, when the Premier, Thomas Playford, took appropriate steps to free South Australia's electric power generation from the whims and caprices of the NSW coal miners. The decision was made to construct a power station of 90 megawatts capacity at Curlew Point near Port Augusta. Within 12 months, the designed capacity was increased to 270 megawatts. It proved to be one of Playford's greatest achievements.

During this period, too, both the Commonwealth Railways and the South Australian Railways again experimented with the use of the coal in their steam locomotives, either on its own or in conjunction with heavy furnace oil. It helped out in an emergency, but its continued use as a locomotive fuel was out of the question.

In the meantime, large tonnages of coal were railed to the Adelaide metropolitan area for use at the Osborne power station. This movement, which went on for about 13 years, involved as much as 300,000 tonnes per annum.

At this time, the railway from Telford to Terowie, 385 kilometres long, was narrow gauge and of light construction, the section from Telford to Quorn being owned and operated by the Commonwealth Railways. The remaining 230 kilometres from Terowie to the power station were heavy duty broad gauge. South Australian Railways T class locomotives were used over the whole of the narrow gauge portion of the route, and even though they worked as twin units the gross load between Telford and Quorn was as little as 671 tonnes, while the payload of coal was only 447 tonnes.

Crew working involved an empty movement from Quorn to Beltana, a distance of 191 kilometres and, following on a rest period of at least eight hours, the crew would work to Telford, leave the rake of empty wagons, pick up a loaded one and return to Beltana — a round trip of 80 kilometres. After another rest period, the crew would work a loaded train to Quorn, where SAR staff would take over the running to Terowie. There the coal would be transferred to broad gauge vehicles and on-railed to the Osborne power station.

At times, as many as 17 coal trains operated weekly in each direction. Indeed, during the livestock season, when there was a mass movement of cattle from Central Australia, the number of trains of all description totalled 28 up and 28 down, a fantastic load to put on such a light railway.

Another of Playford's many achievements. — and perhaps his master stroke — was in persuading Senator Collings, Federal Minister for the Interior, to agree not only to the extremely low freight rate of one halfpenny per ton mile (0.255 cents per tonne kilometre) for the carriage of coal from Telford to Quorn, but for this rate to apply in perpetuity.

The initial demand for Leigh Creek coal at Port Augusta, estimated at 1.2 million tonnes per annum, was patently beyond the capacity of the narrow gauge line. It would have required 55 double-headed coal trains per week in each direction. The subsequent decision to increase the generating capacity at Port Augusta to 270 megawatts, requiring not less than 2 million tonnes of coal annually, put the matter beyond question. Quite obviously, an operation of this magnitude demanded a solidly constructed standard gauge railway with easy grades and curves.

In the 1870s, alternative routes for the Port Augusta to Government Gums railway were considered; one entirely west of the Flinders Ranges, and the other crossing them in three places. The western route was favoured by Surveyor General Goyder, but a subsequent Royal Commission expressed a preference for the alternative, and this was the route adopted.

During the 1939–45 war, the CAR was subjected to an extremely heavy traffic load, which produced two postwar legacies. One was the existence of a substantial railway establishment at Quorn, and the other a precarious situation in respect of the condition of locomotives, rollingstock and track. So while Quorn was equipped to handle large tonnages of Leigh Creek coal, the existing railway would be unable to carry a large and sustained traffic in coal.

The Commonwealth Railways Comissioner, P.J. Hannaberry, had no difficulty in deciding that the construction of a heavy duty standard gauge railway, with easy grades and flat curvature, was imperative. He also submitted that, because South Australia had always taken the view that the conversion of the CAR and indeed its extension to Darwin should be part of any national standardisation plan, the Leigh Creek line could well come within its ambit. However, when the Rail Standardisation Division did enter the discussions, Hannaberry very quickly changed his mind and was determined that the whole project should be a Commonwealth Railways undertaking.

There were certain undertones to his decision. The Commonwealth Railways was within the portfolio of the Minister for the Interior, while the Rail Standardisation Division reported to the Minister for Transport. In view of then inherent jealousy between Commonwealth Departments, such disharmony was inevitable. Incidentally, the strained relationship between the two departments persisted until 1952, when the Rail Standardisation Division was unceremoniously abandoned and its functions taken over by the

Commonwealth Railways under the banner of the Department of Shipping and Transport.

The Commonwealth Railways undertook trial surveys to determine the most favourable route for the new railway. What became known as the western route departed from the narrow gauge line at Copley, 10 kilometres south of Telford, and deviated west of the Ranges, bypassing Beltana and rejoining the existing railway a few kilometres north of Parachilna. The two lines then ran parallel for 27 kilometres to Brachina, where the standard gauge again deviated to the west and headed in a more or less straight line to Stirling North.

Prima facie, this route offered such advantages from a railway point of view that investigation of an alternative appeared unnecessary. Nevertheless, a second trial survey was conducted to see what improvements might be made substantially along the narrow gauge route, with its 1 in 50 grades and 141 m (7 chain) curves. Between Telford and Brachina, it followed the western alternative, but thereafter it proceeded through Quorn to Stirling North, though with a great deal of regrading, as well as deviations between Mern Merna and Hawker and between Hawker and Wilson. A deviation was also contemplated between Quorn and Stirling North, but this was abandoned in favour of the use of assistant locomotive power. However, considerable curvature improvement would still have been necessary on this section.

The comparison was overwhelmingly in favour of the western route. It was 14 kilometres shorter; its ruling grade of 1 in 150 contrasted strongly with the 1 in 120 from Telford to Quorn with bank engine working beyond; the curvature of 60 chains (1207 m) radius was infinitely better than that of 10 chains (201 m) on the route through Quorn; and the estimated construction cost was substantially less. It was also found later

Stirling North - Leigh Creek Standard Gauge Railway Alternate Routes

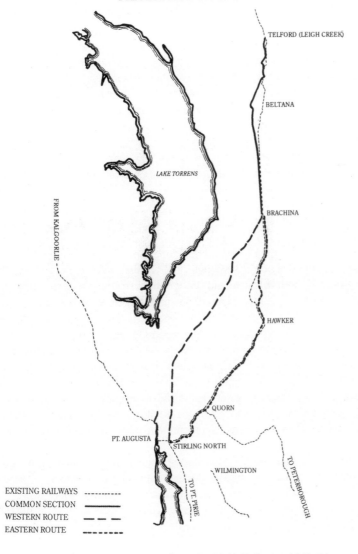

EXISTING RAILWAYS
COMMON SECTION
WESTERN ROUTE
EASTERN ROUTE

The Leigh Creek Standard Gauge Railway Commission. Left to right: Mr J.A. Fargher, Mr Justice A.A. Wolff and the author

Marree, South Australia. Official opening of the standard gauge railway extension from Leigh Creek, 27 March 1958. (*Photo:* J.H. Sykes)

that a 1 in 180 grade could be achieved on the western route without any significant increase in earthworks.

Operationally too, this route offered advantages, not only because of its shorter length and heavier train loads, but also because the eastern route would have involved either doubling — that is, breaking the train into two parts and surmounting the steep grade in two movements — or an assistant engine between Quorn and the Summit, a distance of eight kilometres.

Hannaberry had previously submitted proposals to the Commonwealth Government for the purchase of diesel electric locomotives of American manufacture for use on the Trans Australian Railway, and no doubt also contemplated their use on the Leigh Creek railway. However, in the late 1940s the Chifley Government imposed severe restrictions on expenditures involving U.S. dollars and this implied an indefinite postponement of the acquisition of diesels.

At about this time, a number of Mikado type standard gauge steam locomotives became available in Australia. They had been built by the Clyde Engineering Company Pty Ltd, and had been intended for China, but to appease possible objection by the recipients they were designated the MacArthur type. However, the Communist takeover in China prompted the authorities to withdraw their offer and the Commonwealth Land Transport Board sought to sell the locomotives locally. The South Australian Railways bought ten units, converted them to broad gauge and designated them the 740 class.

The Commonwealth Railways also purchased ten, classified as L class.

As events turned out, and particularly as the result of the Menzies Government's success in 1950 in negotiating a substantial loan in the United States and so facilitating the purchase of diesel units, these steam locomotives were not used to any marked extent by the Commonwealth Railways. The SAR, however, made extensive use of them and they were in traffic for many years.

In the light of their having acquired the MacArthur locomotives, the Commonwealth Railways based their economic studies of the alternative routes for the Leigh Creek standard gauge railway on the assumption that this type of power would be used. Those studies indicated that annual operating savings of the order of $257,000 and capital savings of $1,956,000 would be effected if the western route was adopted. In view therefore of the longstanding agreement between the Commonwealth and South Australian Governments in respect of the freight rate on coal between Telford and Quorn — and which, it was logical to assume, would apply to Stirling North when the Port Augusta power station became operative — there appeared to be an irrefutable case for its adoption; and such a recommendation, was made to the Federal Government.

This recommendation, if adopted, would have meant the inevitable demise of Quorn as a large railway centre. At that time, there were 313 railway employees stationed there, who with their families represented a total of over 750 people, or slightly more than 40 percent of the town's population. The South Australian Government, especially Messrs Malcolm Mcintosh and R.H. Chapman, Minister of Railways and Railways Commissioner, were concerned not only in respect of the economic damage to Quorn that would result from the adoption of the western route, but also of the possible prejudicial effect that it might have on any standardisation proposals for the Peterborough Division of the SAR.

Therefore, while the State desired the transport of large quantities of coal at minimal cost to itself, it also sought to maintain the status quo of Quorn and the Peterborough Division as a whole. But as both Commonwealth and State legislation would be necessary before any railway works could commence, an impasse seemed likely.

On 29 May 1950, a discussion took place in the Prime Minister's office in Canberra. In addition to Mr Menzies, the Commonwealth was represented by Senator George McLeay, Minister for Shipping and Transport, Philip McBride MHR, Pat Hannaberry, and the author. Representing South Australia were Messrs Playford, McIntosh and Chapman. It was apparent that Playford, while not wanting to prejudice Quorn, was primarily concerned with the movement of large quantities of coal, and at a low cost to the State. However, McIntosh and Chapman argued bitterly against the western route. They were opposed just as bitterly by Hannaberry, who throughout the whole conference received only tacit support from his Minister. In fact, except for Menzies, who maintained a neutral though sympathetic stance, not one word was offered on his behalf.

But Hannaberry was quite capable of presenting his case without assistance, and I feel sure that his performance that afternoon so impressed the Prime Minister that his subsequent representations for a share of the US dollar loan, with which to purchase diesel electric locomotives, were viewed sympathetically.

The Canberra conference achieved nothing. However, Playford and Hannaberry held their own talks a few months later, and from these came the idea that the stalemate might be resolved by a Royal Commission, whose determination as to the route to be adopted would be binding on both parties. This proposition was acceptable to both the Commonwealth and the State, and the enabling legislation enacted by both Parliaments.

As there was no dispute over that portion of the railway north of Brachina, Bills were drafted for the authorisation of the Brachina to Leigh Creek North Coalfield Standard Gauge Railway. After assent, construction on this section started in mid-1951.

The Royal Commission consisted of His Honour Mr Justice A.A.Wolff of the Supreme Court of Western Australia, as chairman, together with Mr J.A. Fargher and the author, nominated by the South Australian and Commonwealth Governments respectively. It sat from June 1951 to June 1952, there being a total of 49 sitting days as well as a number of inspections, and the findings were submitted precisely one year after its first sitting.

Justice Wolff was no stranger to railway problems. In the 1940s he conducted an enquiry into the Australian Standard Garratt locomotives on behalf of the Western Australian Government. During the Leigh Creek railway Royal Commission, a Belpaire firebox was mentioned, something normally alien to anyone but a steam locomotive man, but on this occasion His Honour sketched its outline and passed it to Fargher and me for confirmation.

Fargher — at that time Assistant to the SAR Commissioner — and I were both placed in delicate situations. In our substantive positions, we were subordinate to our Commissioners, who had expressed diametrically opposite views regarding the route that the railway should take. It was difficult therefore to disregard entirely the loyalty that we owed them. Nevertheless, we tried to maintain a strictly objective stance, for which, in the long term and in different ways, we both suffered as a consequence. Once, during a lunch break between sittings, Hannaberry, in an angry outburst, threatened me with dismissal.

Despite the strain under which we laboured, especially during the last month when we were consolidating the estimates while the chairman was drafting the report, not at any time did we allow our disagreements to descend to a personal level. Out of this experience there developed a mutual respect and trust which, in later years, resulted in the establishment of a close and harmonious working relationship which lasted until Fargher's retirement in 1966, and continued on a personal basis until his death in 1977.

The two parties were represented by eminent counsel: the Commonwealth by Messrs F. Villeneuve-Smith KC and J.L.Travers, and the State by Messrs A.J. Hannan and R.R. St.C. Chamberlain. However, while not questioning the qualifications or professional standing of either the Chairman or counsel, my close association with this and a number of other investigations has convinced me that, where technical or economic matters are to determined, it would be preferable if legal personnel were excluded.

In the Leigh Creek railway enquiry, the chairman had the good sense to rely on Fargher and me when railway engineering matters were in dispute; but it was obvious that counsel on both sides were floundering for most of the time. On a number of occasions, it was necessary for the cross-examination of witnesses to be taken over by Fargher and me, because it was patent that counsel had no idea of what it was all about.

South Australia's opposition to the western route was based on four things.

First, it claimed, and with some justification, that, in its estimates for construction, the Commonwealth had underestimated the figures for bridging and housing on the western route and had overestimated those for earthworks on the route via Quorn. During the course of the Royal Commission, and without any prior advice to the Commonwealth Railways, South Australian Railways Commissioner Chapman arranged for check surveys to be made of certain deviations proposed for the eastern route, as well as typical creek crossings on both routes. This intervention into Commonwealth territory without prior notice did not enhance the relationship between the two railway administrations.

Second, it maintained that, using MacArthur locomotives, it would not be possible on either route to work a coal train from Telford to Stirling North in one shift. If the movement could not be achieved in one shift and the operation split into two, then, on the eastern route, Quorn could be the change-over point and so remain a railway centre, and in this way the town's economy would be unimpaired. On the other hand, two shift working on the western route would mean that the Commonwealth's estimates for train crews and housing would be too low.

The SAR had had extensive experience with this type of locomotive, its design being fundamentally that of its 700 class; and its officers were adamant that one shift working could not be achieved. Hannaberry was equally adamant that through working was practicable; and he went so far as to decide that, even on the Quorn route, this would be done. This meant that, in his view, Quorn was doomed as a railway centre irrespective of the alternative adopted. One of Hannaberry's characteristics was to achieve what he had set out to achieve, but this decision worried both his traffic officers and me.

Third, Chapman argued that the use of diesel electric locomotives, the ultimate adoption of which was inevitable despite the current restrictions on US dollars, would result in the operational savings on the western route being reduced to such a degree that they would be outweighed by the disaffection to Quorn and the Peterborough Division in general, if the latter were quantified. He maintained therefore that the economic studies should be based on the use of diesel power.

Fourth, the State claimed that the possible economic damage to Quorn and the Peterborough Division, particularly after standardisation, had not been given adequate consideration. Subsequent events proved that, commercially, Quorn died with the passing of the railway. In the same way, the Peterborough–Quorn narrow gauge line fell into desuetude to such a degree that, in later advocacy for further rail standardisation works in South Australia, this section was excluded.

The Royal Commission decided that it would consider the matter on the basis of diesel electric motive power. Estimates were prepared accordingly, the Commonwealth on the premise of the use of twin locomotives on both routes, but in the case of the eastern route with special working over the steep grades between Quorn and Stirling North. On the other hand, South Australia submitted the proposition that, by taking advantage of what was known as the short term rating of the locomotive, it would be possible to haul a train of 2500 tonnes gross up the grade out of Quorn, without either load reduction or additional engine power.

The Commonwealth challenged this working on the grounds that the effort required of the locomotive to lift a load of this magnitude over the steep grade would be beyond the normal limits of friction between the wheels and the rail. The sittings of the Commission then developed into a debate on the subject of adhesion between wheel and rail. Many days were spent in argument, ranging over the entire gamut of the theory of friction, from basic physics on the one hand to treatises by Russian scientists on the other. Unfortunately it also became a contest between the proponents of the virtues of the General Motors locomotives compared with the English Electrics — this by the Commonwealth and State authorities, and not by the makers themselves, both of whom were especially careful to keep out of the dispute.

Professional reputations were now at stake. Both parties became emotional and descended to personalities. Justice Wolff was inclined to cut short the argument, feeling that the proposition submitted by F.H. Harrison, Chief Mechanical Engineer of the SAR, had not been proved wrong. However, knowing that the Commonwealth had some damaging evidence still to produce, I was able to persuade him to let it proceed for a little longer. Finally, Harrison's case collapsed under cross-examination when he was obliged to admit that the locomotive manufacturers themselves had stated that, should a train with a load calculated for a 1 in 120 grade stop on a 1 in 54 grade, such as that from Quorn to the Summit, it could not be started again.

The Royal Commission found that, after evaluating the disaffection to Quorn, the western route was to be preferred on the grounds of both capital and operating costs. Shortly after the release of its report, enabling legislation was passed by both the Commonwealth and South Australian Parliaments, and work on this section of the railway got under way. Traffic over the new line from Telford commenced in June 1956. The line was extended to Marree in 1958, something well justified in the light of the heavy movements of cattle by rail from the Strzelecki and Birdsville tracks.

South Australian Railways Commissioner Chapman was deeply affected by the Royal Commission's finding for no other reason than he considered the retention of the route through Quorn to be in the best interests of South Australia. He was upset by the bitterness that had crept into the enquiry, particularly as he was in poor health at the time. There is no doubt that the whole business contributed to his death less than a year later. He was then 63 years of age.

For my own part, the Royal Commission had its debits and its credits. I had to shoulder an excessive work load. I had not been relieved of my substantive duties as Chief Civil Engineer for the Commonwealth Railways, so it was not uncommon, during a hoped-for weekend break in Port Augusta, to be met on my arrival there with a multitude of matters requiring consideration and decision. Sadly too, my relationship with Hannaberry deteriorated. On the credit side, however, not only was I given the rare opportunity of sitting on a Royal Commission, but out if it grew a professional and personal rapport with Jack Fargher which proved to have been the most fortuitous feature of my entire career.

The new line was laid with rails weighing 94 pounds per yard (46.63 kg/m), welded into 270 feet (82.3 m) lengths and heavily ballasted with 10 inches (254 mm) of crushed stone under the sleepers. However, material shortages—structural steel and sleepers in particular — were even more pronounced than they were during the war years. In view of the time factor, those shortages called for some dramatic compromises.

The shortage of steel and of steel fabricators led us to standardise the bridge spans using imported broad flange beams, including the welding of two beams together, one on top of the other. This was an unorthodox procedure and neither design-wise nor economically the most preferred.

Sleeper supplies were even more critical, and those of suitable Australian hardwoods were simply not available. The author held private but unfruitful discussions with importers. Enquiries were also initiated into the possible use of concrete sleepers on the Leigh Creek railway, but the cost was quite prohibitive Finally, Commissioner Hannaberry — who never seemed to have relinquished what was now my substantive position of Chief Civil Engineer — ordered untreated sawn karri sleepers from Western Australia. In view of the Commonwealth Railways' experience with karri sleepers on the CAR between Oodnadatta and Alice Springs, one can only assume that he felt that there was no other option. On the other hand, he might well have sought support from South Australian Premier Playford in an endeavour to exert pressure in the right places, either to obtain suitable timber sleepers or to have the cost of concrete ones subsidised.

I did not see the completion of the railway, having left the Commonwealth Railways in April 1954, but my five years' association with it — from the trial surveys, the Royal Commission and the first three years of construction — led me to the conclusion that the whole project should properly have been one for a separate organisation. Hannaberry's determination to undertake it unaided placed not only an almost impossible load on the Civil Engineering Branch's limited resources, but it also resulted in the diversion of many of them away from essential maintenance work. Indeed, apart from the greater part of the concrete work and for the supply of ballast, both of which were undertaken by contractors most often using equipment provided by the Branch, all other activities — surveys, earthworks, tracklaying, lifting and packing, communications and administration — were carried out departmentally on a day labour basis.

A consequence of this extra load was that the activities of the Branch were near to breakdown. With one or two exceptions, it was only the loyalty of the engineering and administrative staffs, who worked interminably long hours, that prevented this from happening.

Departure
On 8 February 1954, I tendered my resignation from the position of Chief Civil Engineer for the Commonwealth Railways, a decision that had been inevitable for some time but which was brought to a head when Commissioner Hannaberry issued a policy directive which left me no other option.

I held a sincere respect for Pat Hannaberry in a number of areas. However, his impatience, impetuosity, prelidection for a fight, as well as his proneness to personal vendettas, made life difficult — indeed, at times embarrassing — for those associated with him. But perhaps the underlying reason behind my resignation arose from the fact that, even after his appointment as Commonwealth Railways Commissioner, he seemed determined not to surrender his former personal control of the day-to-day workings of the Civil Engineering Branch. This went so far as his actions in bypassing me as Chief Civil Engineer, and giving instructions direct to employees of the Branch. It went even further, to the extent that, without any prior intimation to or consultation with me, he placed orders, among other items, for heavy earthmoving plant and rail welding equipment. This last action resulted in some panic when he realised that the generating capacity of the departmental power plant at Port Augusta was insufficient to service it. It was a situation of which I was already aware, and I had taken steps to ascertain the availability of similar plant, but with its own in-built power generator.

It was a sad situation, because I held a high admiration for many of Pat Hannaberry's achievements.

In spite of the circumstances leading to my resignation, I retain many fond memories of my five years with the Commonwealth Railways, as well as Doreen's and my associations with Port Augusta.

The nature of the job was in effect an extension of my hands-on career with the WAGR, particularly during the Depression. It also gave me the opportunity to know another wide stretch of inland Australia, and it resulted in my earlier love for WA's Murchison now being shared equally with that for the old Ghan country.

And from the initial welcome that we received from arrival at Port Augusta and through our five years' residence there, to the public farewell we received on our departure, I have fond memories of our sojourn in what was, without doubt, the most friendly of the many places in which Doreen and I lived during our 60 years' itinerant married life.

9 South Australian Railways, 1954–73

The Adelaide railway station building. Completed in 1928, since 1985 it has housed Sky City Casino. The corner office on the first floor was formerly occupied by six successive Railways Commissioners

Once again my appointment, this time to the South Australian Railways, was somewhat unusual, but fortuitous.

A couple of months after I had tendered my resignation from the Commonwealth Railways, the South Australian Railways advertised locally and interstate inviting applications for the position of Assistant to the Railways Commissioner, a post rendered vacant by J.A. Fargher's appointment to the top position. I submitted an application and had the good fortune to be offered the vacancy.

Except for the Commonwealth Railways, and for F.J. Shea's appointment as Chief Mechanical Engineer for the SAR in the early 1920s, it was quite unusual for an officer to join a railway administration at the level that I did. It seems,

The author being greeted by his predecessor, J.A. Fargher, on the occasion of his appointment as South Australian Railways Commissioner, 4 October 1965 (*Photo:* South Australian Railways)

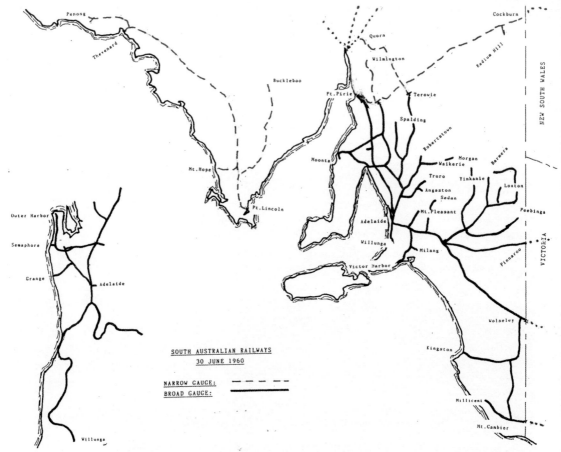

SOUTH AUSTRALIAN RAILWAYS
30 JUNE 1960

NARROW GAUGE: - - - - - -
BROAD GAUGE: ——————

North Terrace–Glenelg passenger train in Jetty Road, Glenelg. The train was replaced by an electric tram in 1929 (*Photo:* Port Dock Station Railway Museum)

however, that Fargher, although only 53 years of age at the time, looked ahead to his possible successor and saw that his best qualified senior officers were of a similar age. Perhaps therefore the fact that I was nine years his junior might have acted in my favour.

My advent might well have invited resentment

from the existing railway staff, but if any such feelings did exist, they were not made apparent to me. Indeed, it was the start of a 19 years' harmonious working relationship which, in retirement, developed into a number of lasting friendships.

Origins and Development

It started on 18 May 1854, and the last traces of the South Australian Railways disappeared on 1 March 1978, just 79 days short of its 124th birthday. The story of its demise is recorded later in this chapter.

Seven factors appear to have influenced the pattern of railway development in South Australia. They were:
- The provision of a blue water outlet for the River Murray traffic at Port Elliot, Milang and Morgan, the last indirectly through its rail connection to Port Adelaide.

- The discovery of copper ore at Kapunda, Burra Burra and Moonta.
- The tapping of the immediate hinterlands of the small outports around the coastline, in particular, Beachport, Kingston, Port Wakefield, Wallaroo, Port Broughton, Port Pirie and Port Augusta. This was possibly the principal factor behind the uncoordinated pattern of railway development in the earlier years.
- The establishment of an intercapital rail link with Victoria.
- The provision, in association with the Silverton Tramway Company Ltd, of a rail connection to Broken Hill at a time when New South Wales declined to do so.
- The grand concept of a north–south transcontinental railway.
- Agricultural development.
- Individually and collectively, these factors must have had a major influence, not only on the pattern of development, but also on the proliferation of gauges.

The disabilities associated with multi-gauges were recognised a long time ago. In the SAR Annual Report of 1889, the fallacy of having two gauges was pointed out to government. One wonders what the railways commissioners of that period would have said had they realised that, at the time of its demise 79 years later, the State would have been blighted with not two, but three different gauges, and this as the result of purported rail unification!

There might have been some justification for the adoption of the narrow gauge for the north–south and Port Pirie–Broken Hill railways — and, in later years, for those on Eyre Peninsula. The proposed line from Port Augusta to Darwin, over 2000 kilometres long, would have traversed for the most part arid country offering very little potential rail traffic, while that serving Broken Hill was dependent on a risky mining venture. Both projects must have been challenging undertakings for the impoverished and lightly populated colony.

Therefore, and as a result of these circumstances and decisions, at 30 June 1900 — and excluding the Darwin to Pine Creek railway — the SAR consisted of 816 kilometres of broad and 1978

Steam hauled passenger train in Semaphore Road between Glanville and Semaphore. The service ceased in 1978 (*Photo:* Port Dock Station Railway Museum)

kilometres of narrow gauge tracks, in all, a total of 2794 kilometres, but in four divisions based on gauge. They were:

• A relatively small broad gauge section, 816 kilometres long and extending from Terowie and Morgan through Adelaide to the Victoria border and with a branch to Victor Harbour and Milang.
• An extensive narrow gauge system starting from Hamley Bridge and extending to Moonta; from Kadina to Brinkworth; from Balaklava to Gladstone and Laura; from Terowie to Quorn; and from Port Pirie to Cockburn; in total 861 kilometres.
• The Quorn–Oodnadatta section, 769 kilometres long, of the proposed north–south railway.
• The south eastern division of 318 kilometres from Wolseley to Mount Gambier, Beachport and Kingston.

To its credit, South Australia took steps to minimise its problems of gauge, and, in the 1920s, broadened the lines from Hamley Bridge to Moonta, from Kadina to Brinkworth, and from Balaklava and Gladstone. Later, it undertook similar action in respect of the narrow gauge division in the south-east and opened successive broadened sections between 1950 and 1960.

For the most part, new construction post-1900 was confined to agricultural development, and which — including all that on Eyre Peninsula — was undertaken during the first 30 years. In fact only three new lines totalling 69 kilometres — Redhill to Port Pirie, Cutana to Radium Hill, and from Kowulka to Kevin — were completed during the next 24 years leading to my joining the SAR on 3 May 1954.

After taking into account the transfer of the Port Augusta–Oodnadatta railway to the Commonwealth, some minor line closures, and new construction, at that date the SAR amounted to 4127 kilometres, made up of 2569 kilometres broad gauge (as far south as Naracoorte), and 1558 kilometres narrow gauge (Northern Division 607 kilometres; South Eastern Division 175 kilometres; and Eyre Peninsula 776 kilometres).

During my 19 years with the SAR, new construction was limited to 115 kilometres: 8 kilometres broad; 47 kilometres standard; and 60 kilometres narrow gauge. The first covered two small suburban lines; the second between

Cockburn and Broken Hill bypassing the former Silverton Tramway; and the third, a more direct route between Thevenard and Kevin to facilitate the movement of increasing rail tonneages of gypsum and salt. On the other hand, there were 10 line closures totalling 229 kilometres, of which six were of broad gauge and four narrow. They were:

Broad Gauge: Grange to Henley Beach, Eudunda to Morgan, Hallett Cove to Willunga, Cambrai to Sedan, Balhannah to Mount Pleasant, and Sandergrove to Milang.

Narrow Gauge: Millicent to Beachport, Wandilo to Glencoe, Kapinnie to Mount Hope, and Cutana to Radium Hill.

With some justification at the time — and particularly in respect of the Port Augusta–Darwin proposal — the early lines in South Australia were constructed to very light standards, not only in respect of rail weights, but also in the matters of ballast and of narrow gauge sleeper dimensions. However, this policy persisted into the 1920s and resulted in continuing restricted axle loads, very light locomotive power, low operating speeds and vexatious maintenance problems.

Main line operations were improved substantially between 1922 and 1930, during the commissionership of W.A. Webb, who was recruited from the United States with the objective of rehabilitating the South Australian railway system. He proceeded to introduce heavy and powerful steam locomotives, which necessitated the strengthening of the main line tracks and structures.

Unfortunately, his departure in 1930 coincided with the onset of the Depression, an agonising period for South Australia, which suffered more than any other state. Webb's successor, C.B. Anderson, and the latter's Chief Engineer, R.H. Chapman, were forced to effect economies on all sides, which in hindsight appear to have been more stringent than were necessary.

Nevertheless, the contribution made by the SAR to the war effort was meritorious, particularly in the matters of munitions factory design and construction, the manufacture of armoured fighting vehicles, munitions and aircraft components. A pleasing legacy from this was that the Islington railway workshops became possibly the finest heavy industrial machine shop in Australia.

But reverting to the former obsession with light construction, by the beginning of the 1950s, more than one-third of the SAR tracks consisted of rails weighing not more than 50 pounds per yard (24.8 kg/m). Indeed, 41 pounds per yard (20.34 kg/m) and 35 pounds per yard (17.36 kg/m) were still in place in a number of areas; while, even as late as in 1970, the Waikerie and Peebinga branch lines were still of 41 pound rails, and that to Kapinnie predominantly of 35 pound. And, to compound the problem, some of the main lines were inadequately ballasted and most of the branch lines lacking it entirely. However, any criticism of those early standards of construction should be tempered with the realisation that almost all of the railways built in the 20th century were designed to open up lands to agriculture; lands of which a substantial proportion was at least only marginal.

Fargher, who succeeded Chapman as Railways Commissioner, and who had been his lieutenant for 30 years, set about to improve the position, and laid down minimum annual inputs of rails, sleepers and ballast. But even these proved to be insufficient, and the minima were increased in subsequent years.

At the time of Fargher's appointment in 1953 as Railways Commissioner, the broad gauge locomotive fleet consisted of 99 units of heavy steam power put into service after 1926. It consisted of the 500, 520, 600, 620, 700, 710, 720, 740 and 750 classes, supplemented on the minor light branch lines by 30 Rx locomotives originally purchased between 1886 and 1895, but rebuilt between 1900 and 1913.

On the other hand, services on the narrow gauge were still operated by T class locomotives purchased between 1904 and 1917. In 1952 and as an emergency measure, the SAR acquired six Australian Standard Garratt units and designated the 300 class. However, these locomotives were built as a wartime emergency measure, and possessed some inherent weaknesses which resulted in their universal rejection as a permanent proposition. Then, in 1953–54, the SAR obtained 10 Beyer Garratt locomotives for use on the Broken Hill ore traffic; and they were a worthwhile acquisition until superseded by diesel electric motive power. Webb had also introduced a number of self-propelled petrol driven rail cars for use on both the broad and narrow gauges, and which were retained until the early 1950s. While they might have been considered satisfactory when purchased, latterly they were deemed both slow and uncomfortable.

After World War II, the Australian railways looked into the merits of diesel electric motive power and the SAR, along with other systems, negotiated with the Clyde Engineering Company Ltd in respect of the purchase of locomotives designed and constructed by the Electro Motive Division of the General Motors Corporation, but assembled in Australia on locally built underframes. However, postwar restrictions

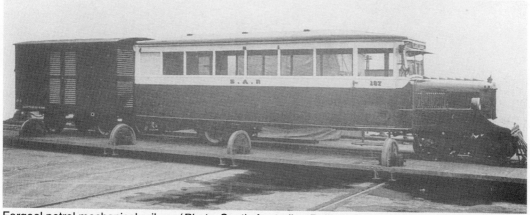

Fargeol petrol mechanical rail car (*Photo:* South Australian Railways)

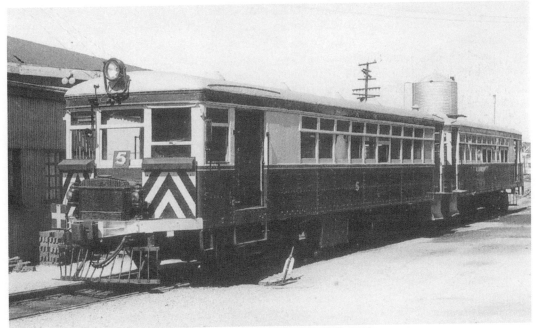

55 model petrol mechanical rail car (*Photo:* South Australian Railways)

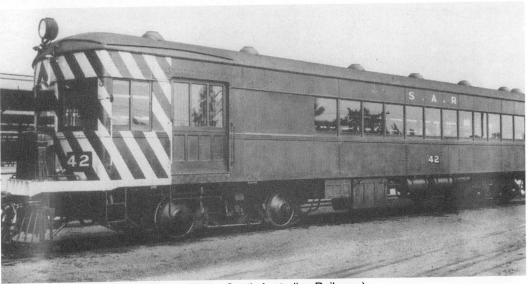

75 model petrol mechanical rail car (*Photo:* South Australian Railways)

on dealings involving US currency led to what appeared to be an indefinite postponement; whereupon Railways Commissioner Chapman and his Chief Mechanical Engineer Harrison decided to build their own, using power units, generators, traction motors and control equipment supplied by the English Electric Company of Great Britain. This courageous decision resulted in the SAR's main line flag bearer, Number 900 — the Lady Norrie — making the first scheduled diesel electric hauled train service in Australia on 12 September 1951.

Replacement of the 55 and 75 model rail cars on the longer routes by modern diesel powered units was also planned, and after some teething problems, as well as delays arising out of the

250 class diesel hydraulic rail car (*Photo:* South Australian Railways)

300 class diesel hydraulic rail car (*Photo:* South Australian Railways)

inability of a war-ravaged European manufacturer to meet his commitments in respect of the supply of transmissions, by the early 1950s the first of the 250 class diesel hydraulic rail cars entered traffic. These cars, with their blue livery and named after native birds — the flag bearer being christened the Quail — were also designed and built at Islington. They were the first of a number of self-propelled rail cars of world standard which were constructed in Australia and introduced into the nation's railway systems over the next 20 years.

Suburban passenger stock was also unattractive. Archaic side loading carriages were still in use on some services, and even the end loading vehicles built shortly before World War II were obsolete by current standards.

Electrifiction of the suburban system had been contemplated immediately after the war; and, based on the level of wartime patronage, it would have been economically viable. However, the

400 class diesel hydraulic rail car (*Photo:* South Australian Railways)

520 class locomotive, Duchess of Gloucester, heading an ARHS special train near Eden Hills, South Australia, April 1970 (*Photo:* Ian Hammond)

Westbound narrow gauge ore train near Huddleston, South Australia, December 1969 (*Photo:* Ian Hammond)

T class locomotive, Wilmington line, South Australia (*Photo:* Ian Hammond)

The Lady Norrie, the first diesel electric locomotive in scheduled service on the Australian mainland (*Photo:* South Australian Railways)

The Overland in the Mounty Lofty Ranges (*Photo:* South Australian Railways)

subsequent drop in passenger numbers by more than 75 percent caused the postponement and eventual abandonment of the proposal. Instead, in 1954 incoming Railways Commissioner Fargher directed that designs be prepared for a no-nonsense utilitarian diesel hydraulic rail car for suburban use. Out of this, the 300 class, or the Red Hen, was born.

The introduction of the Red Hen fleet, with their rapid acceleration, high top speed, flexibility of operation, and the fact that they did not require any expensive catenaries, might well have meant the abandonment for all time of the electrification of the Adelaide suburban services. However, the State Government announced plans in the early 1970s for the electrification of at least part of the suburban system. This decision must have been made on emotive rather than on economic grounds as even a doubling of the patronage at that time would still have left it below the wartime figures, and only one tenth of that of Sydney.

The SAR also pioneered the introduction of new long-distance locomotive-hauled passenger rollingstock on its eastern and western intersystem services.

In 1949, air-conditioned sleeping roomette and twinette sleeping cars of a standard not excelled in this country at that time — or indeed in most other countries — were placed in service on The Overland, the jointly owned overnight passenger train operating between Adelaide and Melbourne. Their design and construction, which was a major triumph for the Islington workshops, was extended over the years to include first and economy class coach cars. By 1970, club cars were added to The Overland, and modern air-conditioned coach cars introduced into the Adelaide to Port Pirie section of the Adelaide to Perth transcontinental service.

That might well summarise the situation in respect of the South Australian Railways at the time of my appointment as Assistant to the Railways Commissioner in May 1954.

Despite a number of notable achievements, the South Australian Railways did have some problems of its own. They included a small but somewhat complicated commuter service feeding six suburban terminals, but with a relatively low patronage.

Despite corrective action taken over the years, in 1954 the mainland system consisted of two narrow and one broad gauge divisions, and to this should be added the isolated Eyre Peninsula division.

As a result of the railway system being developed as an instrument of development, opening up of the land to primary production,

'Down' goods train, Mount Lofty Ranges, May 1980. Twin 930 class locomotives (*Photo:* Ian Hammond)

Narrow gauge ore train near Mannahill, South Australia, March 1969. Twin 830 class locomotives (*Photo:* Ian Hammond)

One of the last narrow gauge ore trains, near Yunta, South Australia, January 1970. Standard gauge bridge in the background. Twin 830 class locomotives (*Photo:* Ian Hammond)

less than 40 percent of the railways on the mainland could be deemed trunk routes and the remaining 60 percent feeder lines, carrying vital though low density traffics. The compact nature of the railway network in South Australia was such that its average length of haul for freight and livestock was only about one half of that of the other state railways.

Nevertheless, in terms of financial control and employee output, the SAR was no less efficient than were its sister systems. Indeed, the budgetry control procedures established by the SAR after World War II were adopted, to a substantial degree, by them. It is also to Fargher's and his predecessors' credit that, except for one short period in the late 1920s, the SAR operated at all times within the parameters laid down by government.

Concurrent with his decision to introduce the Red Hen rail cars, Fargher also initiated a long-term programme for the complete dieselisation of motive power. It was probably his greatest achievement as Railways Commissioner, even though it was not completed during his term of office. But even more noteworthy was the fact that he implemented it, as well as his other rollingstock improvement programmes, within the constraints of his normal loan funds allocations. At no time did he request special grants for the purpose.

In 1954, the main line diesel fleet consisted of ten 900 class 1760 hp broad gauge locomotives, while orders had been placed for ten 750 hp transfer units. In that year too, tenders were invited for the supply of six broad gauge locomotives of about 1800 hp. In December 1955, Number 930, the first of the Goodwin-Alco units, entered service. This was the forerunner of a fleet of main line locomotives — of varying horse power and of both broad and narrow gauges — of Goodwin-Alco manufacture to which the SAR confined its purchases. In this way, a great deal of flexibility was achieved, especially in the matter of spares.

Special mention should be made of the 830 class, 950 hp general purpose locomotives which were used on the branch and lightly trafficked lines. It was with some apprehension that these units, with their 11.43 tonnes axle load, were placed in running on the 41 pounds per yard (20.3 kg/m) tracks in the Murray Mallee and on Eyre Peninsula; but they proved to be ideal for

these light lines. Their riding characteristics were outstanding, due to their tri-mount bogies. To see them operating to Yinkanie and Peebinga, and on the Port Lincoln Division — where the two strands of fencing wire that passed for rails were contorted into unbelievably crooked alignments — was a revelation, not unmixed with a degree of incredulity that anything could stay on such tracks.

Of recent years, the most significant occurrence affecting the South Australian Railways was the action by Sir Thomas Playford in 1964 in eliminating all forms of freight transport regulation in South Australia. The full ramifications of his action became apparent in January 1966, shortly after I had succeeded Fargher as Railways Commissioner.

In 1964, the Broken Hill mining companies made yet another of their periodic attempts to achieve a reduction in the rail freight charges on the carriage of lead and zinc concentrates to Port Pirie. When they threatened to divert the traffic to road, something that they could do under the Privy Council's interpretation of Section 92 of the Constitution, Playford accepted a recommendation from Fargher that a road maintenance tax be imposed. But in doing so he took steps to free intrastate freight traffic from any controls whatsoever. This decision meant that, at that time, South Australia was probably the only state or province anywhere in the world without some form of transport regulation. The lifting of controls resulted in the railways' share of the State's transport task dropping alarmingly and prejudicing the Department's financial position. Indeed, its share of the grain, manure and livestock traffic was reduced by up to 57 percent.

The Hoop Iron Railway

The employees called the Eyre Peninsula system, rather affectionately, the 'hoop iron' railway. It was an apt description. The first time that I saw the tracks on the isolated narrow gauge Port Lincoln Division, I exclaimed: 'I don't believe it!' I had come across a piece of 'main line' on the later abandoned section between Wandana and Kowulka that was so buckled that the motor inspection car, with its three-metre long wheelbase, could not traverse it and we had to get the permanent way gang to pull it into a less distorted alignment before we could move on. The next day, on the Kapinnie track, I found a length of rail — not steel but iron, and weighing only 35 pounds per yard (17.4 kg/m) — with 30 centimetres missing from its head.

This isolated rail network was, in some ways, unique. Not only did it fill a specific and clearly defined task, without which neither the agricultural nor the mining activities on Eyre Peninsula could function efficiently, but its operations bordered on financial viability. Cereal growing did not gather momentum until the start of the 20th century, but after many years of steady but unspectacular development, its post-World War II growth was dramatic and it accounted for about 40 percent of the State's cereal production as well as very high tonnages of gypsum and salt. It had two shipping ports served by rail and over 30 inland grain storages.

Railway construction on Eyre Peninsula began in 1907 and, except for a major deviation of the route between Thevenard and Penong, was completed by 1926. The lines extended from Port Lincoln to Kapinnie and Penong in one direction, and to Buckleboo in the other. Ostensibly for economic reasons, like most of the other agricultural lines in South Australia, the railways were built to very light standards; indeed, they were fragile. The heaviest rails weighed only 50 pounds per yard (24.8 kg/m); most of them only 41 pounds per yard (20.34 kg/m); and those on the Kapinnie branch line 35 pounds (17.4 kg).

Train movements inevitably gave rise to two gambles. One, would the train get there? Two, having got there, would it get back? With every kilometre that the train proceeded on its forward journey, so did the odds against its returning unscathed lengthen. Between Kimba and Buckleboo, the light crippled rails were so distorted, both vertically and horizontally, that a speed limit of 15 km/h applied throughout. The two hours that it took to travel the 36 kilometres at this speed seemed interminable, and on the return trip the sight of Kimba just around the last curve used to prompt a sigh of relief.

But this was nothing compared with the Kapinnie branch, where a ride at any speed beyond walking pace was hazardous. For the entire 23 kilometres there and the entire 23 kilometres back, the speed was restricted to 8 km/h, really too high for the track as it then stood. The only alternative would have been to close the line, which was something that politicians the world over were too scared to do. Near Kapinnie, where it crossed a swamp, the line, with its light, corroded and broken rails and its rotten sleepers, was, in places, under water.

Derailments, broken rails, broken draw gear, uncouplings and track damage from wet weather was the diet upon which the Port Lincoln railwaymen subsisted. They were all past masters at the art of rerailing vehicles and Jesse Averis, the locomotive foreman, was a grand master. The ingenuity displayed was outstanding, and this characteristic extended right through the ranks. The men would set to work on the repairs without waiting for the boss to arrive. The way too in which the train crews rode their locomotives, especially the firemen on the steam engines, who had to shovel coal while maintaining their footing on the lurching, bucking and swaying footplates, would have evoked spontaneous admiration from a rough rider.

However, the lines lost a large measure of their precariousness when, in 1966, it became apparent that there would be a dramatic increase in grain and gypsum production on Eyre Peninsula, and that the railways would be called upon to handle similarly increased tonneages. With sympathetic government support, steps were taken to strengthen the tracks and to acquire diesel electric locomotives and rollingstock. These actions transformed the Port Lincoln Division to one of a standard at least equal to the task likely to be imposed on it.

There are several railways in this country whose functions are less significant than this one, but which are afforded greater publicity and credibility. It is a pity that its achievements are not more widely known. For reasons of its vital service to the activities of a very productive sector of South Australia's economy, its isolation, and the pioneering spirit and resourcefulness displayed by the entire railway staff on the Division, the Hoop Iron Railway was my favourite among those of the South Australian Railways. I rank it alongside Western Australia's Murchison and the Commonwealth's original Ghan Track.

Washaways, Port Lincoln–Buckleboo railway, December 1966 (*Photos:* Alf Francis)

The River Murray Floods

After my earlier experiences of standing waist-deep in a flooded creek at Wurarga in Western Australia, salvaging sleepers that had been caught in a flash flood; after some spine-tingling section car rides over washouts on the Central Australia Railway; and after wading chest-deep through the torrent that was Stoney Creek near Oodnadatta, it was like old times to be in South Australia's Riverland in August 1956. There, the River Murray provided us with a few moments of excitement.

The Renmark irrigation project, started in 1888, is as old as its counterpart Mildura. The other Upper Murray irrigation schemes in South Australia — Cadell, Waikerie, Barmera, Loxton, Berri and places in between — were pioneered in the following decade, but it was the resettlement of returned servicemen from the 1914–18 war that provided the greatest stimulus to its expansion.

Initially, transport to and from Adelaide was by rail to Morgan — to which the railway reached in 1878 — and then by road along the north side of the river, or by the river itself. In later years,

railways were constructed, radiating out from Tailem Bend through the marginal wheatlands south of the Murray. The line to Paringa, on the south side of the river opposite Renmark, was completed in 1913; and those to Waikerie and Loxton in 1914. However, it was not until 1927, when a large lift-span rail-road bridge was built, that the railway reached Renmark. A year later it was extended to Barmera while a branch line from Wanbi to Yinkanie — which, inexplicably, stopped a few kilometres short of the river — was opened.

Rationalisation of services by Australian National over recent years resulted in the closing of three of these lines, and the concentration of rail traffic to and from the Riverland at Loxton.

But to return to 1956. For 12 months the river had been high, but during that winter and after heavy falls of rain in the south-eastern part of the continent, it started to border on the critical. The highest recorded flood level at Renmark had been 29 feet 5 inches (8.96 m) in 1870, but this was exceeded on 16 August 1956 when it topped 29 feet 6¼ inches (9.06 m). But it did not stop there.

River Murray Floods, 1956. Rail shuttle service at Paringa. (*Photo:* Robyn McIntosh)

River Murray Floods, 1956. The railway between Renmark and paringa. The submerged Renmark–Paringa road was on the left-hand side (*Photo:* Robyn McIntosh)

River Murray Floods, 1956. Road Bridge over Bookmark Creek (*Photo:* Robyn McIntosh)

River Murray Floods, 1956. Rising floodwaters at Morgan railway station (*Photo:* Bob Sampson)

River Murray Floods, 1956. Aerial view of Morgan station under water (*Photo:* Bob Sampson)

River Murray Floods, 1956. Murray Bridge goods yard under water (*Photo:* Murray Bridge Historical Society)

River Murray Floods, 1956. Murray Bridge goods yard under water (*Photo:* Murray Bridge Historical Society)

Four days later it reached a new high of 30 feet 7 inches (9.32 m).

Renmark lies between the main river channel and an anabranch known as Bookmark Creek. With both streams at flood level, the town was virtually an island with two points of access. The Murray was spanned by the high-level rail-road bridge at Paringa, three kilometres to the south-east; and, while the railway embankment leading to it was clear, the vehicular approach

was submerged under several metres of water.

The South Australian Railways instituted a shuttle piggyback service between Renmark and Paringa, using a 55 model rail car for both motive power and passenger accommodation, and a drop-side rail wagon for the transport of motor vehicles and heavy equipment. It was a push-pull operation, the wagon being hauled in one direction and pushed in the other. As the railway formation became increasingly waterlogged, the condition of the track deteriorated, and at one stage it was necessary to suspend even this slow shuttle service. (It should be mentioned here that, after the 1956 crisis, the roadway level was raised to that of the railway. Consequently, it would now be above any prospective future flood.)

The railway formation also became the dry-land refuge for the hundreds of snakes that infested the river banks, and their habit of seeking sanctuary under the head of the rail meant that one had to be extremely careful when kneeling down with one's eyes at rail level to squint the track. I had one or two close encounters.

At the other end of the town, where the railway to Barmera ran parallel with Renmark Avenue — the main outlet to the west — there were two separate but contiguous rail and road bridges over Bookmark Creek. Both were awash to girder level and their continued safety was doubtful. Indeed, in the case of the road bridge, the roadway was kept clear of the flood waters only by the continual dumping of earth on top of the decking. This build-up of soil eventually amounted to about 30 centimentres and superimposed a heavy deadload on the structure.

On 15 August, when things appeared to be approaching crisis point, I went to Renmark, both to look after the Railways' interests and to see what further assistance we might be able to render the community. Being unable to obtain accommodation there, I booked in at the Berri Community Hotel, at that time a single-storey building on the river front. My room was in the front of the house, and looked out across the road and a small stretch of lawn to an earth levee about two metres high. It was with some apprehension that I went to bed at night, knowing that, just across the road, the river level was more than a metre above my recumbent person. The levee bank held.

The Renmark people were all for breaching the railway formation leading to the Paringa bridge, believing that it was causing a dangerous bank-up of flood water. It took a great deal of argument to convince them that the water level on the downstream side of the bank was only 18 centimetres lower than on the upstream side, and that little if any relief would result from blasting a gap in it. More importantly, should the breaching

of the bank be followed by the collapse of the bridges over Bookmark Creek — and this could not be ruled out — Renmark would be completely isolated. At that time, every ferry across the River Murray in South Australia was out of action due to the high river level and bridges at Murray Bridge and Paringa were the only river crossings in South Australia still open.

When I arrived at Renmark, there were no floodwaters near Renmark Avenue, except of course Bookmark Creek itself, but the situation changed dramatically within an hour. It had been decided by those fighting the flood to abandon some protective works upstream from the bridges. This allowed the water to creep through the vineyards and orange groves, and to bank up against the formation of the railway to Barmera. As this meant that the railway was the only barrier between the floodwaters and the road on the south side of the line — and which was the alternative to the now submerged Renmark Avenue — we set about strengthening the formation.

Twelve days earlier, on Saturday 3 August, there had been a landslide in a railway cutting near National Park in the Mount Lofty Ranges, and the line had been cleared by loading the debris on to a work train. As this material had not yet been unloaded, the train was sent forward to Renmark, where it was used to reinforce the bank. The train was then kept there to bring in spoil with which to keep the water away from the station yard.

The situation at this time was so critical that George Turner, the stationmaster and whose house abutted the river channel, loaded most of his furniture into a railway van and sent his family away to drier climes.

As the river level continued to rise, the residents faced up to the eventuality of having to evacuate the town. It was planned to do this by train, so Theo Rogers, Assistant to the General Traffic Manager, and Don Watson, Train Controller, were posted there to supervise the operation. A 14-car train, with a locomotive under steam 24 hours a day, was kept on stand-by. Fortunately, total evacuation was not necessary, although more than 1400 people, mostly women and children, did in fact move out by motor vehicle.

Despite the number of breaks, including a

major one on the night of Sunday 19 August, when Angove's distillery was threatened, the dykes held firm. The people of Renmark, backed up by the entire state, held even firmer. It was an amazing example of community spirit.

Obviously inspired by the manner in which the locals set about helping themselves, volunteers flocked to the Riverland from the city. On the evening of 19 August, five young men called in for tea at the Berri Community Hotel. They were from Kadina, 330 kilometres away. After having played football on the Saturday afternoon, they had driven their truck to Renmark, to spend Sunday loading and carting filling for the levee banks. Then, after tea, they drove the 330 kilometres back to Kadina. There was no thought of payment, even for petrol.

Renmark's pride and joy was its crash gang. It consisted of about 20 young men on permanent stand-by in case of a break in the retaining banks.

They spent their free time relaxing, but when a crisis did arise they threw themselves into the breach, literally, acting as buttresses against which sandbags, or even sheets of iron, would be placed preparatory to the tipping of spoil.

Further down the river, the passenger platform at Morgan and the goods yard at Murray Bridge were inundated and had to be abandoned until the water subsided. Following the flooding at Morgan, the rail service was terminated at Lanosa, a siding a short distance away.

The final touch of excitement occurred at the normally dry Cookes Plains, on the main line to Melbourne and 40 kilometres south of Murray Bridge. On 8 September, a strong wind caused back-up water from Lake Alexandrina — several kilometres away — to break over the line and to cause some concern to the crew of The Overland. To prevent the scouring of the railway formation

"WELL, IF WE DON'T PUT THE FARES UP HOW CAN WE PAY FOR THIS NEW PLAN TO FIT 'EM WITH RUBBER TYRES AND FOUR-WHEEL DRIVES?"

Cartoon by Norm Mitchell in the *Adelaide News*, 1968, when the South Australian Railways were experiencing a spate of derailments

and, possibly, a minor but potentially serious washaway, we constructed a revetment of old sleepers on the face of the low embankment over which the railway crossed the flat plain, and weighed them down with railway rails so that they would not be washed on to the permanent way by wind-blown flood waters.

Amid the excitement and the anxiety aroused by the floods, there was a feeling of exhilaration, not only at having played some part in what was a magnificent community effort, but also at having challenged nature and not lost.

Derailments

There used to be a delightful children's book called *Tootle* (Little Golden Books), which was about the village of Lower Trainswitch, where the little locomotives were taught to be big ones. Among their lessons were whistle-blowing, stopping for red flags, hauling the diner around curves without spilling the soup and, most important of all, never leaving the rails no matter what.

Tootle should be a textbook for every budding locomotive but, unfortunately, most of them do not seem to have been aware of its existence.

Apart from the inevitable and frequent ones that plagued the Port Lincoln Division before the tracks were upgraded, in the latter part of the 1960s, the South Australian Railways suffered a number of serious freight train derailments which, in addition to problems such as delays and damage, led to embarrassment arising from the political gamesmanship which followed a state election which saw the defeat of the Dunstan Government and its replacement by that of Steele Hall, supported by the casting vote of the Speaker, an independent.

No doubt with the incoming government's precarious hold of office in mind, the new Minister — and with no thought of prejudicing the railways — used the derailments as a vehicle towards his own end. He even went so far as to visit one particular derailment without informing me of his intention to do so, at the same time ensuring that his presence there was photographed. The resultant publicity arose, not from the derailment itself but from the fact that the Minister had visited it.

This series of derailments occurred south of Tailem Bend, all but one on the main line to Melbourne, and they followed the lifting of freight train speeds from 50 to 60 miles per hour (80 to 96 km/h) on that section of track. However, they took place at speeds of less than the former maximum of 80 km/h; and, contrary to all recognised criteria, it was the bogie wagons that left the track while the four-wheeled ones on the same trains did not.

Another disturbing feature too had arisen. Dogspikes driven into new hardwood sleepers were being bent outwards and the gauge widened after only two days in the track. It appeared obvious that there was some external force at work, and this could have come from the rollingstock.

Eventually the Government set up an independent Board of Inquiry, its members comprising professors in civil and mechanical engineering, and a company director with a background in chemical engineering. The SAR welcomed the composition of the Board. We were convinced that there was something associated with the bogies that was contributing to the mishaps. Otherwise, why did four-wheeled vehicles — which were notorious for their disposition to derailment — stay on the rails while bogie ones did not?

The Board did not see it that way, and was highly critical of the standard of the permanent way. However, Lance McLean, at that time Assistant but later Chief Engineer for the South Australian Railways, had always been convinced that there was something in the bogie wagon suspensions that was contributing to the derailments. As a result of his insistence, a series of tests of rail-wheel interaction was undertaken in association with the University of Adelaide. Some of those tests revealed lateral thrusts on the rails exceeding 16 tonnes, a circumstance that we felt warranted a review of bogie design. Initially, the idea was not supported by the other railway systems, the general attitude being that the simple solution to the problem lay in heavier rails and stronger track. However, subsequent experience seems to have vindicated the South Australian view, and more thought has been given to bogie design and vehicle suspension over more recent years.

It was a very embarrassing time for the railway

administration, and it was not helped in any way by the parliamentary opposition's use of the occasion to mount an attack on the Government. However, I feel that, in the long run, the South Australian Railways' contention was correct.

Two years later, and very shortly after the opening of the new standard gauge railway between Port Pirie and Broken Hill, we experienced one or two derailments brought about, not by any civil or mechanical weaknesses, but by teething troubles associated with the consolidation of a new track. The fact that it is a regular problem where new railways are concerned did not stop ministerial interference once again. This time it was an appeal to the Federal Minister for Shipping and Transport who, in turn, arranged for the Commonwealth Railways to inspect the line. It was a ludicrous situation. Here was I, a former Chief Civil Engineer for the Commonwealth Railways, yet the current incumbent was called upon to report on the new standard gauge line; and all this while the inspecting authority itself was not free from its own derailment problems, but which rarely aroused publicity. We of the SAR never saw any report that might have been submitted, but, more likely, the Commonwealth Railways was embarrassed at having been called upon to undertake such an inspection. The whole affair developed into nothing more than an illustration of uninformed and unqualified intervention.

Political Footballing

The use of a public utility for points scoring against government—no matter how autonomous that instrumentality might be — seems to be endemic in the political arena, and the railways appear to offer a field for such an opportunistic strategy. There are several reasons for this. As an undertaking that has both commercial and social obligations to fulfil, while at the same time involving a heavy drain on the public purse, the railways cannot win. On the one hand, they are admonished for their cost, while, on the other, any proposals to adjust services — particularly passenger ones — in line with falling patronage is met with howls of protest.

The SAR did not escape such attacks. Indeed,

three instances of blatant political footballing occurred towards the end of the 1960s.

In an endeavour to free the railways of certain uneconomic and unpatronised activities, late in 1967 I suggested to Frank Kneebone, Minister of Transport in the Dunstan Government, that I prepare a report to him on the possible rationalisation of the system. With this he agreed, and in January 1968 I submitted a report which recommended that action be taken in certain areas.

This included the closing of some sparsely trafficked lines where such action would not prejudice local business; the elimination of certain country passenger services and their replacement with coordinated road-rail ones; the underwriting by the Government of expensive but socially necessary operations; and the definition of a transport task for which the Department should aim at viability and on which its level of efficiency could be assessed. The objects were twofold. First, it was meant to point out that certain of the railways' services were not being used, and that a substantial saving of public funds — even at that time of almost zero inflation estimated at almost $1 million per annum — could be achieved by their elimination or modification. Second, it was intended to bring home to the community that, if it desired the retention of all of the services offered by the railways, it had better change its attitude and patronise them. No doubt because of the impending state election, Frank Kneebone gave no official indication of his government's reaction to the proposals. Significantly, however, they were not rejected; on the contrary, it was leaked to me that the recommendations were not unacceptable.

The Dunstan Government was defeated, and one of the first actions of Murray Hill, on becoming Minister of Roads and Transport in April 1968, was to gain the incoming government's concurrence with the report and to make a public announcement that its recommendations would be implemented forthwith. This, I think, gave rise to a great deal of the subsequent reaction. Previously, we had effected changes and terminated uneconomic services by proceeding quietly. In this instance, however, the ministerial announcement led to the belief that all measures would be implemented at once. Naturally, the political, industrial and community outcries were vociferous. The new government came in for a great deal of unwarranted criticism and abuse, which it accepted as its responsibility, and did not try to pass it off on to me as Railways Commissioner. Throughout the entire controversy, Frank Kneebone refrained from indulging in any criticism or abuse, to maintain that gentlemanly demeanour that made it such a pleasure to work with him.

In my view, the only criticism that might have been justified was Hill's precipitate announcement. Another factor too might have been Steele Hall's undisguised antipathy towards the SAR, which he had demonstrated from the very first day that he entered the Parliament. It is not unlikely therefore that many Labor Party members, not being aware of the circumstances under which the proposals were submitted, interpreted their adoption as yet another anti-railways move by the incoming Premier.

The second instance concerned off-peak suburban passenger services. Being conscious of the fact that railway finances were a continued source of worry to the Government, we were always looking for ways whereby some relief might be achieved. About 18 months after the first episode, I directed that, among other management studies, an investigation be made into the implications of eliminating off-peak and Sunday suburban passenger services. Actual counts had revealed that, on some trains, the staff outnumbered the passengers. Prima facie therefore, this in itself justified the study. However, the implications were also to include the social effects on the community, as well as the economics.

Because of the number of the facets involved, the modus operandi to be followed in the investigation was circulated in printed form among the senior officers concerned. Inevitably, a copy of the memorandum found its way into the hands of the Australian Railways Union, thence to the Parliamentary Opposition, who raised it in debate as a matter of urgency. At this stage, Murray Hill was entirely unaware of the existence of the study; it was purely an intra-departmental exercise which, like many others, was a responsibility of management, and would not have been referred to him unless subsequent action seemed warranted. Naturally, both Steele Hall and Murray Hill were caught unawares.

The third was only a minor incident, but was used in an attempt to attack the incumbent government with little thought of its effect on the standing of the railways.

Late one afternoon there was a minor derailment of a rail car at a suburban station. Neither vehicle damage nor passenger injury was incurred, but for a couple of hours single line working over a short section of normal double track was necessary. The manner in which the incident was handled by the railway staff, both in train working and public relations, was so good that, having been on the spot throughout the incident, next day I saw fit to congratulate all concerned. But that did not prevent a newly elected member of parliament — a former railway employee who, a couple of years later, became Minister for Transport following a change of government — from delivering a trenchant criticism of the way in which the incident was handled. His attack was grossly unfair but, in this instance, I had the opportunity to defend the railway employees' efforts.

Royal Commissions and Inquiries

Following the lifting of transport regulation of freight transport in South Australia in 1964, there was a dramatic drop in the tonnages carried by rail, and this despite the concurrent imposition of a road maintenance tax.

A comparison between the five year periods before and after the lifting of controls — namely 1959–64 and 1965–70 — showed that the proportion of the State's wheat production carried by rail dropped from 67 percent to 50 percent; that for barley from 69 percent to 42 percent; and that for manures from 69 percent to 59 percent. Over the same periods, the amount of livestock moved by rail fell by a massive 57 percent. These losses had a devastating effect on the viability of a number of branch lines which were constructed for the very purpose of promoting and serving agricultural development.

When the Labor Government assumed office in 1965, it tried to reintroduce transport control, and presented to the Parliament a Bill that provided for a fair measure of freedom but, in certain instances, the issue of a permit would have to be subject to the payment of a fee based on the load carrying capacity of the road vehicle. Monies received from this would have been paid into a Railway Improvement Fund. The Bill passed the House of Assembly but was rejected by the Legislative Council.

Following this, the Minister of Transport, Frank Kneebone, sought to establish a Royal Commission to enquire into all forms of transport, except air, in South Australia, and whether some from of control would be desirable. However, the terms of reference were wide and opposition from the road transport industry to the reinstatement of any form of control was strenuous; and the Broken Hill mining companies attempted to use the Royal Commission as a vehicle whereby they could complain about the rates charged for the movement by rail of lead and zinc concentrates to Port Pirie. In such circumstances the railways became virtual defendants.

We in the railways were operating without any advantages in a highly competitive field; indeed, in some respects at a disadvantage, because we were obliged to publish our rates. At one stage during the hearings I submitted certain costing data to the Commission, and asked that it be treated as evidence in private. This was strongly opposed by the other parties; but I was prepared to face charges of contempt for refusing to disclose the information. Fortunately, that circumstance did not arise.

The Royal Commission — which consisted of retired Magistrate Joe Nelligan, Auditor General George Jeffries and Tom Shanahan, a prominent and highly respected primary producer — reported to the Government that, in its opinion, some form of transport control in South Australia was desirable. However, neither that government nor any subsequent one took steps to impose it. Indeed, the reverse was the case.

On 9 February 1968, less than one month before the state election, the South Australian Road Transport Association held a dinner to mark its jubilee. At that function Don Dunstan, who had become Premier following Frank Walsh relinquishing the position in anticipation of his impending retirement, caused something of a sensation when he announced that his government would not reintroduce transport control. This was quite at odds with his party's avowed policy, the Government's legislative proposals two years earlier, and the findings of a Royal Commission set up for the very purpose of investigating the matter.

The Premier's announcement was greeted by his hosts with tumultuous applause. I do not think that it would be over cynical to suggest that the approaching election, and the presence at the dinner of his political opponent and arch rival, Steele Hall, prompted Dunstan — apparently without party approval — to reverse his government's policy. Indeed subsequent discussions with some members of the Government revealed that they too were dumbfounded by the Premier's declaration. The final outcome was that the Royal Commission achieved nothing more than to confirm a principle.

In its report the Royal Commission recommended that periodical reviews be made of the performance of the South Australian Railways, and in the early 1970s Minister of Transport Virgo appointed a committee of three, chaired by an engineer from the Highways Department, to do so. At the first — and in fact the only — meeting between the committee and SAR Heads of Branches, I offered full cooperation, but from that moment virtually all contact with the administration ended.

Obviously, the intent of the Royal Commission was that these reviews were to cover such matters as financial and operational performances, movements in passenger patronage and freight tonneages, load factors on individual main and branch lines and the retention or abandonment of lines and services. In all of these matters, we had ample statistics and costs to enable them to make reasoned judgments.

However, the Committee appeared to have an entirely different view of its task. It ignored our offer of cooperation and, without any prior notification, even to officers from the grades of stationmaster, maintenance engineer and locomotive foreman upwards, went about inspecting the system and seeking comments from employees at the very lowest end of the work chain.

The level of their investigations and the uninformed tenor of their reports barely warranted comment. For instance, one report criticised the railways for not having sold some old rails left alongside the track. Had they enquired, they would have been told that experience had proved that better returns were achieved by offering larger quantities of used rails than from casual and spasmodic sales.

In another interim report, they drew attention to the fact that, although a certain siding had been closed to traffic, it had not been pulled up. The facts were that, on my instructions, labour was not to be diverted away from essential track maintenance just to pull up the siding until such time as the material was required for use elsewhere, or where it should be removed for reasons of safety.

For over nine months, the Committee pursued its investigations without making even one contact with either my senior officers or me. Eventually, I had to seek out the chairman and to express my dissatisfaction at his and his members' lack of communication.

Naturally, the Committee's criticisms, even though confined to inconsequential matters, were afforded publicity. In reality, the whole exercise was a waste of time, and gave weight to the adage that everybody is a railway expert — except the railwayman himself.

The Dunstan Government was defeated in the 1968 election. On its return to office in 1970 it made substantial cuts to the railways' allocations in its next two annual budgets. In 1971/72 the reduction was set initially at $900,000 or just over 2 percent, and with it came the direction that the saving was to be implemented without any curtailment of staff numbers, train services or track rehabilitation. Such a contradictory instruction could only have arisen from a fear of adverse union reaction to any diminution of their work opportunities, because when I told Geoff Virgo that one of the avenues for economy was the elimination of some poorly patronised train services to the River Murray and Murray Mallee towns he exclaimed, 'But the Tailem Bend boys would not stand for that!'

A few months later, in a detailed report to the Minister, I drew the Government's attention to an alarming drift in railway finances, and again recommended that action be taken in a number of areas.

Cabinet reacted to the report with some concern and, as the Minister put it to me, 'to placate the

unions', the problem was referred to a joint union-department committee, chaired by Mr Ron Loveday, formerly a Minister in the Labor Government.

After investigation — which was both objective and cooperative — the committee supported all but one of my recommendations. Despite this, the Government did precisely nothing. Early in 1973. I was questioned by the Commonwealth Grants Commission, at its Adelaide hearings, as to what action had been taken following my submission and the joint committee's endorsement of virtually its entire content. However, I was unable to indicate what, if any, action had been taken. Nor do I know whether the Grants Commission took this into account when assessing South Australia's position.

Having been associated during my career with three Royal Commissions, I can only subscribe to the commonly held concept that they are established by governments for one of three reasons. One, to find a scapegoat. Two, being afraid, for political reasons, to make a decision, you pass the problem on to a Royal Commission to make it for you. Three, to achieve your objective, not through the parliamentary process, but by submitting the matter to a Royal Commission, under terms of reference so framed as to give it little or no option as to its findings. Cynical comment perhaps, but difficult to deny.

The Festival Theatre and the Railways

The Adelaide Festival Theatre complex, opened in 1974, is a magnificent addition to the city's cultural life, but its construction did involve one or two railway tribulations,

In 1969, at which time there was no final decision in respect of the location for the theatre, Town Planner, Stuart Hart contacted me to say that the Premier, Steele Hall, favoured the area occupied by the City Baths and the Railways Institute, and had directed him to pursue the matter with me.

The Railways Institute was housed for the most part in what was initially the Cheer-Up Hut, a social and welfare centre for servicemen, and taken over by the Railways at the end of hostilities.

Its activities were financed approximately 60 percent by direct staff contributions together with other fundraising. Not only did the Institute cater for the social, recreational and sporting needs of railway employees — and in doing so constitute an inestimable stimulus to staff morale — but also was it responsible for conducting courses of study in railway safe-working rules and other essential practices and procedures.

On an area adjoining to the Cheer-Up Hut building were some galvanised-iron single-storey buildings which, in the 1920s, were occupied by railway staff during the construction of the existing station building, and which was called affectionately 'Tin Town'.

I told Stuart Hart that the SAR would cooperate in every way possible but, at the same time, would not want our current activities or future developments prejudiced. This would include continued access to railway property as well as possible future underground extension of the suburban commuter system as envisaged by the consultants to the Metropolitan Adelaide Transport Study.

Shortly afterwards, the Cheer-Up Hut site was adopted and the architectural firm of Hassell and Partners commissioned to prepare plans for the Festival Theatre project. Some months later — by which time the Dunstan Labor Government had replaced Steele Hall's LCL one — it was brought to our attention, purely by accident, that the designs included a plaza at theatre level which left not more than eight feet (2.44 m) headroom to the road under it and leading to the station concourse This would have denied access to the concourse or the platforms to fire engines, ambulances, motor buses or road freight vehicles

Fortunately, our protestations led to the provision of alternative though not altogether satisfactory access; but it was not achieved without a heated and acrimonious confrontation between Dunstan and me.

Earlier, and while he still remained Minister for Roads and Transport, Murray Hill displayed serious concern for the future of the Railways Institute and went so far as to obtain cabinet approval to authorise me to commission Hassell and Partners to prepare preliminary plans for a New Institute building, to be sited west of the theatre complex and to a design that would conform with its general concept. However his successor's attitude was less sympathetic, and, until its demise following the transfer of the non-urban rail activities to Australian National, the South Australian Railways Institute was unable to obtain satisfactory accommodation.

Demise

On Friday 1 December 1972 — the eve of the Federal election that witnessed the election of Gough Whitlam as Prime Minister — Gilbert Seaman, South Australian Under Treasurer and with whom I enjoyed a cordial working relationship, telephoned me and said: 'There's going to be a change of government in Canberra tomorrow, and the State will want to hand over all but the suburban train services to the Commonwealth. What would be the best way to do this?'

I replied that I would think it over and let him know.

About one hour later I did so and suggested that the Commonwealth should assume ownership of all facilities held by the SAR, and that it be asked to operate a suburban service under charter from the South Australian Government. This arrangement would obviate any problems associated with staff dispositions as well as the dual use of assets.

No doubt, Seaman's thoughts on the subject were prompted by a number of things. He would have been aware of what might be described as continued gutlessness on the part of the Government in that, while it vehemently opposed my recommendations of January 1968, it did not respond to its own self-initiated Royal Commission's recommendation that some form of transport control be re-established. In addition, it had not reacted to the content of my more recent submission regarding railway finances — and this in spite of the fact that the Loveday chaired committee had endorsed the recommendations.

One can only assume that the eagerness with which the State Government sought to hand over South Australia's non-urban services and facilities was indicative of either a lack of determination to tackle the problem itself, or a fear of union disapproval.

Charles Jones, the incoming Federal Minister for Transport, seemed hell-bent on taking over the state railways whatever the cost, and under inducements which prompted Peter Nixon — who succeeded him in 1975 following the defeat of the Whitlam Government — to say that the Commonwealth 'had been taken to the cleaners!'

The final demise of the South Australian Railways took place in three phases.

On 18 April 1974, the State Government established the State Transport Authority to control transport operations in the State and to integrate the Adelaide commuter services.

Then, on 1 July 1975, the Commonwealth assumed financial responsibility for the non-metropolitan railways and services; and finally, on 1 March 1978, management and responsibility for them were transferred to the Australian National Railways Commission. However, that transfer was not just a straightforward handover. It involved an extraordinary state election.

When in 1975, a Bill authorising the transfer was passed by the House of Assembly but defeated by the Legislative Council, the Parliament was dissolved and an election called. The Dunstan Labor Government survived by a hair's breadth when, amazingly, it nominated as Speaker a newly elected Independent Labor member, on his very first day in parliament. His casting vote kept the Dunstan Government in office.

As was to be expected — and with justification on purely financial grounds — Australian National took steps to eliminate or to reduce certain services, something which on more than one occasion I sought unsuccessfully to do. However, unlike the SAR, the ANR did not have to take into account the social or regional implications of such actions.

Consequently, one is inclined to argue that, had the State Government of the day shown more determination, it could have remodelled the system in keeping with its social and developmental objectives, something which AN had neither the need, the authority, nor the inclination to do.

South Australian Railways started on 18 May 1854 and ceased as a separate entity on 28 February 1978, but its achievements should never be forgotten. They included:

- The Goolwa to Port Elliot railway, the first public railway in Australia, even though its motive power was in fact equine.
- The first publicly owned railway in the British Empire; that between Adelaide and Port Adelaide.
- The Darwin to Pine Creek and the Port Augusta to Oodnadatta railways, the initial sections in the grand concept of a north–south transcontinental railway.
- Its gesture, together with the Silverton Tramway Ltd, in providing a rail connection to Broken Hill at a time when its mother state of New South Wales declined to do so. But for this action, Broken Hill would have died of thirst in its infancy.
- The introduction into the Australian railways of large steam locomotive power.
- The installation of the nation's first train control system.
- The honour of placing into scheduled service on the mainland of Australia the first main line diesel electric locomotive.

The greater part of the negotiations leading to the transfer of the non urban activities to the Commonwealth took place after the termination of my active duties on 30 March 1973, but the alacrity with which the State Government seized on the Whitlam offer did influence my decision to retire on the eve of my 63rd birthday. There were, however two other reasons,

Perhaps the most telling one was an amendment to the Australian Railways Commissioner's Act that was made in 1971. To that time, the Commissioner possessed a substantial degree of freedom, something vital when operating in a competitive and commercial transport field.

However, in 1971, the Act was amended by the addition of a clause which provided that, notwithstanding any other provision in the Act, the Commissioner and the officers and employees of the Commissioner shall be subject to the control of the Minister, and, in the exercise of the powers, functions, authorities and duties conferred or imposed on the Commissioner, his officers or employees, they shall comply with the directions, if any, given by the Minister,

Taken literally, this amendment empowered the Minister to bypass the Commissioner and give instructions directly to an officer or employee. While such a circumstance did not arise during the remainder of my term as Railways Commissioner, in one or two cases — and these in the industrial relations arena — it was a near thing.

Furthermore, under the Act as amended, the Commissioner could be sued following a Ministerial direction either to him or to an employee, and in respect of which he totally disagreed, but which he would have to defend in court. It was potentially an untenable situation.

The other reason leading to my decision has already had some reference in this chapter. If the Railways Commissioner is obliged to operate within the parameters of his budget, yet, at the same time, is prevented from doing so under ministerial directions as to where and when both services and maintenance shall or shall not be varied because 'the Tailem Bend boys would not stand for that', then he would be unable to fulfil his obligations, and especially so in matters of safety, levels of service and finance.

Therefore, with these things in mind, I tendered my resignation after a most rewarding 19 years with the South Australian Railways,

I would be remiss if I did not express my appreciation of the extremely harmonious relationship that pervaded not only the SAR, but also the entire State Public Service. Such was the mutual trust between government departments that deals were regularly negotiated by word of mouth.

It was this trust and cordiality — as well as Fargher's gesture in offering me the position in the first place, and for which I owe him an eternal debt — that led me to reject any any possible thoughts of moving elsewhere.

So, on Monday 3 May 1954, after 27 years on the wallaby, 20 different postings and 25 changes of domicile, I settled down and commenced the final 19 years of an unforgettable 46 years' railway career.

10 My Standardisation Story

Australia's rail gauge mess has been nothing short of disgraceful, and it is to the everlasting discredit of those responsible. It has been a farrago of procrastination, parochialism, interstate jealousies and political bloody-mindedness. All this capped off by hindrance on the part of Canberra-insulated public servants whose function appeared, for the most part, to be confined to paper shuffling but who, despite their remoteness from the action, sought to impose their obstructive philosophies on the states. And, finally, when at last something was done, we were still left with three gauges, a dozen breaks of gauge — which, at one stage, included two three-gauge stations only a few kilometres apart — and a half-baked standard gauge system that one could be pardoned for suggesting had been designed specifically to ensure that complete unification could never be achieved.

Both the United Kingdom and the United States — each with a far greater length of track than Australia — were able to unify their gauges during the closing years of the nineteenth century. But in this country we have only fiddled with standardisation, and in doing so have left the nation with a seemingly insoluble proliferation of rail gauges.

More recently, some of the residual impediments have been removed by the simple expedient of closing a number of branch lines. But do not such actions constitute a tacit admission of earlier dereliction or indecision? Indeed, the fact that we have failed to achieve at least a substantial degree of standardisation when presented with a heaven-sent opportunity to do so remains the one big disappointment of my railway life.

Starting with an insignificant contribution in 1929, followed by continued association from 1944 until retirement in 1973, I am most likely the only person still living who had a part in the Clapp enquiry of 1944–45; consequently, I feel that my experiences and thoughts should be recorded.

The Multi-Gauge Catastrophe

In 1901, when the Commonwealth of Australia was established by the Federation of the six states — each a crown colony in its own right — apart from the North Australia Railway, there was, on the mainland, a total of 20,600 route kilometres of public railway, and of three gauges; broad gauge (1600 mm), standard gauge (1435 mm), and narrow gauge (1067 mm). Breaks of gauge existed at five locations: Wallangarra (Queensland), Albury (New South Wales) and at Wolseley, Hamley Bridge and Terowie (South Australia). All were dual gauge stations; in total ten gauges.

By 1945, and following upon main line construction between Kalgoorlie and Port Augusta, Kyogle and South Brisbane, Ivanhoe and Broken Hill, Redhill and Port Pirie, and between Port Pirie and Port Augusta, together with other railway developments in all states, the length of public railways on the mainland — and again excluding the North Australia Railway — had increased to 42,300 route kilometres, and the breaks of gauge to 13, namely Wallangarra and South Brisbane (Queensland); Albury, Tocumwal, Oakland and Broken Hill (New South Wales); Wolseley, Mount Gambier. Terowie, Gladstone, Port Pirie and Port Augusta (South Australia); and Kalgoorlie (Western Australia).

Of these, Port Pirie, now the eastern terminus of the Trans Australian Railway and the western one for the narrow gauge from Broken Hill, could claim the dubious distinction of possessing what was probably the world's only triple gauge station, thus bringing the number of gauges involved to 27.

Then, by 1984, after Adelaide had been connected to the Sydney–Perth standard gauge railway, the narrow gauge Ghan line replaced by a standard gauge one from Tarcoola to Alice Springs, and a number of little used branch lines closed, although the route kilometres had fallen to 38,300, the national system still consisted of three gauges, and the number of transfer stations reduced by only one. Moreover, while Port Pirie had lost its three-gauge station, two others were created in its place — at Gladstone and Peterborough — and these only 66 kilometres

apart! And to add to the farce, two adjoining branch lines — from Gladstone to Wilmington and from Peterborough to Orroroo — were left as isolated narrow gauge appendages to the standard gauge main line.

This scandalous situation followed the expenditure of huge sums on what were purported to be standard gauge projects in Western Australia, South Australia and between Sydney and Melbourne. The position would have been even worse had not Western Australia, at its own cost, converted to standard gauge the narrow gauge lines stretching from Leonora in the north, through Kalgoorlie and down to Esperance on the south coast. Subsequent action by Australian National in abandoning some lines in South Australia has, operationally, eliminated the triple gauge stations of Gladstone and Peterborough.

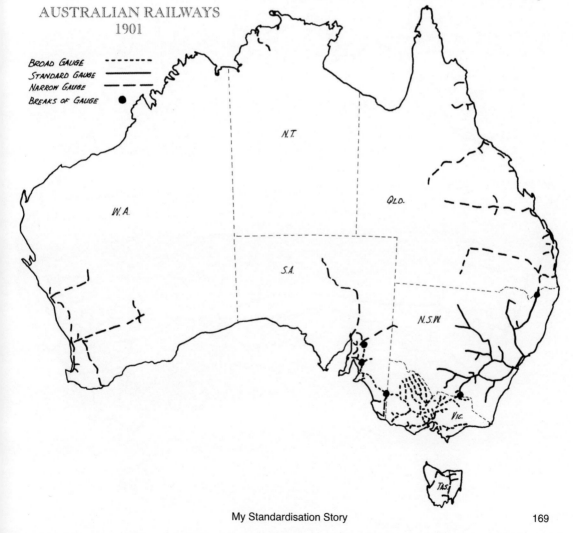

AUSTRALIAN RAILWAYS
1901

BROAD GAUGE
STANDARD GAUGE
NARROW GAUGE
BREAKS OF GAUGE

N.T.

QLD.

W.A.

S.A.

N.S.W.

VIC.

TAS.

However, the fact remains that such a mess would not have been created, nor would there have been such a waste of money in building those two stations, had the Commonwealth Government been less intransigent and had shown more consideration for the wishes of the states.

Since that time, there have been two developments; the standard gauge connection between Adelaide and Melbourne, and the completion of the Alice Springs–Darwin rail link.

So, today, after more than 100 years of Federation, we are left with 33,500 route kilometres of public railways on the mainland, still of three gauges — 4000 broad, 15,100 standard, 14,100 narrow and 300 dual — together with ten operative breaks of gauge and three inactive ones on account of the cancellation of services. The former are Brisbane (Queensland), Wodonga, Melbourne, Maryborough, Dunolly and Ararat (Victoria), Adelaide (South Australia), and Perth, Northam and Merredin (Western Australia); while the other three are Heywood (Victoria), and Pinnaroo and Wolseley (South Australia). In all, the gauges involved still total 26. It represents anything but standardisation.

The Standardisation Saga

The story of the initial rail gauge blunder in Australia is well known. Suffice it to say that the blame should be shared equally by the colony of New South Wales and the Parliament of Westminster. Primarily, New South Wales was at fault when, in 1853, it changed the gauge of its railways from 1600 mm to 1435 mm without first

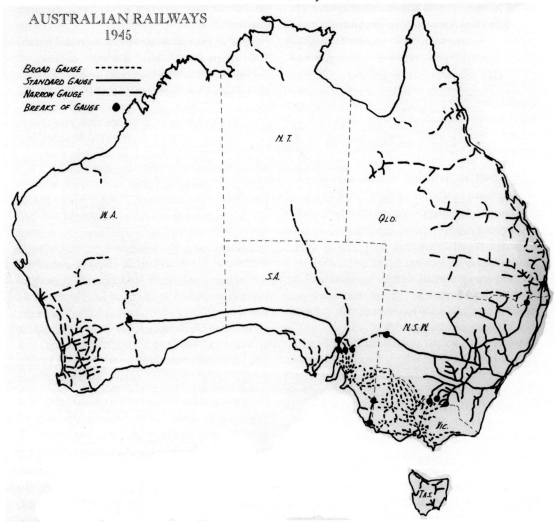

AUSTRALIAN RAILWAYS
1945

BROAD GAUGE -------
STANDARD GAUGE ———
NARROW GAUGE — — —
BREAKS OF GAUGE ●

Australian Railwayman

informing either Victoria or South Australia. The British Government too was remiss in that, while it had strongly recommended to the colonies in 1848 that they adopt a unified rail gauge, in the space of only five years it equivocated and ignored an appeal by Victoria to withhold consent to New South Wales' change of mind.

The introduction of the 1067 mm narrow gauge compounded the original blunder, but, particularly in the cases of Queensland and Western Australia, there might have been some mitigating circumstances. With their vast distances and limited populations, they were obliged for economic reasons to build their railways to minimum standards. Their decisions might also have been abetted by the degree of independence and unconformity so characteristic

of the two states, then as now. Moreover, Perth is separated from Adelaide, its nearest neighbour, by over 2500 kilometres of forbidding country, and any thought of a railway linking up the two cities 100 years ago would have been barely comprehensible.

South Australia's early contribution to the gauge chaos, as well as its opposition to standardisation in the years leading up to World War II, also merits condemnation. Not only did it build its railways to two gauges — 1600 mm and 1067 mm — but also did it do so haphazardly. Its small broad gauge division was sandwiched in between two narrow gauge ones. On the other hand, its adoption of the narrow gauge for the north–south transcontinental railway might have been warranted. The only means of communication

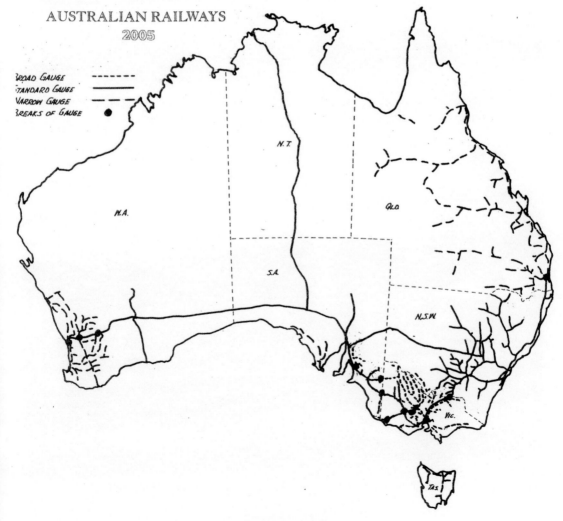

AUSTRALIAN RAILWAYS
2005

BROAD GAUGE
STANDARD GAUGE
NARROW GAUGE
BREAKS OF GAUGE

N.T.

W.A.

QLD

S.A.

N.S.W.

VIC.

TAS.

Gauge widening, Mount Gambier, South Australia, 1953 (*Photo:* C.R. Stewien, SAR)

Gauge widening, Millicent, South Australia, 1955 (*Photo:* South Australian Railways)

Australian Railwayman

The Trans Australian lounge car, 1918 (*Photo:* The Rose Stereograph Company)

Luncheon stop for west–east Transcontinental train, Eurelia, South Australia, c. 1920. The refreshment room is in the goods shed to the right (*Photo:* South Australian Railways)

All that remains of the Eurelia refreshment room, 1991 (*Photo:* the author)

Riverton, South Australia, luncheon and dining stop for east–west passengers, 1917–37. Also the scene of a fatal shooting in 1921 (*Photo:* the author)

between north and south was by long circuitous sea routes around either the western or eastern sides of the continent; yet, following its courageous act in constructing the Overland Telegraph, it was inspired to contemplate a railway linking Adelaide with Darwin. Sparsely populated and impoverished, the colony had no option but to build the railway to narrow gauge.

To its credit, South Australia did attempt, of its own volition, to eliminate a great deal of its narrow gauge. In the 1920s it converted to broad gauge a number of lines north of Adelaide. Then, during the latter years of World War II, it decided to broaden the narrow gauge division in the south-east of the State. It may be argued then, that South Australia did what it could to rectify some of its gauge deficiencies, and to create a broad gauge system conformable with that of its Victorian neighbour.

That, in brief, is the sad history of the origins of our rail gauge disaster; but it was not our greatest railway mistake. Indeed it pales into insignificance compared with the post World War II blunder when the opportunity to unify the greater part of the national rail network was torpedoed. That this happened represents a blot on our railway history. The chance will never come again.

The attention of government to the disabilities associated with the proliferation of gauges was drawn by railway administrations as long ago as 1857, and again in 1889, by the New South Wales and South Australian Railways Commissioners. Further weight was given to their representations in 1911 by Lord Kitchener, who expressed the opinion that the multiplicity of rail gauges in this country would more likely assist the invader than it would the defender. Kitchener's view was supported by the Australian War Railway Council and the Inspector-General of the Australian Military Forces, but the politicians did nothing more than to arrange for the preparation of estimates for conversion.

Prior to Federation, the New South Wales, Victorian and South Australian Governments discussed the question of a unified gauge, and directed that estimates be prepared. Subsequently, the Railways Commissioners submitted figures which showed that, despite the fact that there was approximately 30 percent more broad gauge track than standard, it would have been substantially cheaper to convert to the standard gauge. When, a few years later, the Trans Australian Railway was being planned, a majority of the Commissioners reaffirmed their support for the 1435 mm gauge, even though it would have meant the introduction of a second gauge into Western Australia and a third into South Australia, a situation not welcomed by either state. Nevertheless, the standard gauge was adopted.

With the completion of the Trans Australian Railway in 1917, the 5592 kilometre route from Perth to Brisbane virtually followed the coastline. The full journey involved six nights' travel, five breaks of gauge and nine different trains.

Gauge transfers took place at Kalgoorlie, where passengers changed from narrow to standard gauge; back again to the quaint antique narrow gauge at Port Augusta for the section through the Pichi Richi Pass to Quorn and beyond to Terowie; to broad gauge as far as Albury on the Victoria–New South Wales border; to standard gauge once again to Wallangarra on the Queensland border; and finally back to narrow gauge for the remaining 358 kilometres to Brisbane. In addition, there were changes of trains at the capital cities of Adelaide, Melbourne and Sydney.

Passengers travelling to and from Western Australia had the dubious and unique experience of being served dinner on the westbound journey, and luncheon on the eastbound by white aproned waitresses in a converted goods shed at Eurelia, on the narrow gauge section between Terowie and Port Augusta. It would have been one of the most primitive features of any transcontinental train journey in the world, and must have stunned international travellers. The other meals on the Port Augusta–Adelaide section — luncheon westbound and dinner eastbound — were served in the station building at Riverton, 101 kilometres north of Adelaide.

Riverton achieved a notoriety of sorts when, on the morning of 22 March 1921, a Russian named Tomayoff ran amok with a rifle and fired indiscriminately at passengers from the southbound Broken Hill Express, who were breakfasting there. Five persons were injured, two, including Percy, Bloomfield MLA from Broken Hill, fatally.

The first apparent positive step by government to unify the gauges was taken in 1920, when the Commonwealth and State Ministers established a Royal Commission to enquire into rail standardisation. However, it would not be too cynical to suggest that this bore all the features of a delaying tactic, because, following receipt of the Commission's report, one State Premier was reported to have said: 'The sooner we get the gauges unified the better; but this is not the time to do it.' The Royal Commission, in its report issued in 1921, submitted the following estimates:

(A) Convert all railways on the mainland of Australia to standard gauge; $114,400,000.

(B) Provide a standard gauge line from Brisbane to Fremantle, together with the conversion all broad gauge lines in South Australia and Victoria; $43,200,000.

Estimate (B) was to be achieved by means of:

1. An independent standard gauge railway from Fremantle to Kalgoorlie, where it would link up with the Trans Australian Railway.

2. A standard gauge line from Port Augusta to Adelaide via Redhill. (At that time, the SAR broad gauge extended only as far as Long Plains, 76 kilometres north of Adelaide and 95 kilometres short of Redhill.)

3. Conversion of all broad gauge lines in South Australia and Victoria, plus the narrow gauge section from Terowie to Peterborough in South Australia.

4. The construction of a 1435 mm gauge railway from Kyogle in New South Wales to South Brisbane, thereby providing a standard gauge link between Sydney and Brisbane.

Not unexpectedly, the Royal Commission's report prompted an outbreak of that disease so endemic to Australia — interstate jealousy. Victoria and South Australia rejected the proposals and for some incomprehensible reason South Australia sought to retain the antediluvian narrow gauge route through Quorn and Terowie. A Draft Agreement between the Commonwealth and the five mainland states lapsed because of South Australia's intransigence.

But at least some positive action did ensue. In 1924, agreement was reached between the Commonwealth, New South Wales and Queensland Governments for the construction

of the Kyogle–South Brisbane standard gauge railway and the line was opened in 1930. This small step was the first in the often dreamed-of but seemingly unachievable Brisbane to Fremantle unified rail link. It also eliminated one break of gauge and reduced the overall distance by 162 kilometres.

The next hopeful but unfulfilled sign of progress was evidenced in 1926, when the Commonwealth and South Australia agreed to provide — in association with the extension of the Central Australia Railway to Alice Springs, either by narrow gauge from Oodnadatta, or by a new standard gauge line from Kingoonya on the Trans Australian Railway — a standard gauge connection between Port Augusta and Adelaide. Under the Agreement, the Commonwealth would finance the construction of a 1435 mm gauge railway from Port Augusta to Redhill (the terminus of the broad gauge since 1925), together with the addition of a third rail to Adelaide. Concurrently, the State would meet the cost of a third rail over the Redhill–Port Pirie section of the new standard gauge, thus providing dual gauges between Adelaide and Port Pirie. While the Oodnadatta–Alice Springs part of the Agreement was implemented, that covering the Port Augusta–Adelaide section was allowed to lapse.

In 1929, when the Kyogle–South Brisbane project was nearing completion, the Railways Commissioners decided to upgrade Section (B) of the 1921 Royal Commission's estimate, namely, the provision of a standard gauge link between Brisbane and Fremantle, together with the conversion of all broad gauge lines in Victoria and South Australia. The revised figure for the whole project, including the Kyogle–South Brisbane section, amounted to $50,402,000, an increase of 16.7 percent over the 1921 estimate.

The next step in the standardisation saga was something of a regurgitation of the 1926 proposal. In 1937, the Commonwealth Railways' standard gauge was extended from Port Augusta to Port Pirie and South Australia's broad gauge from Redhill to Port Pirie. One break of gauge was eliminated; the slow and circuitous narrow gauge section through Quorn to Terowie removed from the transcontinental route; and a saving of about eight hours effected. However, the decision to retain the broad gauge south of Port Pirie meant that another opportunity to extend the standard gauge into Adelaide was passed up. It also resulted in the creation at Port Pirie of the world's only three-gauge station.

It would have been marginally cheaper to have built the 42 kilometres of track between Redhill and Port Pirie to standard rather than to broad gauge; while substantial saving would have been achieved had the Port Pirie station been limited to two gauges instead of three. Those savings would then have gone a long way towards the cost of converting the Adelaide–Redhill line to standard gauge. And, while the cost of the Redhill–Port Pirie broad gauge railway was met in its entirety by the State, it is reasonable to assume that, had the standard gauge been extended to Adelaide, the Commonwealth would have contributed 20 percent of the total cost, as had applied to the Kyogle–South Brisbane project. Indeed, had the 1926 Agreement been implemented, the Commonwealth would have met the entire cost.

Without apparent justification — indeed incomprehensively — South Australia claimed compensation for the alleged loss of revenue that followed the shortening of the route between Port Augusta and Adelaide, and for the next 20 years received from the Commonwealth an annual recoup of $40,000.

It took until 1984 before the standard gauge reached Adelaide. It could have been realised 50 years earlier, and had this been the case a lot of the friction and frustration suffered by South Australia during the postwar years — when its attitude towards standardisation changed and it enthusiastically sought its implementation — might have been avoided.

The completion of the Port Augusta–Port Pirie–Redhill project saw rail standardisation recede into virtual oblivion until the outbreak of hostilities in the Pacific.

The Clapp Report

If ever any evidence was needed to justify the establishment of a unified rail gauge in Australia, it was provided during the years from 1942 to 1945, when the war came very close to home. Indeed, Kitchener's prophecy proved all too true.

In 1942, the mainland railways consisted of nine transportation islands, seven separated by their gauges, and two isolated. The seven were: Queensland; New South Wales; Victoria's and South Australia's broad gauge; the narrow gauge division in the south-east of South Australia; the contiguous narrow gauge systems of the Commonwealth, South Australia and the Silverton Tramway; the Trans Australian Railway; and Western Australia. The two isolated ones were South Australia's narrow gauge Eyre Peninsula division and the Northern Territory's fragile and highly vulnerable North Australia Railway from Darwin to Birdum. Perhaps, too, one should add the Port Hedland–Marble Bar line in Western Australia's north-west, and that from Normanton to Croydon in far north Queensland.

The problems were not confined to the physical transfer of personnel and equipment, in themselves expensive in manpower and transit time. They included the imbalance between the capacities of locomotives and rollingstock on the different gauges; delays in the turnround of equipment at transfer stations; and, more importantly, the lack of flexibility in the use of such equipment throughout the country. At one stage during the war, the build-up of loading awaiting transhipment was so great that the railway authorities were forced to decline to accept any more until the backlog had been cleared. At that time too, the army was obliged to defer the movement of as many as two troop trains a day and it is no exaggeration to say that the railway system in Australia was on the verge of collapse. This situation must have jeopardised General MacArthur's plans for an early offensive against the Japanese.

During those years too, there was concern that enemy action might interfere with the movement by sea of iron ore from Whyalla in South Australia to Newcastle in New South Wales, and thought was given to the standardisation of the narrow gauge line from Port Pirie to Broken Hill. This would have provided a safe and unified rail link from Port Augusta — only about 70 kilometres from the source of the ore in the Middleback Ranges — to the eastern seaboard. Once again, South Australia would not cooperate, and the idea was abandoned.

However, in 1944 the first really positive steps were taken to create a unified and integrated rail network throughout Australia. Given a longer term of office by the then incumbent Federal Minister for Transport, and less of the bureaucratic obstructionism and jealousy that have marked Commonwealth–State relations since Federation, it might well have been achieved.

The man behind it was E.J.Ward, at that time the firebrand of Australian politics. A fiery speaker and a bitter opponent of anything non-Labor, in 1941 he was appointed Minister for Labour and National Service in John Curtin's first Ministry. He then moved to the Transport and External Territories portfolio, and in this capacity he served under Prime Ministers Curtin and Chifley until 1949. Revered by his constituents and reviled by his political opponents, to Ward must go the credit for the achievement of at least some gauge unification in this country.

In March 1944, after only a few months as Minister for Transport, Ward persuaded Cabinet to agree to a comprehensive inquiry into the standardisation of the nation's railways. No doubt his appreciation of the transport mess into which wartime Australia had sunk prompted that action.

His selection of Sir Harold Clapp — successively Chairman of the Victorian Railway Commissioners, Chairman of the Aircraft Production Commission and Director General of Land Transport — was a master stroke. He was Australia's greatest railway personality. Although 69 years of age at that time, his mental capacity, energy and drive were unimpaired. Tall and lean, with a stern and normally unsmiling face, he did in fact possess a sense of humour. It was told that, when addressing a group of Victorian railwaymen, he said:

'I know what you fellows call me behind my back. My brother has a farm at Ouyen. One day, he called in at the railway station and found the stationmaster and porter cleaning up the place. When my brother asked them what they were doing, the stationmaster replied: "Didn't you know? The Bloody Disease is coming up tomorrow on inspection."'

As Directors of Mechanical and Civil Engineering, Clapp chose F.J. Shea — Director, Aircraft Maintenance Division of the Aircraft Production Commission, but whose substantive position was that of Chief Mechanical Engineer for the South Australian Railways — and W.D. Chapman. However, Fred Shea did not stay long with the Rail Standardisation Division, resigning to become Engineering Manager for the Clyde Engineering Company Limited.

Wilfred Chapman, with who I had a great deal of contact, was a remarkable man, having achieved distinction in military, academic and professional spheres. Graduating Master of Engineering, he started his railway career in Victoria. After having served as a commissioned officer in the Machine Gun Corps in World War I, in the 1939–45 conflict he rose to the position of Chief Superintendent of Design in the Master General of Ordnance Branch. He was possessed

Sir Harold W. Clapp, KBE
(*Photo:* Victorian Railways)

Hon. E.J. Ward, Minister for Transport and External Territories, 1944 (*Photo:* L.J. Dyer Collection)

Brigadier W.D. Chapman

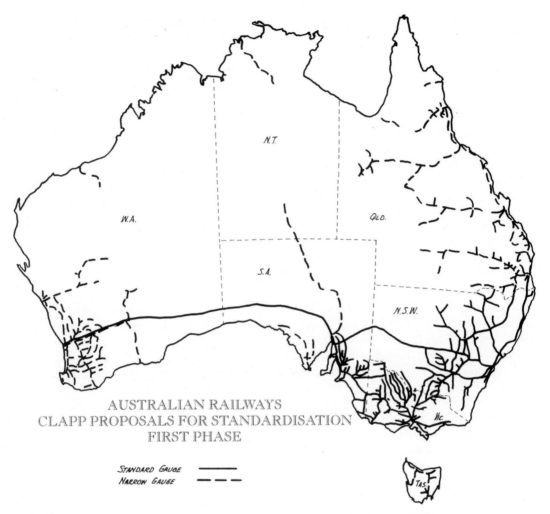

AUSTRALIAN RAILWAYS
CLAPP PROPOSALS FOR STANDARDISATION
FIRST PHASE

STANDARD GAUGE ———
NARROW GAUGE — — —

of a delightful personality, a capacity to get on with people, and a willingness to cooperate. The shabby treatment that he suffered at the hands of the Commonwealth when, in 1952, the Standardisation Division was unceremoniously and surreptitiously phased out, appalled those who knew him and had grown to love him. Indeed, he was not informed personally of the decision. It was a disgusting episode.

Ward displayed outstanding drive and enthusiasm, as well as an understanding of the problems involved. Like Clapp and Chapman, he was both tolerant and cooperative in seeking to meet the wishes of the states. It was an attitude vastly different from that shown by the Commonwealth in later years when work actually started.

Ward and Clapp also developed a rapport that augured well for the ultimate success of the project. When addressing the Perth Chamber of Commerce and Manufactures in 1945, Sir Harold paid a warm tribute to Mr Ward, and when his remarks were greeted with laughter he went on:

'You, may laugh. I did until I knew him. He is one of the most knowledgeable men that I have known. Mr Ward was raised in a tough atmosphere and educated himself. I laughed at him, and no doubt he laughed at me, until we started working together, but no one knows better than Mr Ward what this plan means to Australia.'

Despite the early lack of agreement between the Commonwealth and the States, I remain convinced to this day that, had Ward remained Minister for a few more years, standardisation of the major part of the national rail network would have been achieved.

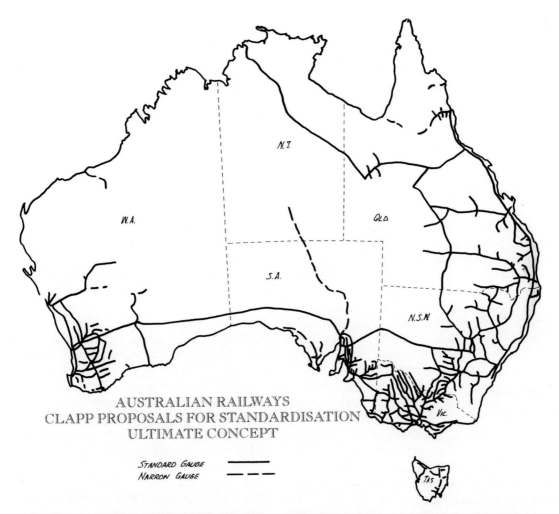

AUSTRALIAN RAILWAYS
CLAPP PROPOSALS FOR STANDARDISATION
ULTIMATE CONCEPT

STANDARD GAUGE ━━━━━
NARROW GAUGE ━ ━ ━ ━

Clapp's report, dated 24 March 1945, was and remains the most comprehensive review of rail standardisation ever produced in this country. Its recommendations, in order of priority. were:

(1) An independent standard gauge line from North Fremantle to Kalgoorlie in Western Australia; Conversion to standard gauge of all broad and narrow gauge lines in South Australia, (except those on Eyre Peninsula); the acquisition and conversion of the Silverton Tramway Company's line from Cockburn in South Australia to Broken Hill in New South Wales; and the conversion of all broad gauge lines in Victoria.

(2) Construction of a standard gauge railway from Bourke in New South Wales to Longreach in Queensland; thence the conversion of the narrow gauge lines to Townsville in the east and Dajarra

in the west, together with associated branches.

(3) Construction of a standard gauge railway from Dajarra to Birdum in the Northern Territory, and the conversion of the narrow gauge line from Birdum to Darwin.

The proposals, which did not include the railways in Tasmania, were estimated to cost $153,502,000 at 1944 rates.

Clapp also proposed that, subsequent to agreement being reached between the Commonwealth and the States regarding these three phases, plans and estimates be prepared for the conversion of most of the narrow gauge lines in Western Australia and Queensland, at estimated costs of $95,000,000 and $140,000,000 respectively. Significantly, he was of the opinion that the conversion of the Central Australia Railway from Port Augusta to Alice Springs be deferred indefinitely, because he considered that the Bourke–Dajarra–Darwin line offered both economic and strategic advantages.

Release of the report immediately revived the interstate jealousies so characteristic of Australian life, and which are never dormant for very long. With one exception, its recommendations were received with either open hostility, lack of enthusiasm, or only qualified support.

Queensland, always something of a lone star state, would have no part in the plan; while New South Wales, realising that, per-capita-wise, it would be called upon to meet the major part of the cost while benefiting from only minor improvements within its borders, displayed a noticeable degree of indifference. Victoria, while going along with the recommendations, expressed some concern that the shorter routes from Sydney to Adelaide and Perth via Broken Hill and bypassing Melbourne, would have an adverse effect on its rail traffic and revenue.

On the other hand, South Australia, formerly an opponent of virtually everything pertaining to standardisation, exhibited a complete change of heart and was the only state to show any real enthusiasm. But it too had one objection. It demanded the conversion of the Alice Springs line and its extension to Darwin, thus fulfilling its long-cherished dream of a north–south transcontinental railway. No doubt with Queensland's opposition to any standard gauge works in that state in mind, Mr Ward agreed.

However, despite the high priority given by Clapp to the North Fremantle–Kalgoorlie proposal, and its vigorous sponsorship by Ward, it was received with outright hostility by the Western Australian Government, a Labor one led by Mr F.J.S. Wise. Before leaving Perth for Canberra to attend a standardisation conference, Wise made a statement to the press in which, in belligerent terms, he announced that, 'I am not going to be pushed around by anyone in the eastern states'. Had the State Government endorsed the Clapp plan in 1945, a great deal of the agony suffered by the WAGR over the ensuing 15 years might have been avoided. However, in the final analysis Western Australia received preferential treatment in the matter of rail standardisation.

Because of Queensland's and Western Australia's rejection of the proposals, the Railway Standardisation Agreement Act of 1946 — which was introduced into the Federal Parliament on 31 July, and received Vice Regal Assent on 15 August — covered only the Commonwealth, New South Wales, Victoria and South Australia. In his second reading speech, Mr Ward said: 'After full examination of the facts, the Commonwealth Government has come to the conclusion that the standardisation and modernisation of our railway system is an essential defence work. Whilst the project is advanced by the Commonwealth primarily as being necessary for defence purposes, it cannot be overlooked that the economic gains resultant from the adoption of uniformity in gauges and railway equipment would be tremendous.'

Robert Menzies, Leader of the Opposition, paid a high tribute to Sir Harold Clapp — with whom he had enjoyed a close relationship during his term as Minister of Railways in Victoria before entering Federal politics — but cast doubt on the priority given to rail standardisation vis à vis other demands, such as water conservation, power generation, shipbuilding and fishing. He also felt that the non-participation of Queensland and Western Australia compromised the efficacy of the project. Finally, Menzies said: 'Speaking on behalf of the incoming government, I say that we shall reserve judgment'. (A Federal election was imminent but, contrary to Menzies' prediction, the Chifley Government was returned.)

Before the end of the year, both Victoria and South Australia had passed complementary legislation, but New South Wales declined to do so. Finally, after a lapse of three years, New South Wales was told that, unless advice was received by 30 September 1949 that it was prepared to introduce the necessary legislation, the Commonwealth would assume that it did not wish to ratify the Agreement and that, in the circumstances, immediate steps would be taken to negotiate another one with the other two states. No satisfactory reply was received.

Despite Western Australia's rejection in 1945 of the Clapp proposals, it was not averse to seeking funds under the guise of standardisation when it thought it advantageous to do so. In

1947, following a change of State Government, the incoming Minister of Railways, H.S. Seward — who nurtured a longstanding hatred of the railways — instituted a Royal Commission into the WAGR. Early in 1948, and following receipt of the Commission's unjustifiably scathing report, the Government thought that it could achieve rehabilitation on the cheap if it now agreed to standardisation. Neither Chifley nor Ward fell for the ploy, and told Western Australia to put its own railway house in order before standardisation could be considered.

Again, in 1950, the Commonwealth was asked to provide funds under the standardisation formula for the reconstruction of the Fremantle–Kalgoorlie line to 1435 mm standards, but with the gauge remaining at 1067 mm for the foreseeable future. Any faint hope of success that this request might have had disappeared when the Westland, carrying Minister for Shipping and Transport George McLeay, Commonwealth Railways Commissioner Pat Hannaberry, and the author to Perth for discussions on the proposition was delayed for about four hours at Bullabulling, a remote siding 68 kilometres west of Kalgoorlie, following the collapse of the brick arch on the locomotive.

In 1949, Mr (later Sir Thomas) Playford, no doubt sensing the imminent defeat of the Chifley Government, took advantage of Ward's conciliatory attitude towards those states favouring standardisation and negotiated an Agreement which provided for:
(a) The State to convert to standard gauge all of its broad and narrow gauge lines except those on Eyre Peninsula.
(b) The Commonwealth to:
(i) Convert to standard gauge its lines from Port Augusta to Alice Springs and from Darwin to Birdum
(ii) Construct a standard gauge railway from Alice Springs to Birdum; and
(iii) Take steps to acquire the Silverton Tramway from Cockburn to Broken Hill and vest it in the South Australian Railways Commissioner.
Under the financial provisions of the Agreement, the Commonwealth would meet 70 percent of that portion of the project to be carried out by the State, and 100 percent of its own commitments. Also, and most significantly, the Commonwealth agreed to accept as a standardisation debit the cost of the conversion to broad gauge of the narrow gauge division in the south-east of South Australia. The only condition attached to this was that the ultimate conversion to standard gauge would be at State cost. Such an eventually did then and even now seems remote, because not only does it imply the standardisation of the entire broad gauge systems of both Victoria and South Australia, but also the fact that Australian National closed those lines some years ago.

In view of the strong rapport that existed between Chifley and Playford, one wonders who made the initial approach on this occasion. However, the manner in which the negotiations were conducted at Commonwealth level was typical of Canberra bureaucracy at that time. They were handled by the Rail Standardisation Division of the Department of Transport — of which Ward was Minister — while, for some strange reason, the Commonwealth Railways had since 1917 been part of the portfolio of the Minister for the Interior (formerly the Minister for Home Affairs). Commonwealth Railways Commissioner Hannaberry was unaware of the 1949 discussions with South Australia, and this led to some inter-departmental bitterness which spilled over when, following the advent of the Menzies Government later that year, responsibility for the Commonwealth Railways was transferred to the Minister for Shipping and Transport. The new Minister, Senator George McLeay, took early steps to wind up the Rail Standardisation Division and to add its functions to those of the Commonwealth Railways. This seemed to be a logical decision, but the shabby way in which it was done reflected little credit on those responsible.

When Hannaberry assumed his new res-ponsibilities, the only state with which he had to deal was South Australia, and, unfortunately, there was a deterioration in the cordiality between Commonwealth and State that had prevailed previously. This could be attributed not only to the manner in which the Agreement with South Australia had been negotiated, but also to some residual bitterness which arose during the dispute over the route to be adopted for the Stirling North–Leigh Creek standard gauge railway.

One of Hannaberry's first actions after taking over the Rail Standardisation Division's activities was to question certain costs incurred in the gauge widening in the south-east of South Australia. E.J. Watson, Chief Engineer for the SAR and I, as Chief Civil Engineer for the Commonwealth Railways, were delegated to resolve the dispute. We had no difficulty whatsoever.

Another matter that arose was the intrusion into the standardisation debate of Mr W.C. Wentworth, MHR for the Federal seat of Mackellar and something of an amateur railway buff. Brilliant but unconventional, Bill Wentworth sometimes riled Prime Minister Menzies, who appointed him Chairman of the Government Members' Rail Standardisation Committee. In the light of Menzies' earlier lukewarm attitude towards standardisation, one is inclined to asssume that it was nothing more than a ploy to neutralise a member who had the capacity to embarrass him.

However, Wentworth took the job seriously and came up with a modified plan that would link all capital cities by standard gauge. His Committee recommended the construction of independent standard gauge lines from Albury to Melbourne, from Adelaide to Port Pirie, and from Kalgoorlie to Perth, as well as the conversion of the narrow gauge railway from Port Pirie to Broken Hill. Unfortunately, its members were so obsessed with intercapital working and passenger travel that they ignored completely any consideration of the local and bulk traffics which constitute by far the greater part of rail business in this country.

Not to be outdone, the Labor Opposition established a similar committee which came up with virtually identical recommendations.

Over the years, Bill Wentworth tried very hard to see the achievement of some measure of rail standardisation in Australia. However, his train-buff approach to the problem and entire disregard for anything but intercity working virtually wrecked any chance that there might have been in achieving a national unified gauge. The final outcome has been a continuation of the proliferation of gauges, the attempted solution of which seems to have been the closure of a number of branch lines and the diversion of vast tonneages of bulk commodities from rail to road, something that should never have been allowed to happen. Now that the capital cities have been appeased, this tragic mistake will never be corrected.

During the first seven years of the 1950s, the only actual work that came within the ambit of rail standardisation — and that the outcome of the cosy deal between Chifley and Playford in 1949 — was the ongoing conversion to broad gauge of South Australia's narrow gauge division in its south-east. Then, in 1958, two standardisation proposals were put forward. One was approved and the other rejected.

Authorised under the Railway Standardisation (New South Wales and Victoria) Act of 1958, work commenced two years later on the construction of an independent standard gauge line between Albury and Melbourne. It opened in 1962 and at long last the two major cities of Sydney and Melbourne were linked by a common gauge.

On the other hand, when, in 1958, South Australia sought, in terms of its 1949 Act, to proceed with the standardisation of its narrow gauge Peterborough Division, it was met with outright hostility from the Commonwealth. It took another five years, an unsuccessful appeal to the High Court, and an opportunistic decision by the Commonwealth Government in the atmosphere of a Federal by-election, before approval was granted — but only for the conversion of the Port Pirie–Broken Hill line, and not for the whole division as sought by the State.

Three years later, Western Australia — whose violent opposition to Clapp's 1945 proposals was possibly the vital factor leading to the abandonment of his visionary plan, and who tried to have the rehabilitation of its narrow gauge system financed under the standardisation formula — was given preferential treatment. In 1961, and with the development of the Koolyanobbing iron ore deposit north east of Southern Cross providing the impetus, approval was received for the construction of a standard gauge railway from Kalgoorlie to Kwinana, south of Fremantle. Work started shortly afterwards and, in 1968, a standard gauge connection with the eastern states was established.

Finally, in December 1969, the unbroken

unified rail link between east and west was forged when the unnecessarily delayed standardisation of the narrow gauge section between Port Pirie and Broken Hill was completed, the first through freight and passenger trains travelling over it in January and in February 1970. But for Commonwealth prevarication, this would have happened nearly two years earlier.

The next step was not initiated with rail standardisation in mind. The fragile narrow gauge Central Australia Railway from Port Augusta to Alice Springs was prone to extensive flood damage and, with it, to lengthy delays to traffic — especially so after the advent of diesel electric locomotives, whose low-slung traction motors could not cope with even a minimal flow of water over the rails. The Commonwealth Railways therefore proposed and received approval for the construction of a new standard gauge line from Tarcoola — on the Trans Australian Railway 415 kilometres west of Port Augusta — to Alice Springs. Except for the fact that it started from Tarcoola instead of Kingoonya — 79 kilometres to the east — the new railway followed the route proposed during the 1926 discussions surrounding the extension of the Central line to Alice Springs. Construction started in 1975 and when the line was officially opened in 1980 it became an integral part of the north–south transcontinental railway concept.

The euphoria surrounding the official opening was such that it prompted Prime Minister Fraser and Northern Territory Chief Minister Everingham to make optimistic predictions that they would see its extension to Darwin. However, no substantial action was taken by either government to meet those predictions. Indeed, we had to wait another 24 years before the 130-year-old dream of a north–south transcontinental railway became a reality — and that as the result of action by private enterprise!

The standard gauge connection to Adelaide had to survive years of inaction followed by Commonwealth intransigence until 1984, when the first standard gauge passenger train ran between Adelaide and Crystal Brook on the Sydney–Perth transcontinental railway.

South Australia submitted a consolidated proposal for the standardisation of the broad and narrow gauge lines north of Adelaide. However, the Commonwealth would have nothing to do with the proposal, even though its own consultant's plan for a standard gauge line in isolation was blown to pieces by the State's response to it. Consequently, and abetted by the subsequent transfer of the SAR's non-urban activities to Australian National, the final outcome was the provision of an independent line from Crystal Brook to Adelaide and, with it, disaffection to the adjacent broad gauge rail system. This was countered by the new owners by the simple action of closing lines and cancelling services, diverting from rail to road the transportation of vast quantities of bulk commodities.

The last phase in the standardisation saga — and certainly the death knell of any chance of unifying Australia's rail gauges — occurred in 1996, when Adelaide and Melbourne were linked by standard gauge. It may satisfy some long distance passengers, but will it obviate their changing trains at Adelaide and Melbourne? In any case, current trends indicate that except for once-only tourists — most of whom travel at social welfare subsidised special rates — long distance passenger travel will be diverted more and more to air.

The sorry story might well be illustrated by comparing the situation today with that of 1944, when Clapp made his inquiry. In 1944, the mainland network consisted of 42,300 route kilometres and of three gauges, with 13 breaks of gauge. Today, the corresponding figures are: 33,500 route kilometres, still with three gauges, and with 10 operative breaks of gauge.

These figures do not indicate any improvement. The obsession in some quarters with intercapital working and the establishment of independent standard gauge lines in the midst of other gauges has disaffected vital local traffics. This problem has been 'solved' by the simple but damaging procedure of closing branch lines so essential to the prosperity of local agriculture.

The financial provisions of the Rail Standardisation Agreement Acts were also something of a confidence trick. Under the Agreements, the Commonwealth made funds available out of capital — on which of itself it does not pay interest — and the states were required to pay, out of revenue, 30 percent of that cost, plus interest, in 50 equal annual instalments. However, when taking the interest into account, they are in fact obliged to pay more; in reality, nearer to 80 percent. This was yet another imposition on the states, and it explodes the myth that the Commonwealth bore the greater part of the cost.

Over the critical years of World War II, Australia's war expenditure averaged $2.86 million per day. At that rate, the cost of Clapp's first phase of standardisation would have been met by four and a half days' war expenditure per annum over the planned conversion period of seven years. His ultimate plan, scheduled over 17 years, would have represented only three and three quarter days' such expenditure each year. And, after all, the Bill for the Agreement Act was introduced into the Federal Parliament as a defence measure.

What a comparatively cheap price it would have been to pay! It is now too late. Had President Truman dropped the bomb a few weeks earlier, standardisation would not have cost us one cent.

So ends the tragic story of Australia's rail gauge mess. Surely, it has been our greatest railway mistake.

The responsibility for the mess goes back to the New South Wales colonial administration and to Westminster, but their culpability was compounded by Queensland, Western Australia and South Australia building its railways not only to two gauges, but also to no orderly pattern.

However, deserving of the greatest censure are those responsible for the subsequent failure to achieve a uniform gauge railway system — or even a satisfactory modified one — when the opportunity arose. Among the most blameworthy would be:

• F.J.S. Wise, Labor Premier of Western Australia during the 1940s, and H.S.Seward, Minister for Railways in the McLarty Liberal-Country Party Government that followed. Wise must be condemned for his violent opposition to the Clapp recommendations, in which he was in effect abetted by Seward's anti-railway phobia. The actions of these two men eliminated for all time the possibility of a uniform and integrated rail system in Australia, because they provided New South Wales and Victoria with an excuse to opt out.

• Politicians, both Federal and State: the former for their stubborn and dictatorial stance, and their inability to appreciate the wishes of the states; the latter for their parochialism. The Commonwealth's attitude in the later years was in distinct contrast to that shown 20 years earlier.

• The Commonwealth Department of Shipping and Transport, whose officers assigned to the project were entirely unqualified in transportation matters. Indeed, successive appointees to the position of Comptroller of Rail Standardisation came from the Commonwealth Treasury. Instead of limiting their activities to the financial functions associated with those of Comptroller, they seemed to buy into all sorts of matters, including engineering, and at times made decisions far beyond their mandate — certainly beyond their expertise — and without consultation. While these things did not of themselves prevent the start of the project, their restrictive attitude towards rail standardisation matters in general — and, in particular, their inclination to impose their views on the states — must have played a part in the non-fulfilment of Ward's and Clapp's grand design.

• South Australia. Had its attitude in the 1920s and 1930s not been so negative, Adelaide would have been linked to the east–west standard gauge 50 years earlier.

• Despite his undoubted enthusiasm for railway matters, Bill Wentworth's intrusion into the debate, and his advocacy for nothing more than intercapital links, doomed forever any chance of an integrated standard gauge rail network being achieved. It is a pity that he ever became involved.

The author was actively associated with rail standardisation projects in both Western Australia and South Australia — starting in a very minor way in 1929 and with heavy involvement from 1944 onwards. It would be appropriate Therefore if his reminiscences in relation to those states should be recorded.

Western Australia

The Western Australian standard gauge story, at

least that prior to the 1960s, has not yet been told. It goes back to 1903 when, in the Bill authorising the Commonwealth to make laws for a railway between Kalgoorlie and the South Australia border, the State Parliament made provision for Western Australia to build concurrently a railway from Kalgoorlie to Fremantle to the gauge adopted for the Trans Australian Railway. It took 66 years for this to become a reality.

The first positive steps of any kind did not take place until 1929, when the 1921 estimates were upgraded and a survey for a standard gauge railway from Fremantle to Kalgoorlie — to a ruling grade of 1 in 80 — was shared by the State Public Works and the Railway Departments.

George Thornton Smith of the Railway Construction Branch of the Public Works Department was responsible for this section in the 1929 review. His survey followed the Avon River from Northam to its debouchment on to the coastal plain a few kilometres north of Midland Junction, where the stream becomes the Swan. This was substantially the route adopted in the 1960s, when the project finally got under way.

From Midland to Fremantle, the new line was to be located close to the south bank of the Swan River, crossing the Canning River adjacent to the Canning Highway road bridge. The route did not extend as far south as that finally adopted because, in 1929, there was no thought of industrial development in the Kwinana area.

While Thornton Smith was surveying in the Avon Valley, two WAGR engineers, Tom Shackleton and John Shepherd, were given the job of preparing an estimate for an independent standard gauge line between Northam and Kalgoorlie to a ruling grade of 1 in 80.

Particularly over the last 350 kilometres between Merredin and Kalgoorlie, the lay of the land was predominantly a series of north–south ridges with east–west ascents and descents to a natural grade of 1 in 60, and the narrow gauge railway had been constructed to this grade. Where a 1 in 80 grade could not be achieved alongside the narrow gauge alignment, the two engineers undertook trial surveys for deviations. It was at this point that I commenced my 44 years' of on-and-off association with rail standardisation.

The party's return to Perth to complete its estimate coincided with a university vacation. No doubt with the intention of getting me out of his hair, A.G. Lunt, Engineer in charge of the Drawing Office, and one whose interest in engineering cadets was anything but paternal — indeed it was patently contemptuous — bundled me off to Shackleton and

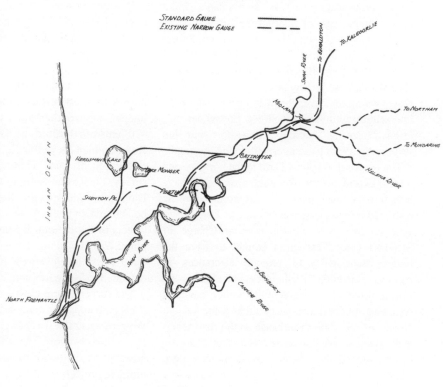

RAIL STANDARDISATION IN WESTERN AUSTRALIA
1945 PLAN TO BY-PASS PERTH

Shepherd. There I spent the whole of the university vacation adding up earthworks figures.

The completion of the 1929 review saw the question of standardisation in Western Australia lapse into oblivion until 1944, when the Clapp inquiry led to its revival, and it stayed active for three years.

In 1944, I joined two engineers — Syd Raynes and Clem Robinson — in the preparation of Western Australia's submissions. Each had a specific task: Robinson's to consolidate the estimates; Raynes' to prepare designs for the Perth station, including a freight yard between Perth and West Perth; and mine to plan the standard gauge from Midland to North Fremantle and into the Midland workshops. It was envisaged that the North Fremantle–Kalgoorlie standard gauge railway would, for the most part, follow the existing narrow gauge route, but with a number of deviations, including that through the Avon Valley.

After running parallel from North Fremantle to a point near the Nicholson Road subway at Shenton Park the standard gauge line would have deviated to the north, through Wembley, then north-easterly across Herdsman's Lake to the intersection of Scarborough Beach Road and Main Street, Mount Hawthorn. Then, taking advantage of a small but significant gully to save earthworks, the line would have turned almost due east to Bayswater, passing south of Dog Swamp and over the Wanneroo Road at its intersection with Walcott Street. Bayswater was to have been the junction with a short spur line serving the Perth passenger and goods terminals.

The proposal to bypass Perth to the north — and which, except for the Wembley area would have been through open country — was prompted by the restricted bridge clearances in the city. However, a year or two later, as Engineer in Charge of Standard Gauge Design, I sought to have the bridges redesigned to provide clearances to national standards. Preliminary calculations by Harold Rowbotham, the WAGR's senior structural engineer, indicated that this could be achieved, but at the cost of some disturbance to the road levels at the Barrack–Wellington Streets corner. However, history proved the whole exercise to have been futile.

Apart from a deviation through vacant land north of the Ashfield industrial area to provide for a marshalling yard, carriage shed and locomotive depot, the standard gauge line would have paralleled the WAGR's and Midland Company's narrow gauge tracks through Guildford and Midland to Upper Swan, where it would turn eastwards and traverse the Avon Valley through Toodyay to East Northam.

Reconnaissance of the Shenton Park–Bayswater deviation demanded a degree of secrecy, because every householder in Wembley was anxious to find out whether his bailiwick was likely to be threatened. The mere appearance of a theodolite or level — or even that of a WAGR motor vehicle — was sufficient to promote an instantaneous kerbside meeting of apprehensive residents.

The story way now be told. All the houses on the eastern side of Marlow Street would have been demolished to make way for the railway, which would have been located in a cutting about five metres deep, and running parallel with the street. The subsequent abandonment of the Shenton Park–Bayswater proposal obviated what would have been a traumatic public brawl.

Despite Western Australia's rejection of his plan, Sir Harold Clapp suggested that surveys be undertaken, particularly in the Avon Valley, and Mr Ward agreed.

Mr Ted Clifford was appointed Engineer in Charge of Standard Gauge Surveys and three parties were established in the Avon Valley; one under George Sutherland, another under Howard Williams and the third successively under Russell Rowe and Ian McCullough.

Subsequent to Thornton Smith's 1929 survey, the Town Planning Commissioner, D.L. Davidson, suggested that flood control measures be undertaken in the Avon Valley to minimise the effects of the periodical floodings of the coastal plain. With this in mind, the 1946 survey covered three possible elevations for the railway, and extended to 70 metres above the stream bed.

The surveys were closed down in 1947, when it became apparent that, at that juncture at least, Western Australia was not going to participate in rail standardisation. The effort was not wasted, however, because it became the basis for the ultimate project.

South Australia

Initially opposed to standardisation proposals, South Australia became the only state to endorse the Clapp plan of 1945 in its entirety, although it demanded the standardisation of the Central Australia Railway and its extension to Darwin, something to which Federal Minister of Transport Ward assented.

Then, in 1949, as has already been recorded, the conversion to broad gauge of the narrow gauge south-eastern division of the SAR was brought under the financial umbrella of rail standardisation and the broad gauge was opened progressively from Wolseley to Naracoorte in 1950, to Kalangadoo in 1952, to Mount Gambler in 1953, to Millicent in 1955, and finally to Kingston in 1959.

In 1959, when the gauge widening in the south-east of the State was approaching completion, Sir Thomas Playford sought continued standardisation works in South Australia, and made representations to the Federal Government, seeking agreement to proceed with the conversion of the entire narrow gauge Peterborough Division. The State could see some advantages with this work, but not with just the Port Pirie–Broken Hill line. This led to protracted discussions which, in the main, were marked by, a lack of cooperation on the part of the Commonwealth.

Indeed, at about this time, the Commonwealth bureaucracy and the Commonwealth Railways Commissioner seemed to have developed an anti-South Australian Railways paranoia, some of which could have been attributed to the fact that, a few years earlier, the Commonwealth and South Australian Governments had agreed to a freight rate for the movement of Leigh Creek coal over the new standard gauge railway between Telford and the Port Augusta power station at Stirling North. The rate was a favourable one for the State, and Commonwealth Railways Commissioner Hannaberry had fought strenuously against it.

While discussions were going on, we in the South Australian Railways learned by accident that the Department of Shipping and Transport, the Commonwealth Railways and the Broken Hill mining companies had established a joint committee to study the standardisation proposals.

Significantly, the SAR, the instrumentality most vitally concerned, was not invited to participate, nor indeed was it intended that it should even know of its existence.

It is the author's guess that, in an attempt to get something of his own back, Hannaberry invited the mining industry to participate in the committee's deliberations, using as a bait the possibility of reduced freight rates on the carriage of concentrates from Broken Hill to Port Pirie. He was unashamedly envious of the concentrates rate compared with that for Leigh Creek coal.

The Commonwealth would have no part of the State's request for the standardisation of the entire Peterborough Division, and would consider — and this grudgingly — the Port Pirie–Broken Hill line alone. An impasse appeared inevitable. However, in May 1970 Mr (later Sir Hubert) Opperman, who had become Minister for Shipping and Transport, undertook a familiarisation trip over SAR's Peterborough Division. The author clearly remembers Opperman's incredulous comment to Keith Smith — who had succeeded Hannaberry as Commonwealth Railways Commissioner — as he travelled over the Quorn track, where the country was experiencing its best season for years: 'Is this the line you want to close?'

While the discussions were going on, Playford appealed to the High Court, seeking a judgment compelling the Commonwealth to agree to further works in terms of the 1949 Agreement. In due course, the case came before the Court, but, contrary to the opinion given to the State, it was dismissed.

Late in 1960, when Australia was suffering a minor depression, the Commonwealth Government looked to an expanded works programs, including rail standardisation, as one means of encouraging economic activity.

To this end, a conference was held in Canberra in 1961. It was chaired by James Nimmo of the Prime Minister's Department and was attended by seven Commonwealth officers representing the departments of the Prime Minister, Treasury, National Development, Shipping and Transport and Commonwealth Railways. Fargher and I represented South Australia. Incidentally, the disproportionate representation between Commonwealth and State was not unusual;

indeed, it seems to be par for the course whenever Commonwealth–State conferences are held.

Discussion centred around the Broken Hill line, but, despite a measure of harmony, nothing emanated. However, in October 1961 — and most certainly arising out of a degree of self-consciousness at having agreed to the Western Australian project while refusing anything for South Australia — under the Railway Equipment Agreement (South Australia) Act, the Commonwealth consented to provide funds, under terms identical with those applying to standardisation, for South Australia to acquire 12 narrow gauge diesel electric locomotives and 100 ore wagons. Both locomotives and wagons were to be capable of being converted to standard gauge, and at state cost. Further, the wagons, initially of 36 tonnes capacity, were to be enlarged to 56 tonnes when converted to standard gauge.

Late in 1962, Playford proposed that the State reconstruct the narrow gauge track between Port Pirie and the New South Wales border at Cockburn to the ruling grade of 1 in 120 as proposed for the standard gauge line, as well as to standard gauge specifications. He would then approach the Commonwealth for funds and perhaps coerce them into agreeing to conversion. However, before finality could be reached with the Commonwealth, another development took place. I had a hunch that it would.

On 19 April 1963, while deputising as Railways Commissioner while my predecessor, Mr Fargher,

cleared leave, I was summoned by the Premier and informed that the Commonwealth had now agreed to the standardisation of the line between Port Pirie and Broken Hill, and that work should start immediately. It would not be over-cynical to point out that the announcement coincided with a by-election for the Federal seat of Grey.

For the most part, the Port Pirie–Cockburn standard gauge line was constructed alongside the narrow gauge one. There were, however, two major deviations in order to achieve a ruling grade of 1 in 120 in the westbound, or loaded, direction. They were between Paratoo and Ucolta and between Yongala and Jamestown; while, included in the project was the conversion to broad gauge of the 23 kilometres section of narrow gauge between Terowie and Peterborough.

Three major station yards were involved in the standardisation works; Port Pirie, Gladstone and Peterborough. The narrow gauge was eliminated at Port Pirie, reducing it from a three- to a two-gauge station. On the other hand, the introduction of standard gauge into Gladstone changed it from a reasonably uncomplicated two-gauge yard into a complex three-gauge one; and, although a break of gauge had been eliminated at Terowie, Peterborough was relegated from being a single gauge station to one involving three. Consequently, South Australia's former notoriety of possessing a three-gauge railway station was duplicated — and this the outcome of a costly standardisation project.

Tracklaying new standard gauge line at Port Pirie–Broken Hill, South Australia (*Photo:* South Australian Railways)

Tracklaying new standard gauge line at Port Pirie–Broken Hill in 1969 (*Photo:* South Australian Railways)

Tracklaying new standard gauge line in 1969 (*Photo:* South Australian Railways)

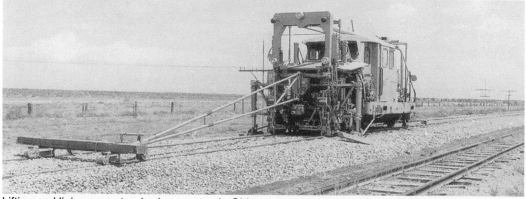

Lifting and lining new standard gauge track. Old narrow gauge line in the foreground (*Photo:* South Australian Railways)

Standardisation? Peterborough, South Australia, triple gauge yard under construction in 1969 (*Photo: South Australian Railways*)

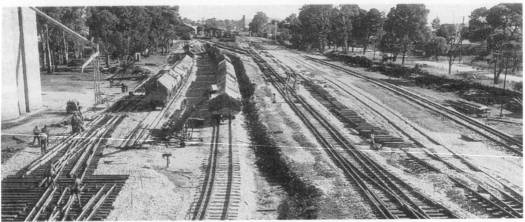

Standardisation? Gladstone, South Australia, triple gauge yard under construction in 1969 (*Photo: South Australian Railways*)

It was a ludicrous situation. Had the decision to proceed with the Adelaide–Port Pirie standardisation been taken at that time, a great deal of the work carried out at Port Pirie would have been avoided. In any case, it became redundant when the Adelaide connection was made. In the same way, the conversion of the Gladstone–Wilmington line concurrently with the Broken Hill project could have been financed out of the money saved by limiting the Gladstone

station yard to two instead of three gauges. Indeed, the cost of the multi-gauge signalling alone would have gone a long way towards meeting the expenditure.

The State asked for substantially less than its entitlement under the Agreement for standard gauge locomotives and rollingstock, but that did not stop the Commonwealth from declining to accept even those reduced requests. It even extended to the financing of the joint ownership of the Indian Pacific. South Australia's share of the cost came within the ambit of the 1949 Agreement, a fact not denied by the Commonwealth, but which it ignored — by intent, one is led to assume — and the State was obliged to meet its share under less favourable financial terms. It became obvious that those administering the project at Commonwealth level were envious of the terms negotiated with Ward. However, with the taking over of the non urban assets of the SAR, the Agreement lapsed.

Another instance of the Commonwealth's attitude was in the manufacture of standard gauge rollingstock. Tenders were called for the supply of all new rollingstock. In every case but one, that submitted by the Mechanical Branch of the SAR was the lowest. However, that did not meet with unqualified approbation from the Department of Shipping and Transport, the inference being that success by a government undertaking in open competition with private industry was something akin to heresy. But that did not stop the Commonwealth from asking the SAR to manufacture some standard gauge brake vans for Western Australia, because their price was so very much lower.

It would have been possible to complete the Port Pirie–Cockburn section by the end of 1968, and indeed initial planning provided for this. However, the work had to be slowed down because of the delay in finalising negotiations over the line from Cockburn to Broken Hill, and the need to retain a work force to undertake tasks on 'D day', when the standard gauge would be extended through Silverton Tramway territory to Broken Hill. The circumstances surrounding the conversion of this 56 kilometre privately owned length of track constitutes a saga of its own which is recounted later in this chapter.

Back in 1958, when Playford sought Commonwealth approval for the standardisation of the Peterborough Division, Railways Commissioner Fargher looked further ahead to its integration with a standard gauge connection to Adelaide. He propounded a scheme which involved the conversion of all lines on the Peterborough Division, and, concurrent with the provision of a standard gauge to Adelaide, the conversion of

the broad gauge between Gladstone, Snowtown and Wallaroo. With a standard gauge line from Adelaide to Port Pirie, the rail distance to Sydney would have been 89 kilometres longer than that through Terowie and Peterborough. The Snowtown–Gladstone standard gauge link would have reduced that discrepancy to 35 kilometres. At the same time, conversion of the line to Wallaroo would have eliminated the transfer of superphosphate at Gladstone. In fact it would have reduced that station from a two gauge to a single gauge one, and not increased it to three gauges as eventually happened. In addition, there existed a heavy rail traffic in sulphuric acid from Port Pirie to Wallaroo and, unless the branch line was converted, a hazardous transfer operation would be necessary at Snowtown.

At my April 1963 meeting with the Premier, he too looked beyond the immediate project and talked about a standard gauge connection to Adelaide. On his office wall hung a large map of South Australia, and on this he drew a rough line from Adelaide to Crystal Brook, and said that the junction for the standard gauge should be there,

Being aware of Fargher's well conceived and comprehensive scheme, I argued for junctions at both Port Pirie and Gladstone. The Premier was not convinced and the Minister of Railways, Norman Jude, who was also present, hinted that Sir Thomas had made up his mind. Subsequently, Playford approached the Prime Minister with his plan and I am convinced that, in the long term, his mention of Crystal Brook prejudiced the ultimate standardisation pattern for South Australia.

The story behind the provision of a standard gauge connection to Adelaide is a sorry one.

As early as March 1964, only 11 months after the Prime Minister had indicated that his Government was prepared to agree to the Port Pirie–Broken Hill project, Sir Thomas Playford approached Sir Robert Menzies seeking his concurrence to further standardisation works in South Australia and, in particular, an Adelaide connection. While not rejecting the proposal outright, Menzies suggested that further investigations be carried out jointly by the Commonwealth and South Australian Railways Commissioners.

Standardisation of the line between Port Pirie

Standard Gauge Pattern North of Adelaide

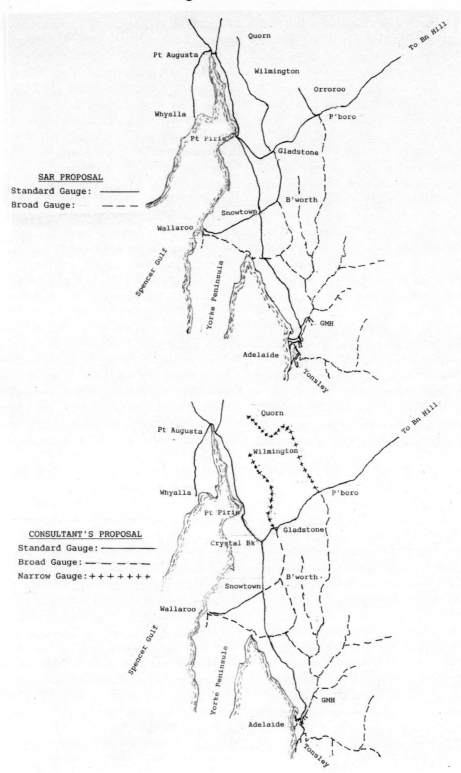

and Broken Hill meant that, while there had been a marked improvement in the operations of that section and in the national railway pattern, the position had worsened in respect of other SAR activities.

Whereas, formerly, there had been a three-gauge station at Port Pirie and two-gauge ones at Gladstone and Terowie, there now existed a two-gauge station at Port Pirie and three-gauge ones at Gladstone and Peterborough. Moreover, instead of having a compact narrow gauge Peterborough Division, the SAR was left with two narrow gauge lines (those to Wilmington and Quorn) as separate and isolated appendages. The State wished to correct that situation, at the same time hoping that it would obtain a standard gauge connection to the Adelaide metropolitan area, but in a form not prejudicial to its intra-system movements.

At this juncture, the author, then Assistant to the Railways Commissioner, undertook a personal study and analysis of every freight and livestock movement over the lines north of Adelaide during the 1963/64 financial year in order to determine what the position would be under seven alternative rail patterns for the provision of a standard gauge connection between Adelaide and the Sydney–Perth transcontinental railway. In the absence of a departmental computer at that time, the study involved many hours of tedious analysis,

The seven alternatives were:

(1) Convert Adelaide–Port Pirie.

(2) Convert Adelaide–Redhill.
Construct new standard gauge Redhill–Crystal Brook.
Close Redhill–Port Pirie.

(3) Convert Adelaide–Port Pirie.
Convert Snowtown–Gladstone.
Convert Gladstone–Wilmington and extend to Quorn.
Close Peterborough–Quorn or alternatively convert Peterborough–Orroroo and close Orroroo–Quorn.

(4) Convert Adelaide–Redhill.
Construct new standard gauge Redhill–Crystal Brook.
Close Redhill–Port Pirie.
Convert Gladstone–Wilmington and extend to Quorn.

Close Peterborough–Quorn or alternatively convert Peterborough–Orroroo and close Orroroo–Quorn.

(5) Convert Adelaide–Port Pirie.
Convert Bowmans–Kadina.
Convert Wallaroo–Snowtown–Gladstone.
Convert Gladstone–Wilmington and extend to Quorn.
Close Peterborough–Quorn or alternatively convert Peterborough–Orroroo and close Orroroo–Quorn.

(6) Convert Adelaide–Port Pirie.
Convert Kadina–Snowtown–Gladstone with independent standard gauge Wallaroo–Kadina.
Convert Gladstone Wilmington and extend to Quorn.
Close Peterborough–Quorn or convert Peterborough–Orroroo and close Orroroo–Quorn.

(7) Construct independent standard gauge Adelaide–Port Pirie.

The study showed that, at the 1965 level of costs, the conversion in isolation of the Adelaide–Port Pirie line would have increased annual operating costs by $121,000, while the corresponding figure for an independent standard gauge line would have been $255,000. On the other hand, Alternative No. 6, which was Fargher's comprehensive scheme, would have meant a saving of $169,000 per annum. In other words, the Fargher proposal was more attractive to the tune of at least $290,000 per annum at 1964 rates. Four years later, nine alternatives were considered and, once again, the economics strongly favoured the comprehensive scheme, which on this occasion also provided for standard gauge connections to industries in the Adelaide area.

This information was conveyed to Keith Smith, who had succeeded Hannaberry as Commonwealth Railways Commissioner in 1960. On 3 March 1966, he forwarded to me for comment the draft of a report which, he told me, he proposed to submit to the Minister for Shipping and Transport. In it, he stated:

'As a result of the initial analysis and consultation with the South Australian Railways Commissioner, it became clear that the construction of an Adelaide Port Pirie standard gauge railway in isolation from several associated interconnecting lines of 5 foot 3 inch [1600 mm] gauge would add substantially to operating difficulties and costs to the State railway system when the South Australian northern railway division was considered as a whole. It is true that the standard gauge construction would provide access to eastern and western states, but as far as the Railway department was concerned the operation of numerous transfer stations that would be made necessary by the imposition of a single standard gauge railway running from Adelaide to Port Pirie in the body of a broad gauge system would outweigh any likely financial and physical benefits to be derived.'

That was the first time in all the years of negotiations regarding standardisation that anyone associated with the Commonwealth had made reference to and recognised the injurious effects that a standard gauge in isolation would have on South Australia's intrastate operations. However, in the long term, it did not influence the Commonwealth Government's thinking.

Mr Smith went on to outline the scheme 'which in the view of the South Australian Railways Commissioner and myself will contribute most to the overall economic operation of the State railway system in the interim period before full standardisation in the state can be achieved'.

It was in effect the plan proposed by my predecessor, and which envisaged, in conjunction with the conversion of the Wilmington and Quorn narrow gauge lines, the standardisation of certain broad gauge ones north Adelaide — including that between Adelaide and Port Pirie. At the 1965 level of costs, the proposal would have shown a financial advantage of $200,000 per annum over that for an independent isolated standard gauge connection to Adelaide.

However, the Commonwealth was not convinced and, in that year, suggested that consultants be commissioned to report on the matter. The State had no option but to agree, but it was given little if any say in the framing of the terms of reference, the short list of consultants to be approached, or the final selection of the consultants themselves. The latter's report of March 1970 did not surprise us. Even before the study commenced, we had been pre-conditioned by the Commonwealth as to what to expect.

The consultants recommended, as we had expected, the construction of an independent standard gauge line from Adelaide to Crystal Brook, with connections to Gillman (Port Adelaide) and the Pooraka livestock trucking yards. No other standard gauge connections in the Adelaide metropolitan area were contemplated. They did recommend, however, the conversion at minimal cost the Snowtown–Wallaroo section. At the 1970 level of costs, the proposals were estimated at $35 million.

The suggestion that a new railway be constructed, rather than the conversion of the existing heavy duty broad gauge one, was, to say the least, amazing. It could have been prompted only by the consultant's ignorance of the techniques of conversion, something with which the SAR had been familiar since the 1920s. Economically, the independent line — even with the Wallaroo connection — represented one of the most unfavourable of all the possible alternatives.

In essence, the Adelaide–Crystal Brook standard gauge railway in isolation would have meant little more than the shifting the transfer stations from Port Pirie and Peterborough to Adelaide, and this at a cost of $35 million. We had always assumed that the Port Pirie line would be converted. It was set up for such an operation, not only in respect of the track structure, but also because the railway network north of Adelaide was admirably suited for the alternative routing of traffic during the conversion period. Therefore, on learning that the Commonwealth was prepared to accept the consultant's plan, we in the SAR looked at how far the cost of an independent standard gauge line would go towards fulfilling our comprehensive proposals if conversion, rather than new construction, was adopted.

We came to the conclusion that everything sought by the SAR, including standard gauge from Gladstone and Wilmington to Quorn, from Peterborough to Orroroo, to Mile End and essential points in the metropolitan area, including General Motors Holdens at Elizabeth and Woodville and to Chrysler Australia (now Mitsubishi) at Tonsley, could be achieved at a cost, at 1970 rates, nearly $5.5 million, or 15.7 percent, less than that quoted by the consultants for the Adelaide Crystal Brook independent line alone. It would also have represented comparative operating savings in excess of $200,000 per annum. At current cost levels, the amounts of $5.5 million and $200,000 would approximate $44 million and $1.6 million respectively.

In April 1970, I reported in detail to the South Australian Minister of Roads and Transport and recommended that the State reject the consultant's proposals, because they would be inimical to the long term operations of the South Australian Railways. In fact, I went further and argued that it would be preferable to do nothing rather than to accept the plan which, in my opinion, was prejudicial to the State's interests. The Premier, Steele Hall, would not accept this, his attitude being that, as the Commonwealth was prepared to go only as far as the Adelaide–Crystal Brook line, it would be a waste of time asking for anything else — and this despite the fact that considerably more standardisation could be achieved for substantially less money.

Within weeks, the Hall Government was defeated in a state election. The incoming Labor Premier, Don Dunstan, and his Minister of Transport, Geoff Virgo, on learning of the existence of my report and its advocacy for something better, took immediate steps to press the Commonwealth to agree to the scheme propounded by the SAR, and which had been conceived only after exhaustive studies of factual data. It was also the one supported by the Commonwealth Railways Commissioner in his report of March 1966.

This led to a reopening of negotiations at Ministerial level. The new Minister for Shipping and Transport, Peter Nixon, appeared to display a more sympathetic approach than did his predecessor, Ian Sinclair, and offered a compromise which went a little way towards meeting the State's wishes. It allowed for standard gauge access to Mile End and certain industries, but it still excluded the conversion of the narrow gauge lines remaining on the Peterborough Division. Oddly too, the Commonwealth persisted with its demand that, instead of converting the broad gauge line between Adelaide and a point near Redhill, whence a new route would be followed to Crystal Brook, an independent standard gauge

track be constructed on a parallel alignment. This could only be interpreted as a face-saving gesture.

That was the situation at the time of my retirement in March 1973. Naturally, I should make only passing comment on what has happened since then, but this I must say: South Australia, the only state to show any consistency in its attitude towards rail standardisation, has not achieved its just entitlement. Sir Robert Menzies was not alone in his political opportunism when, in April 1963, he made public the decision to proceed with the work between Port Pirie and Broken Hill. On 3 May 1974, the then Prime Minister, Gough Whitlam, announced that the Adelaide–Crystal Brook would go ahead. Significantly too, he made that announcement during the course of a Federal election. It should have been made 11 years earlier.

In December 1975 and following the defeat of the Whitlam Government, Nixon again assumed the Transport portfolio; and he deputed Dr Stewart Joy to report of the Adelaide–Crystal Brook proposals. When his report of December 1976 supported the concept of conversion rather than the construction of a new line, one could not refrain from experiencing a measure of satisfaction, indeed of smugness.

The Silverton Tramway

On 20 October 1967, we were the guests of Keith Smith, the Commonwealth Railways Commissioner, at a dinner at Port Augusta to mark the golden jubilee of the opening of the Trans Australian Railway. During the course of the evening, I made the flippant though not altogether hare-brained, prognostication to my interstate colleagues who were also present that there would be a man on the moon before a standard gauge train ran between Sydney and Perth. Neil Armstrong won by precisely seven months.

The feature of the standardisation project that caused the most trouble was the short section of line between the border at Cockburn and Broken Hill, owned and operated by the Silverton Tramway Company Limited.

The disposition of this narrow gauge railway was open to a number of possibilities. In terms of the Silverton Tramway Act of 1886, a New South Wales statute, the gauge of the line was to be

1067 mm; but, by direction of the State Governor, the Company could be obliged to alter it at any time and at its own cost. The Act also provided that, after the expiration of 21 years, New South Wales could purchase the tramway and all of its assets upon payment of an amount equal to 21 times the average divisible profits over the preceding seven years. Calculated on the level of profitability in the 1960s, the purchase price would have approximated $6 million, on a pre-tax basis. Then, under the Railway Standardisation Agreement Act of 1946, the NSW Government would acquire the Silverton Tramway Company's line and, after conversion, vest it in the South Australian Railways Commissioner. However, the Act virtually lapsed and the Agreement was superseded by that of 1949 which stated that 'The Commonwealth shall take all necessary steps to ensure the Silverton Tramway and the locomotives and rollingstock thereon shall be acquired and vested in the South Australian Railways Commissioner'.

We in South Australia were not keen to work into Broken Hill, because we feared the impact on our employees of the lead bonus and other favourable industrial conditions applying there. Previously, there had been moves by our employees stationed at Peterborough and elsewhere to participate in some form of lead bonus because, at both ends of the line, something of that nature did apply. However, our fears were groundless, and the ultimate phasing out of Silverton's main line operations and the working of SAR train crews into Broken Hill proceeded harmoniously. Another reason for our escaping the lead bonus was the fact that, after standardisation, the Silverton Tramway Company continued to act as the mines shunting authority. This meant that the SAR employees were not obliged to traverse the line of lode in the course of their duties, a crucial factor in determining to whom the bonus should apply.

Neither the Department of Shipping and Transport nor the New South Wales Government would appreciate South Australia's position. They did not have any intention of permitting the Silverton Company to remain as a main line operator, or of purchasing it and paying compensation in accordance with the 1886 Act.

Nor did the Commonwealth department feel disposed to fulfil its obligations under the 1949 Agreement to acquire the Tramway and vest it in the SAR Commissioner. On the contrary, they planned to bypass the line by building a standard gauge railway on a new alignment, thus leaving the company with an open ended narrow gauge railway without recourse to any traffic.

As events turned out, they were successful in bringing this about, but only after offering some solace to the company in the form of an ex gratia payment made for 'loss of business'.

The Department of Shipping and Transport's attitude towards the Silverton Company, which bordered on paranoia, was typified by its actions when it was discovered that the southern end of the remodelled Crystal Street station yard in Broken Hill would have impinged on Company territory. Rather than negotiate for the purchase of that small piece of land, the Department decided, without consulting South Australia, to shift the station yard further east. This involved the removal of a whole mountain of mines slimes. The extremely high cost of this action was ignored entirely.

The South Australian Minister of Transport, Frank Kneebone, made frequent overtures to his Commonwealth counterpart in an endeavour to resolve the impasse, because it had become apparent that the SAR would finish the Port Pirie–Cockburn section — as far as would be possible prior to actual conversion day — long before the 48 kilometres into Broken Hill would be completed.

As a preliminary to a Ministerial conference to be held in Sydney on 17 March 1967, Gilbert Seaman, South Australia's Under-Treasurer, and the author held discussions with Commonwealth and New South Wales Railways Commissioners, Keith Smith and Neal McCusker. We could not persuade them to see our point of view.

The Ministerial conference was chaired by Mr (later Sir Gordon) Freeth, Federal Minister for Shipping and Transport. Others present were the Ministers of Transport in New South Wales and South Australia, as well as representatives of so many Commonwealth departments that Health seemed to be the only one not present. However, nothing positive emerged from that conference.

While these negotiations were going on, the Silverton Company reconnoitred an alternative route from Cockburn to Broken Hill which would have entered the latter station through the Company's Railwaytown yard, some one and a half kilometres from but connected to the Crystal Street station. It would also have provided standard gauge access to the trucking yards, the oil depots and other railway clients. The company then submitted a proposition to the Commonwealth that, for a fixed sum, it would construct a standard gauge railway on the new alignment, and hand it over to the New South Wales Government within a period of ten months. A condition of the offer was that compensation, understood to be some $1.25 million less than that calculated in accordance with the 1886 Act, be paid to the Company.

The Silverton proposal was attractive to South Australia. It would have ensured continuity of a rail service to the livestock trucking yards and other local industries; it would have guaranteed an earlier completion of the Sydney–Perth standard gauge rail link; its fixed price seemed reasonable; and, most importantly, it would have represented annual operational savings to the SAR in excess of $40,000.

Negotiations continued, but it was obvious that neither the Commonwealth nor New South Wales would entertain the Silverton proposal, even though it offered substantial savings to the Commonwealth, and operational and commercial advantages to the SAR.

The Commonwealth demanded that a new standard gauge line be constructed free from any contact whatsoever with Silverton territory. A further indication of the paranoia that pervaded the Department of Shipping and Transport at that time was its unilateral action, without consultation with either the SAR or Silverton — and by persons lacking any expertise in railway engineering or transportation — in shifting the existing livestock yards and oil depots sited on Silverton land to a far less satisfactory location.

It was at this juncture too that the Broken Hill City Council thought it appropriate to use the standard gauge project as a vehicle by which it could implement, at no cost to itself, grade separation and the establishment of an industrial area out of town. Prompted no doubt by a feeling of guilt at having delayed for so long the resolution of the Cockburn–Broken Hill impasse, the Commonwealth supported the Council.

It was patently unreasonable for South Australia to be called upon to bear the major portion of the cost of highway and municipal improvements in another state, but it had no option but to do so. Therefore, we located the standard gauge railway on a new alignment which led directly into the New South Wales' Crystal Street station yard.

The Silverton proposal would have permitted standard gauge working to be introduced a year earlier than did actually happen; it would have represented substantial savings in perpetuity in operating costs; and, in the final analysis, it would have saved over $2 million in capital; and this after allowing for compensation to the company in excess of the ex gratia payment eventually made. To me, all of this arose out of a determination in some quarters to have no part of the Silverton Tramway, its route, its terminal, or even any part of its facilities, and to eliminate it from the national rail network, no matter what. Any inherent advantages that might have been gained from their use, or any disaffection that might have ensued to the SAR, were ignored.

That is my standardisation story. It is not a happy one. My long association with it has led me to a number of conclusions. Among them are:

- Had the Ward–Clapp team continued in existence for a few more years, a great deal of additional rail standardisation would have been achieved in Australia, not only to a degree more in keeping with the wishes of the states, but also at a substantiality lower cost.
- Whatever our political affiliations and whatever reputation Eddie Ward might have had as a firebrand, had he held the portfolio of Transport for just a little while longer, the present sorry mess would not have occurred.
- The financial provisions of the Railway Standardisation Agreement Acts were harsher than would appear. After interest was taken into account, the states were obliged to repay nearer 80 percent of the cost, rather than 30 percent.

- The standardisation of Australia's entire mainland railway system would have represented only a few weeks of its wartime expenditure between 1942 and 1945,
- By and large, the Commonwealth possessed neither the experience nor the inclination to appreciate intrasystem operational problems. They were obsessed with intercapital working.
- The Commonwealth adopted a cavalier attitude towards the states, approving only those works that its officers deemed appropriate, and irrespective altogether of any Agreement or the states' rights or wishes. It also set up control procedures which were unwieldy, irritating and an impediment to the efficient implementation of the work.
- With the completion of the Sydney–Melbourne, the Sydney–Perth, the Adelaide–Crystal Brook, the Adelaide–Melbourne and the Adelaide–Darwin standard gauge links in 1962, 1970, 1984, 1996 and 2004 respectively, the realisation of Sir Harold Clapp's concept of a unified and integrated rail network in Australia has receded into oblivion and must surely die.

Indian Pacific Celebrations and Tribulations

Strife of some sort seemed to plague every facet of rail standardisation in Australia. It extended even to the functions planned to celebrate the fulfilment of the century old dream of an unbroken unified rail link between east and west. Three functions were scheduled and all three were threatened. Indeed, one had to be cancelled at the last moment because of a union ban.

At a meeting of the Australian Transport Advisory Council, held at Port Augusta on 19 September 1969 for the purpose of determining the format for the inaugural run of the Indian Pacific, it was decided to hold a spike driving ceremony at Broken Hill to mark the linking-up of the standard gauge tracks.

The Advisory Council was advised that, to permit a ballast train to enter the Broken Hill station yard from the west, a temporary connection would be made on Tuesday 25 November at a point about one kilometre from the station. However, the real link-up would not take place until the weekend of 10–12 January 1970. As the

latter date was deemed to be inconvenient, the decision was made to hold a function on Saturday 29 November.

Prime Minister Gorton and New South Wales and South Australian Premiers — Sir Robert Askin and Mr Steele Hall—would each be invited to drive a dogspike into the track alongside Broken Hill's Crystal Street station, after which the Broken City Council would host an official luncheon.

On Tuesday 25 November, the temporary connection was duly made, and the workmen took the opportunity to hold their own light hearted unofficial ceremony, including the breaking of a bottle of soft drink over the rail. These activities were reported by the local news media in the same carefree manner, and in their right perspective. However, this bit of fun was viewed in an entirely different light by Ian Sinclair, the Minister for Shipping and Transport. Apparently it touched him on a tender spot, because he telephoned Murray Hill, his South Australian counterpart, and threatened to cancel the official function scheduled for four days later.

Fortunately, this extreme action did not eventuate, and the function itself was noteworthy for two contrasting things. On the one hand, there was an entire lack of politics in the speeches by the Prime Minister, Federal Opposition Leader Whitlam, Robert Askin and Steele Hall. But on the other, the local dignitaries turned the occasion into an all-out exercise in pork barrelling.

The Broken Hill City Council had already achieved a great deal of town planning improvements and grade separation at rail standardisation cost. But that did not stop a battery of four or five speakers from using the occasion to press for even more concessions. The blatancy of their intentions was not lost on others; indeed they evoked a very cutting aside from Milton Morris, the New South Wales Minister for Transport, who was seated alongside me at the luncheon.

The circumstances surrounding the second function make quite a story.

Two rather treasured items that I took with me into retirement — and which are now housed in the National Rail Museum at Port Adelaide — were

Unofficial opening of the standard gauge, Broken Hill, 25 November 1969. (*Photo:* Ian Domleo)

Prime Minister John Gorton speaking at the spike-driving ceremony, Broken Hill, 29 November 1969 (*Photo:* New South Wales Railways)

the plaque that was not unveiled at Peterborough on 12 January 1970, and the scissors with which Doreen did not cut a ribbon at the same place on the same day.

Because its geographical situation in the middle of things, and because the terminals of Sydney and Perth offered greater opportunities for festivities, the Port Pirie–Broken Hill part of the standardisation project could have easily been overlooked during the national celebrations associated with the inauguration of the Indian Pacific. Therefore, we in the South Australian Railways decided to hold our own functions on Monday 20 January 1970. In this way, we would be able to give some recognition to the men who had worked on this segment of the national project.

The celebrations were scheduled to start at Port Pirie, where Steele Hall would unveil a plaque and then despatch the first eastbound standard gauge train by the customary method of blowing a whistle and displaying a green flag. The scene

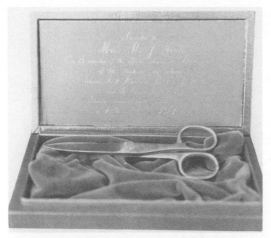

The scissors that did not cut the ribbon and (*below*) the plaque that was not unveiled at Peterborough, 12 January 1970 (*Photos:* Neville Cordes)

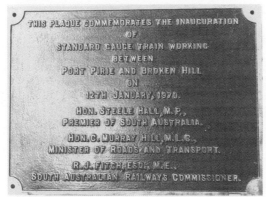

THIS PLAQUE COMMEMORATES THE INAUGURATION
OF
STANDARD GAUGE TRAIN WORKING
BETWEEN
PORT PIRIE AND BROKEN HILL
ON
12TH JANUARY, 1970.

HON. STEELE HALL, M.P.,
PREMIER OF SOUTH AUSTRALIA.
HON. C. MURRAY HILL, M.L.C.,
MINISTER OF ROADS AND TRANSPORT.

R.J. FITCH, ESQ., M.E.,
SOUTH AUSTRALIAN RAILWAYS COMMISSIONER.

would then shift to Peterborough, where this train, together with the first one from Broken Hill and a broad gauge rail car from Adelaide, were to be driven into the station platforms simultaneously by Steele Hall, Murray Hill and me. Immediately prior to this, ribbons stretched across the tracks were to be cut by our wives. Subsequently, a plaque, similar to that at Port Pirie, would be unveiled at Peterborough. Finally, in the evening, an informal buffet was to be held, to which representatives of those employees who had played such a significant part in the project would be invited.

But it did not turn out that way. Feeling against the Hall Government, and arising out of its success over the Dunstan Labor one in 1968, was still running high. It was manifested on this occasion by the railway unions' statement that

neither would Mr Hall flag out the train from Port Pirie, nor would he and Mr Hill be permitted to drive the locomotives at Peterborough. They refused to accept the fact that the driving of the locomotives would be only symbolic, and that the controls would in reality remain in the hands of qualified enginemen.

The attitude of certain SAR employees was in stark contrast to that shown by Commonwealth Railways enginemen at Port Pirie in 1951, when their first diesel electric locomotive was named the Robert Gordon Menzies by the wife of the Prime Minister. Not only did Mrs (later Dame Pattie) Menzies nominally drive the locomotive, but also was she made an honorary member of the Australian Federated Union of Locomotive Enginemen. Commonwealth railwaymen also acted differently in 1960, when Hubert Opperman, the then Minister for Shipping and Transport, flagged away from Port Pirie the Commonwealth Railways' first wildflower special train to Western Australia.

But to return to the SAR standardisation functions, the troubles were not yet over.

Early in December 1969, Glen Moorhead, the General Secretary of the AFULE, together with Rex Matthews and Sylvester Byrne, State Branch President and Divisional Manager respectively, discussed with me the matter of an alternative basis for the calculation of locomotive crew wages, whereby, in some instances, they could be paid in accordance with the distance travelled rather than by hours worked. At the same time, and seemingly as an afterthought, Mr Moorhead intimated that his union had given some preliminary thought to a new scheme for the grading and progression of enginemen and firemen.

On 29 December I again met the union officials and made an offer embodying new principles for the calculation of wages. Five days later the offer was accepted, but at the same time the local division of the union pressed for the proposed new grading procedures, even though they were not as yet official union policy. As the appropriate industrial award covered not only South Australia, but also New South Wales, Victoria and Tasmania, my answer was that, while I would be prepared to discuss the proposition on a four-state basis, I would not do so unilaterally. This did not satisfy the local division of the union, whose members threatened to place a ban on standard gauge working unless I accepted the new grading formula forthwith.

Finally, on the evening of Friday 9 January 1970, less than 60 hours before the celebrations were scheduled to begin, I was informed by Rex Matthews that his members would not agree to the four-state discussions and that, unless their demands were met, they would implement a ban on standard gauge operations as from noon on Monday, 12 January.

There was no doubt that the union expected me to succumb to its threat. This I refused to do, and immediately cancelled all arrangements for the opening ceremonies. In making this decision, I was conscious of the disappointment that would be felt by the many people who had been associated with the project; in particular, the Peterborough railwaymen who, with their families, made up one of the finest communities that one could ever hope to meet.

Apart from the regret that a day on which special emphasis was to have been given to the contribution made by the men who had worked on the project should have come to nought, the union's ban had ramifications outside South Australia. The first 'through' standard gauge freight train was scheduled to leave Sydney on Monday 12 January, and our clients had ensured that it was made up of a representative and appropriately decorated load.

It was dispatched from Sydney's Cooks River depot by Milton Morris in the presence of Neal McCusker and a number of persons prominent in the transport industry. However, the ban imposed by the South Australian enginemen necessitated the train's being diverted through Albury, with gauge transfers at Melbourne and Port Pirie. This fiasco brought the union's action into interstate relief and, with it, widespread criticism from many of the railways' valued clients.

The ban was lifted on Friday, 16 January, after a conference before Commissioner Neill of the Commonwealth Conciliation and Arbitration Commission. Significantly, the question of a new grading procedure for enginemen and firemen was not discussed, nor was it raised again, at least until my retirement three years later. I am now satisfied that I was duped, and that the whole dispute was stage managed for no other reason than to provide the union with yet another means to strike a blow against the Hall Government. Indeed, Harry Neill said to me privately; 'Did you ever really expect that the opening ceremony would be allowed to be held?'

The third and major series of festivities was also menaced. The Australian Transport Advisory Council was advised at its meeting at Port Augusta on 19 September 1969 that, while the line between Port Pirie and Broken Hill would be open for freight traffic on 12 January 1970, some time should be allowed for the track to settle down before passenger trains were permitted to run — and, even then, at reduced speeds. It was agreed therefore that the Indian Pacific service should commence out of Sydney on Monday 2 March 1970 and that the inauguration ceremonies be held during the preceding week. They would start on 23 February with a dinner at Sydney's Wentworth Hotel, followed by a short ceremony on Platform 1 at Sydney Central Station before

Inaugural Indian Pacific run. Dinner at the Wentworth Hotel, Sydney, 23 February 1970. (*Photo:* New South Wales Railways)

Inaugural Indian Pacific run. The Governor-General speaking at Broken Hill, 24 February 1970. (*Photo:* New South Wales Railways)

SAR twin 600 class locomotives being attached to the inaugural westbound Indian Pacific at Broken Hill, 24 February 1970 (*Photo:* W.A. Bayley)

Inaugural Indian Pacific run. The Governor-General, Sir Paul Hasluck, speaking at Port Pirie, 24 February 1970 (*Photo:* National Trust)

Australian Railwayman

Inaugural Indian Pacific in Darling Ranges, 26 February 1970 (*Photo:* Westrail)

Arrival of Inaugural Indian Pacific at Perth, 26 February 1970 (*Photo:* Westrail)

departure in two divisions of the special train. En route, there would be a number of small and informal functions, while three major ones were scheduled for Perth on Thursday 26 February. Once again, however, industrial muscle threatened to intervene when the enginemen in Western Australia sought ways whereby they could use the occasion for their own ends.

Twelve months earlier, locomotive running staff in WA were granted, by agreement, pay rises in line with those awarded to their interstate counterparts. The men also claimed retrospectivity

Inaugural Indian Pacific run. Function at Perth terminal, 26 February 1970 (*Photo:* Westrail)

Eastbound Indian Pacific near Gladstone, South Australia, March 1970. 600 and 830 class locomotives. (*Photo:* Ian Hammond)

First standard gauge freight train near Yongala, South Australia, 17 January 1970. 600 and 830 class locomotives. The first planned Sydney–Perth freight train had to be diverted through Melbourne because of industrial trouble in South Australia. (*Photo:* Ian Hammond)

in respect of the rises, something recommended in April 1969 by the State Industrial Commissioner, but which was not permissible under State law.

As 23 February 1970 approached, the men said that they would place a black ban on the inaugural Indian Pacific if the award was not backdated, even though the State Government had offered to amend its Industrial Arbitration Act in the next session of Parliament to give the Industrial Commission authority to grant a measure of retrospectivity.

However, over the weekend, frantic efforts were made to resolve the dispute. It was agreed that the Chief Industrial Commissioner for Western Australia would act as a private arbitrator, and that his decision would be accepted by both parties. On this basis, the ban was lifted.

Subsequently, the arbitrator ordered the WAGR to pay full retrospectivity back to May 1968 and, in doing so, said: 'In a large industrial undertaking

such as the WAGR, the sum of money involved in this matter is not so great as to deter me from making the order.

'It is loosely expressed as being equivalent to less than half the cost of a locomotive.'

It seems to have been a very odd line of reasoning. The merit of the men's claim might well have been strong; but to equate it to half the cost of a locomotive does not seem to have been a logical basis for arbitration. Would his determination have been the same had the cost been higher?

It was also significant that the ban was not threatened a few months earlier, when through working between Port Pirie and Perth was instituted. Obviously it was saved up for the Indian Pacific opening.

I feel that, in certain Commonwealth political quarters, the view was held that opening ceremonies should go ahead regardless of the

Australian Railwayman

necessity of bowing to industrial pressures, and to their long term implications.

The train left Sydney on time and arrived in Perth 62½ hours later, also on time, but it did not maintain that immaculate performance throughout its journey. Due to speed restrictions over the new track and, more importantly, because the installation of essential signalling equipment for Gladstone's three-gauge station had been delayed by bureaucratic procrastination, two hours' running time was lost between Broken Hill and Port Pirie. Most of this was made up on the Trans Australian section, and then lost again.

But the WAGR — whose standard gauge track had been under traffic for several months and therefore had been consolidated — excelled itself. With the sky the limit in respect of speed, the train had to loiter over the last few kilometres into Perth so as not to arrive ahead of time. It was a tremendous achievement by Western Australia.

However, there was another attack of the spotlight syndrome during the run, which happened to be something of a honeymoon special for Ian and Rosemary Sinclair.

Between Sydney and Port Pirie, the train ran in two divisions which were combined into one long consist for the remainder of the trip. The Port Pirie station was then a dead-end one, meaning that trains entering from either Sydney or Perth reversed direction when departing to complete their journeys. On the occasion of the inaugural train, this reversal movement meant that the Governor-General's car, which was trailing on the first division, would be in the middle of the combined consist from Port Pirie to Perth.

Before we arrived at Port Pirie — indeed during most of the preceding week — I was pressured by Commonwealth officers virtually demanding that, when the two divisions were united, the Vice Regal car be shunted so that it would remain at the rear of the train after it left for Perth. The reason given for this request was that Ian Sinclair wanted to hold a special meeting of the Australian Transport Advisory Council in the lounge car of the Indian Pacific, and that the presence of the Governor-General's car in the middle of the train would prevent newsreel and television cameramen from entering the lounge car to film the meeting.

Approximately six shunting movements would have been involved if the Minister's wishes were to be met, so I told the Commonwealth officers who were pressuring me on his behalf that I flatly refused to shunt the Governor-General and Lady Hasluck around like a truck of livestock at one o'clock in the morning. Further, if the Minister wanted the media to be present at the Advisory Council meeting, then they could detrain at a stop on the Nullarbor, walk along the formation, and rejoin the train behind the Vice Regal car. That is precisely what they did.

11   Perambulations:
Train, Trolley and Armstrong

My railway perambulations were not all confined to Australia, where they stretched from Wiluna in Western Australia to Atherton in Queensland, from Port Augusta to Alice Springs and from Darwin to Birdum in the Northern Territory, as well as from Port Lincoln to Penong on South Australia's Eyre Peninsula. They also included 13 overseas countries.

Neither were they all undertaken in the lap of luxury. Indeed, the various modes of transportation ranged from high speed air-conditioned passenger comfort to those of goods, ballast, construction, breakdown and weed poisoning trains; to thousands of kilometres on motor inspection and on gang section cars; to rail motor quadricycles, muscle-powered Kalamazoo trolleys; down to the ultimate in self-locomotion, the one-man pull tricycle, colloquially known as the Armstrong.

It included riding at night — and in the course of duty — on the footplate of steam locomotives hauling The Trans Australian and the Broken Hill Express at speeds of 96 and 50 km/h respectively; at 32 km/h on the Kurrawang Wood Line in Western Australia; up front with the driver of the first non-stop passenger train to run between Cook and Rawlinna on the Nullarbor Plain; at 160 km/h on British Rail's Intercity between Rugby and Euston; at 100 km/h between Galashiels and Edinburgh; and at 120 km/h on Canadian Pacific's Budd rail car between Windsor Ontario and Toronto. As a passenger, it has included riding at 200 km/h on Japan's Bullet train and on British Rail's High Speed Train; at 150 km/h in a Budd rail car on the Hughes length of the TAR; and at 96 km/h between Nagoya and Kyoto and between Tokyo and Nikko in Japan — an exceptionally high speed at that time for a narrow gauge line.

However, the story would not be complete without reference to my annual inspection trips — first by a locomotive hauled train, but later by rail car — between Yeelanna and Kapinnie on South Australia's Port Lincoln Division. As has been noted earlier, in my opinion the maximum speed of 8 km/h for most of the journey would have been 16 km/h more than should have been allowed. Any consideration of a safe speed would have been purely academic!

Motor section car (*Photo:* the author)

Standard gauge quadricycle (*Photo:* Schiller Collection)

Of the thousands of hours spent on and the thousands of kilometres travelled on those special, normal, privileged and unorthodox modes of rail transport, certain experiences stand out, and for different reasons — speed; luxury; discomfort; the fulfilment of a long-held dream; opportunities rarely available even to the average railwayman; and apprehension.

Those applying to apprehension have been raised earlier. The first was a very close encounter with southbound Train Number 74 between Canna and Tardun in WA. Even a relatively small locomotive assumes gigantic proportions when confronted face to face from a small quadricycle. The second was the perilous condition of the track between Oodnadatta and Alice Springs in 1950 after light but continued rain over a period of weeks. And as for the third, the best that could have been said for the Kapinnie branch on Eyre Peninsula in the late 1960s was that relief replaced apprehension whenever any movement did not involve a derailment.

Perhaps the most exhilarating experience was when, in 1966, I was invited to ride up-front at 160 km/h on one of BR's early Intercity passenger trains between Rugby and Euston. An electrified line, the driver hooked his knee over the dead-man to maintain pressure and rolled cigarettes while the speedometer rose rapidly to 130 km/h before climbing slowly and steadily to 164 km/h (102 mph); and there it remained until approaching Euston. The line was automatically signalled into approximately kilometre sections, and the driver or his observer had to acknowledge each signal by means of cancelling a button in the cab. It was a memorable experience.

France's SNCF pioneered high speed technology, Japan introduced it into regular service and British Rail followed soon after. It was my privilege to experience it as a passenger on Japan's Shinkansen from Kobe to Tokyo and on BR's High Speed Train between Swansea and Paddington. Both rides were comfortable, the UK one slightly the smoother. After setting out quietly from Swansea and passing through the Severn Tunnel, the train settled down to a steady beat and to a constant 200 km/h. The fact that such speeds could be attained on an existing — albeit upgraded — track, was a major triumph for British Rail.

On the other hand, an entirely new standard gauge track, involving modern techniques, was constructed for the Shinkansen, and designed to permit the running of high speed trains at 15 minute intervals. Such was the intensity of the preliminary investigations that it was said that the only technical factor overlooked in the design was the increase in air pressure engendered when two opposing trains crossed in a tunnel.

Train travel in Japan was noticeable for an apparent phobia for cleanliness. Even the platform staff wore white gloves on duty, while passengers seemed meticulous, and yet — and perhaps a strange example of Nipponian contradiction — the toilets, both at stations and in the carriages, were of diabolical design and filthy. Another feature was the sight at every non-urban station stop of a mad dash by passengers on to the platform to buy a small carton of food followed by an equally mad dash back to their seats. Japanese train passengers must have insatiable appetites, because the same passengers appeared to repeat the performance at every stop.

One Saturday afternoon, Doreen and I arrived at Tokyo Central on The Bullet from Kobe, and became hopelessly lost and disoriented in the underground maze when trying to locate the stationmaster's office. We hoped to obtain information regarding our proposed trip next day to Nikko. Fortunately, we were rescued by a Japanese gentleman who had spent some time in Australia and who seemed anxious to demonstrate his fluency in our language. After taking us to the stationmaster's office and engaging in several minutes' rapid fire conversation with his clerk, we were presented with a piece of white pasteboard inscribed with some Nipponese hieroglyphics which provided us with carte blanche treatment all the way to Nikko and back. We were told that the train departed from Uno, a nearby narrow gauge station, and when we asked from which platform it would leave, the reply involved several minutes' hissing and aspirating between our rescuer and the clerk, after which the former turned to us and, with a great degree of pontification, uttered just two words: 'Track three'.

Fleeting reference should be made to some other overseas train trips, some official but most personal. They included Canadian National's

Super Continental from Vancouver to Halifax; The Senator and The Twentieth Century Limited from New York to Washington and Chicago respectively; the Shasta Daylight from Portland Oregon to San Francisco; Le Mistral from Paris to Avignon; the ascent by rail from Interlaken in Switzerland up the mountainside to the Jungfrau in the Bernese Oberland; from Italy's Genoa south through Rome and on to Brindisi, and then north again along the Adriatic Coast to Bologna; and, finally, on the Akropolis Express from Skopje in Yugoslavia to Thessalonika in northern Greece. Brief reference to some of those journeys follow, but special mention should first be made of the outstanding on-time performances of the European trains.

CN's Super Continental fulfilled a long held dream nurtured in childhood by L.M. Montgomery's charming *Anne of Green Gables* — centred around life in Canada's Maritime Provinces — and John Forster Fraser's *Canada As It Is*, wherein, in passing, he described his rail trip through the Rockies riding on the cowcatcher of a massive steam locomotive as it negotiated Kicking Horse Pass. I had the privilege of travelling on The Super Continental twice. Apart from the dynamism of the railways themselves, my outstanding memories of the two journeys include the magnificence of the Fraser River Valley and the superb Canadian Rockies, the Great Lakes, an unforgettable day trip from Toronto to see the Niagara and Horseshoe Falls, the St Lawrence River estuary, and the distinctly different landscape and French-inspired architecture of the Maritime Provinces.

SNCF's Le Mistral must surely have constituted the ultimate in daytime rail travel. Leaving Paris' Gare Lyons daily and making nine intermediate stops, the Mistral covered the 1088 kilometres to Nice in nine hours and five minutes, averaging 120 km/h and maintaining a top speed of 130 km/h for long stretches. The return journey occupied precisely two minutes less. Its riding qualities and passenger facilities were superb, the latter including two restaurant cars, bar, hairdressing salon and secretarial service. It simply oozed Gallic elegance.

But, for sheer beauty, the Swiss and Austrian countryside is superb. The Eurail Book said this: 'If the ride from Spiez to Brig doesn't entrance you, then you may as well pack up and go home because you will see nothing better'. How very true, but that description applies to the whole of the region, including the route beyond Brig to Zermatt with its views of the Matterhorn, and the mostly tunnelled ascent by rail from Interlaken to the Jungfrau. Our extreme favourite was the small village of Kandersteg, midway between Spiez and Brig, which so enthralled us that we detrained spontaneously at the sight of the place and spent an unbelievable half day observing a charming little dairy cow show, with its magnificent and heavily uddered animals.

Final comment on overseas rail travel relates to different circumstances. Having arrived at Dubrovnik in southern Yugoslavia from Vienna — by train to Lubliana and by bus via Plitvice and Split — our onward air journey to Thessalonika was interrupted by industrial trouble and this obliged us to undertake a 17 hours' overnight bus trip through Titograd to Skopje, here to spend the night before travelling to Thessalonika by the Akropolis Express. It was a memorable trip for a number of reasons, none of them scenic. First, the ticket clerk at Skopje station did not or would not comprehend our request for two first class single tickets to Thessalonika. Eventually, and after several minutes of anguished pleading, we were accommodated, but found that every compartment but one was fully occupied. The exception contained one Greek gentleman who spoke no English and, in French said: '*Moi seul*' ('Me only'). Not understanding the implication of his reply we entered his compartment and settled down, something to which he did not object. On the contrary, he was most courteous. I tried unsuccessfully to practise my 50 years-past schoolboy French, but when I showed him my business card, upon which I had written 'Ex-President Chemin de Fer', the floodgates opened and he took charge of everything; express train, customs and currency charges as well as border passport inspections; even to taking us to our Thessalonika hotel in his personally hired taxi. The Akropolis Express might have been a misnomer because its performance was anything akin to that of an express, and it terminated within kilometres of an acropolis, yet this Greek gentleman's gesture turned our journey into an armchair ride.

The entire episode was typical of the cordiality which we encountered on each of our six visits to Greece, something that might have been prompted by two things: the large number of people of Greek origin living in this country, and an everlasting recognition of Australia's contribution towards the defence of Greece in 1941.

Trains; Named, Misnamed and Nicknamed

The imposing names with which some of our trains were invested were in fact the height of over-glamorisation; indeed they were misnamed rather than named. At the same time, the Australian tendency towards nicknaming, satirising and ridiculing has long since found its way into our railway idiom. In a number of instances — the Tea and Sugar and The Ghan for example — the nickname has become the official one.

Of those trains coming within the three categories — named, misnamed and nicknamed — and with which the author became familiar during his working life, some comment would be appropriate.

The Trans Australian, The Indian Pacific, The Overland and The Blue Lake — the last the former overnight sleeping car train which operated thrice weekly in each direction between Adelaide and Mount Gambier — justified their names. The Overland pioneered en suite sleeping car facilities in this country, and possibly worldwide. In his numerous travels overseas right up to the late 1900s, the author did not see any sleeping cars of the type introduced into The Overland in 1950, and adopted soon afterwards on The Southern Aurora, The Trans Australian and The Indian Pacific.

My first experience with The Trans Australian goes back to 1930 when the journey from Kalgoorlie to Port Augusta was undertaken at an unhurried 45 mph (72 km/h) and with equally unhurried good taste. The lack of air-conditioning and reticulated hot water to the compartments was countered in part by the provision of large brown paper bags in which passengers could deposit their hats to protect them from the dust that used to intrude through the necessarily opened compartment windows; and by the supply of a small can of hot water which, of a morning, the conductor would deposit in the corridor outside each passenger's compartment.

The dining car service too maintained a certain level of formality. Male passengers were not permitted to enter the car jacketless, while each diner was allotted a silver serviette ring in which his or her table napkin was preserved between meals. Indeed, their distribution by the senior waiter prior to each meal became something of a ritual. The menus were extensive, that for dinner providing for five courses, together with a selection of fresh fruit. In addition, first class passengers were served after-dinner coffee in the lounge car, as well as traditional afternoon tea with bread and butter and the Commonwealth Railways' renowned sultana cake.

In my experience, four trains — the Kalgoorlie and the Broken Hill Expresses, the Esperance Flyer and the Wiluna Limited — were misnamed.

The Kalgoorlie Express might have been the most important intrastate train in Western Australia, but with a top speed of only 72 km/h and stopping at every station between Northam and Kalgoorlie, it was anything but an express train. From the 1930s, it had good two-berth first class and four-berth second class sleeping accommodation, but previously it was limited to four and six berth compartments, all devoid of individual toilets, hand basins or clothes lockers. The sitting cars were generally of the corridor type, with compartments seating either six or eight persons.

There was an exposed platform at the ends of the sitting cars, and here used to hang a four gallon (18 litre) canvas water bag with an enamel pannikan appended to it by means of a length of dog chain. From this swaying contraption, passengers could decant a drink of water, canvas flavoured and tinted light brown from the swirling dust that had been trapped and held in suspension. During World War II, this train was so heavily taxed that it was not uncommon for some passengers to have to stand in the corridor for the entire 16 hours' journey. On one such nightmarish trip, I was jammed, along with nine

The Kalgoorlie Express at Midland Junction, late 1920s (*Photo:* Westrail)

The Westland, headed by Pr locomotive (*Photo:* Westrail)

Australian Railwayman

others, in a side door compartment designed to seat five persons.

Apart from refreshment stalls at Chidlow, Northam, Cunderdin, Merredin and Southern Cross, breakfast and dinner could be obtained from dining cars, which were attached to the Kalgoorlie Express between Perth and Cunderdin, and between Southern Cross and Kalgoorlie. All of these facilities were operated under franchise by Tom Gorman until the late 1940s, when the Department took them over. The dining cars were positioned in the middle of the train between the first and second class sections, and to attach and detach them it was necessary to shunt the leading section with the passengers still aboard. These procedures could not be looked upon as being in the front line of safe-working practices.

For those passengers not patronising the diner there used to be a mad scramble at Chidlow — one hour's run from Perth — where they would jump off the train and invade the inadequate refreshment stall on the equally inadequate platform. There, lined up three to four deep, they would fight for the opportunity to purchase tea, coffee, meat pies and sandwiches for which railways, the world over, suffer undeserved odium. The 15 minutes that the train spent at Chidlow were hectic, and made the more publicised sorties that used to take place at Albury, when it was a gauge transfer station, seem quite sedate affairs by comparison.

In February 1972, the Kalgoorlie Express ceased to run and its place was taken by the Prospector, a standard gauge diesel rail car of world class.

The Broken Hill Express too was a grave misnomer. Before the line between Port Pirie and Broken Hill was standardised in 1970, the journey from Adelaide involved broad gauge for the first 225 kilometres to Terowie and narrow gauge for the remainder of the 531 kilometres to Broken Hill. Moreover, it stopped at every station beyond Gawler — 29 in all — thus rendering its claim to express status null and void. With maximum speeds of 96 and 56 km/h on the broad and narrow gauges respectively, coupled with station stops and gauge transfer at Terowie, its start-to-stop average speed amounted to only 35 km/h.

The gauge transfer was its greatest disadvantage. Eastbound passengers were obliged to change to the narrow gauge at about 11 pm, but it was even worse on the trip to Adelaide, when the occupants were roused from their bunks at about 5 am to dress and transfer to the broad gauge train. Terowie, on a vast windswept plain, was one of the coldest spots in South Australia and the early morning frosts in the winter months made the transfer quite an ordeal. After standardisation, when the 23 kilometres between Terowie and Peterborough were broadened, the inconvenience was, if anything, aggravated. Passengers were then required to change trains at Peterborough at 4.30 am.

In 1932 it was decided to institute an overnight weekend passenger service between Kalgoorlie and its nearest port, Esperance. Thus was born the Esperance Flyer.

Leaving Esperance on Friday evenings during the summer months and averaging about 35 km/h for the journey, the Flyer would arrive at Kalgoorlie on Saturday morning. It would commence its return trip that same evening, reaching Esperance early on Sunday morning. This enabled Goldfields residents to spend a full week's or fortnight's holiday at this fine seaside resort.

The train had both sleeping and sitting cars; the former were prehistoric. Officially designated the AP class, they consisted of side door vehicles with four 'first' class berths in each compartment. As they lacked even coat hooks, one was obliged to place one's clothes in the small luggage racks located above the upper berths and intended for suitcases, which had to be left on the floor, cluttering up the narrow space between the facing lower seats-cum-bunks. There was a poky little toilet and washroom attached to each compartment; but access to it involved clambering over one of the lower berths while trying to avoid concussing one's head on the upper one.

Many a passenger suffered urinary torture during the night, rather than disturb the passenger in the crucial lower berth, who in all probability was a complete stranger.

A refreshment service did not exist and passengers had to fast and thirst for the 12 hours' journey. Nevertheless, the Esperance Flyer was a popular train with the Goldfields people.

The only way in which the Wiluna Limited lived up to its name was in the matter of speed; it was limited to a maximum of 56 km/h. Nevertheless, it was just as much the lifeline to the Murchison and the Pilbara as was the highly romanticised Tea and Sugar to the Nullarbor. Indeed it served a far wider area and a great many more people. Such was its importance that, in 1937, a senior officer, Bill Okeley, was appointed Traffic Inspector at Cue and given the specific task of getting the train through on time.

Known both in and out of the railways as Numbers 73 and 74, for the northbound and southbound movements respectively, it was the bi-weekly mixed train that used to dawdle over the 966 kilometres between Perth and Meekatharra — and later, over the additional 175 kilometres to Wiluna — at a start-to-stop average speed marginally in excess of 30 km/h. It was after the line was extended to Wiluna that the train received its august title. Taking a very elastic 36 hours for the one-way journey, the Limited provided a passenger service for the pastoral and mining communities extending from Mullewa through Yalgoo, Mount Magnet, Cue, Meekatharra and Wiluna. More importantly, it transported mails, perishables and stores for the whole of the Murchison, and indeed as far afield as Marble Bar, 760 kilometres north of Meekatharra.

Numbers 73 and 74 will always rank high on my list of favourite trains, and for three reasons. One: they were an integral part of the Murchison, my favourite territory. Two: some of the most rewarding periods of my working life were spent there, and those trains provided the only means of communication with things down south. And third: Number 73, on which, after marriage, I took Doreen to our first marital home — the three-roomed hessian house at Cue — was, in effect, our honeymoon special.

Three trains whose nicknames were indicative of their functions, and with which the author had some association, were the Tea and Sugar, the Chaser and the Cabbagee.

The Tea and Sugar would have been the most over-glamorised train in Australia. Having as its one purpose servicing railway employees and their families along the Trans line, its real to claim would have been that, in the light of its duties as well as layovers at major depot stations along the line, its start-to-stop average speed between its terminals of Port Augusta and Parkeston must have made it the slowest train in the world. A fact about the Sugar that is not widely known is that, in its earlier years, live sheep were carried on the train in a special wagon and slaughtered in running by the travelling butcher.

The Chaser and the Cabbagee had wider functions. The former was the goods train that followed The Ghan from Quorn to Alice Springs; while the latter was the fast goods train that operated three times a week ahead of the Broken Hill Express. Both trains were vital to the communities that they served — the Chaser to the Northern Territory and the Cabbagee to Broken Hill and New South Wales' far west — and merit standing at least equal to that of the Tea and Sugar.

Any reference to Central Australia automatically conjures up nostalgic memories of The Ghan. But the warmest memories are not of the standard gauge train that deserted the original narrow gauge route from Quorn through Marree and Oodnadatta. Neither do they include the vehicles imported from Germany in 1952 for the Trans Australian, but subsequently converted to narrow gauge and transferred to the Central Australia Railway, or even the luxury air-conditioned standard gauge train that now spans the continent from Adelaide to Darwin. It is of the original narrow gauge one that commenced running in 1929 when the line was extended from Oodnadatta to Alice Springs — and which saw the birth of The Ghan — that I write.

Initially, there were two Ghans: the Flash Ghan and the Dirty Ghan. The Flash Ghan was the then fortnightly train to Alice Springs, while the Dirty Ghan — the original Oodnadatta mixed — worked on alternate weeks. After World War II, the Dirty Ghan ceased to run and, lacking the necessity for any distinction, the Flash Ghan reverted simply to The Ghan.

Prior to the opening of the Stirling North–Marree standard gauge in 1958, The Ghan used to leave Port Augusta for Quorn on Thursday afternoon;

A northbound Ghan at Marree. The tank in the foreground was supplied with water from an artesian bore (*Photo:* The Port Dock Station Railway Museum)

there, the dining car would be attached. It would then amble along at a steady — and, at times, a definitely unsteady — 32 km/h. Its arrival at Alice Springs approximately 48 hours later was always subject to a degree of speculation. Indeed, twice in 1950 and again in 1953, washaways resulted in its arriving more than seven days late.

Its narrow gauge two-berth compartments, with their straw palliasses passing as mattresses, were small but comfortable; while the second class accommodation was, in general, confined to saloon-type cars with bench seats along the sides. Large wooden louvred shades covered the top halves of the windows to keep out the Centralian sun.

The Ghan's passengers were a cosmopolitan lot: Territorians returning home after a visit to the south; drovers, complete with rolled-up swags, going back after having delivered a mob of cattle to the Adelaide market; stockmen, both Aboriginal and European, aping their American counterparts with their ten gallon hats, gaudy shirts, elastic-sided boots and, occasionally, their guitars; and out-of-works on their way to Tennant Creek or Darwin looking for a job.

As soon as The Ghan left Quorn, the young female passengers, most of whom were having their first look at the Inland, would discard their frocks in favour of jodhpurs, no doubt in an endeavour to appear part of the local scenery. At that time, the craze for jeans had not gripped the thighs and buttocks of our youth; they were still called dungarees, and their wearing confined to navvies.

Part of the local scenery too was the presence

at Marree — where the steam train stopped for one hour while the locomotive was fuelled and serviced — of Bejah Dervish, patriarch of the local Afghan community, and picturesque with his flowing beard, his copious turban and his pantaloons.

One Saturday evening in 1950, an American family of four joined The Ghan at Finke, 228 kilometres south of Alice Springs. The circumstances were unusual.

A United States serviceman named Conte, who had been stationed in Australia during World War II — and in civil life a member of a family acrobatic troupe the Flying Contes — had taken his Australian war bride back to the US, where their two sons were born. However, either homesickness or marital incompatibility resulted in her return to Australia with the boys, where she sought refuge and anonymity on a cattle station out from Finke. However, the deserted husband searched Australia far and wide for his wife and family, eventually locating them in their hideout, but only after assistance from Constable Ron Brown of the North Australian Mounted Police, stationed at Finke at that time. As a passenger on that particular Ghan, I was a silent witness to the little domestic interlude. When I left the Alice to return to Port Augusta, the family was still together; but, whether the reconciliation was permanent, I shall never know.

It may have seemed from the outside that the trip on The Ghan would be a lonely one, but the whole region simply oozed history. Explorers

Ernest Giles, Edward John Eyre, Charles Sturt, John McDouall Stuart, Peter Egerton Warburton and others; pastoralists Thomas Elder and Sidney Kidman; and the AIM's John Flynn had made their mark, and there were historical ruins such as Kanyaka homestead, the Overland Telegraph repeater station at Strangways and the Coward Springs hotel.

Comment of The Ghan would be incomplete without some reference to its little sister up north, the railway immortalised by Jeannie Gunn in her classic *We of the Never Never* (1908). Having steamed from Melbourne to Port Darwin with her husband, she travelled with him to Elsey cattle station, 483 kilometres to the south, and near Mataranka; the first 146 kilometres by train to Pine Creek, and the remainder by horse drawn transport.

Jeannie must have been infatuated by that train journey, describing it as follows: 'At the far end of the train away from the engine the passengers' car had been placed and in front of it a long line of low stacked sinuous trucks slipped along in the rear of the engine, all open to view before us; and all day long as the engine trudged onwards — hands in pockets so to speak and whistling merrily as it trudged — I stood beside the Maluka on the little platform in the front of the passengers' car drinking in my first deep intoxicating draft of the glories of the tropical bush.'

It seems therefore that the *laissez-faire* pervading the train — by virtue of its roller-coaster characteristics more recently nicknamed Leaping Lena — had its origins a long way back.

The North Australia Railway carried an enormous transportation load during World War II, indeed taxing it almost to beyond its capabilities; and Leaping Lena was endowed by the troops with an alternative nomen — The Spirit of Protest — a plagiarism of Sir Harold Clapp's Spirit of Progress, introduced into the Melbourne–Albury run in 1937.

It is sad that the new standard gauge train operating between Adelaide and Darwin should be called The Ghan; even to call it The New Ghan would be inappropriate. This is one time when it is wrong to perpetuate a name. The original Ghan was something unique; it was not even the same when it was modernised and air-conditioned. There will never be another Ghan. It is part of Australia's folklore and should be allowed to rest in peace.

Some years ago, when there was a renewal of enthusiasm for the completion of the north–south railway, Paul Everingham, Chief Minister for the Northern Territory, called for suggestions for a name for the proposed through train and came up with the Maluka, Jeannie Gunn's affectionate nickname for her husband and one far more appropriate to the Top End. Moreover, not only did the Afghan influence not extend much beyond Oodnadatta, but the new railway does not even remotely follow the original route, except for a kilometre or two where it passes through Heavitree Gap.

In Western Australia, we had the Mulga. This was the slow and friendly bi-weekly that worked out of Kalgoorlie, serving the few remaining hamlets as far north as Leonora and, on alternate weeks, Laverton as well. After skirting a breakaway (a small escarpment caused by local subsidence) it emerged from the salmon gum and gimlet country of the Eastern Goldfields and entered the mulga belt — a line of demarcation was known as the Mulga line. Significantly too, it also denoted a change from saline to fresh underground water, and was thought to have been the northern limit of the encroachment of the sea in prehistoric times.

There was a pioneering aura about the Mulga, not unmixed with a degree of nostalgia, passing as it did through so many former goldmining towns, once bustling with activity but now derelict. Following the heavy thunderstorms that occurred from time to time, the mulga country used to blossom into a carpet of pink and white everlasting daisies, interspersed with brilliant patches of Sturt's desert pea. The rains also promoted a prolific growth of grass along the permanent way, which caused problems for the locomotives.

In the winter of 1942, a few months after heavy autumn rains had fallen, the grass alongside the rails almost blanketed them from sight. The grass also tended to lie across the heads of the rails and, abetted by the evening dew, this caused the locomotive wheels to slip uncontrollably.

To minimise such slipping, locomotives were equipped with boxes from which specially dried sand could be directed on to the rails in front of the driving wheels. However, on one of the Mulga's runs to Laverton, the supply of sand was soon exhausted and the driver and fireman were obliged to leave the cab and walk alongside the locomotive for some kilometres up the grade out of Murrin Murrin, and to shovel sand on to the rails.

On the return journey. the rising grade between Scotia and Bardoc proved to be too much, and we passengers in the trailing carriages were subject to a succession of shuddering jolts as the train was allowed to run back over the sanded rails for a short distance and then stopped with a sudden jerk as the engine driver opened the regulator in a vain endeavour to get the driving wheels to grip. When this manoeuvre proved futile, the train had to be halved and taken over the grade in two sections.

Then there was the Berkshire–Tamworth Express, a nickname not so widely known but certainly less flattering than the Mulga.

The overnight passenger trains between Perth and Albany were known departmentally as Numbers 7 and 8, and in the 1960s they were given the exalted title of the Albany Progress. However, Number 8, the northbound movement, did not always enjoy such a glamorous name. Between Albany and Katanning, it was a mixed consist of both passenger and freight vehicles and the custom of its being used to convey all manner of living things — be they biped or quadruped, human, bovine ovine or porcine — led George Fruin, District Engineer at Narrogin and later Comptroller of Stores, to christen it the Berkshire–Tamworth Express. It was an appropriate nickname. It was not uncommon for it to be made up of a long string of loaded sheep vans in front, a number of similarly loaded pig vans in the rear, out of consideration for the passengers, with the passenger cars in between.

Numbers 7 and 8 were once the unwitting cause of a marriage getting off to a bad start, and the ecstacy of a honeymoon shattered. The two trains were scheduled to cross at Wagin, 311 kilometres from Perth, at about 1 am. Wagin was also a refreshment station, where a small stall on a narrow double-sided, or island, platform served passengers from both trains. Early on the morning of Good Friday 1934, the trains crossed at Wagin as scheduled. Among those on Number 7 was a couple who had just been married in Perth and were travelling to Mount Barker, where they would detrain and proceed by bus to the Porongorups for their honeymoon.

The bridegroom tore himself away from his bride of a few hours for what he thought would be a few minutes to buy a cup of coffee; but, before he had finished it, he heard a call for passengers to rejoin their trains. This he did, but, by mistake, he boarded Number 8 instead of Number 7.

His predicament on realising that he was on the way back to Perth while his Easter bride was heading in the opposite direction, was conveyed in unmistakable terms to the train staff on Number 8.

The author, who happened to be on the station at Narrogin when Number 8 arrived there about one hour after the contretemps at Wagin, was an amused but sadly unsympathetic onlooker, as the near hysterical bridegroom sought means to be restored to the arms of his loved one with the least possible delay. What a way to start married life!

And there was also the Snake Gully — abbreviated in time to the Snake — the steam hauled mixed train that operated between Port Pirie and Port Augusta following the construction of the standard gauge line between the two centres in 1937.

The guard's van on the first train, and for a few years afterwards, was an improvised vehicle consisting of a flat wagon upon which a galvanised-iron gabled roofed tent house had been affixed. It was its sheer rusticity that resulted in its being spontaneously dubbed the Snake Gully, locale of the current radio serial 'Dad and Dave'. The nickname remained with the train until 1951, when it was replaced by Budd rail cars.

The Penong Flyer was possibly known by only a few. It referred to the early model petrol powered rail car that used to bounce its way between Port Lincoln and Penong on Eyre Peninsula. Its one claim to passenger comfort was the provision of a small curtained-off section to provide some privacy to mothers breast feeding their babies, particularly indigenous ones. Once a week too it used to haul small trailer vans loaded with perishables brought overnight from Adelaide by the MV *Minnipa*.

I heard its nickname mentioned only once, at a charity ball in Port Lincoln arranged by the local railway unions and at which Doreen and I deputised for the Railways Commissioner and Mrs Fargher. In his address of welcome to the patrons, Perce Puckridge, Mayor of Port Lincoln, stated that Doreen had told him that she had been left standing on every railway station in Australia, and to which he added:

'If she waits for the Penong Flyer, she will have to wait a week.'

But in the realms of appropriate nicknames, the Midnight Horror holds pride of place. It would have been the most notorious train in Western Australia, and I doubt whether it had an equal anywhere.

The Horror was the mixed train that worked on six nights a week between Perth and Bunbury, with a branch connection from Brunswick Junction to Collie. Its primary function was to pick up and set down hundreds of full and empty milk cans at the 25 intermediate stations between Armadale and Bunbury, with the passenger coach trailing the long string of goods vehicles merely an afterthought.

Leaving each terminal at 11.30 pm, the

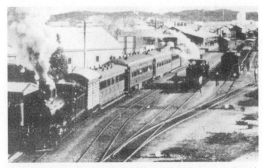

Southern terminus of the Midnight Horror, a local passenger train departing Bunbury in the 1920s. (*Photo:* Westrail)

Midnight Horror would jerk, rattle and shudder its way over the intervening 185 kilometres in the unbelievably slow time of eight hours. Those few passengers who dared accept the challenge of such a journey arrived at their destinations both jaded and unrefreshed. On weekends, its patrons existed almost entirely of men working in either Bunbury or Collie, but whose homes were in Perth.

It was not the first time that I had submitted myself to the tortures of the Horror, but on the night of 11 May 1935 I suffered the train at its worst. I was on transfer from Bunbury in the south-west to Meekatharra in the Murchison, and I was undertaking the first part of the 1150 kilometres journey on the Horror. Stretched out on a vacant seat in one of the side-door dog box compartments in the tail-end passenger car, I was trying to snatch a few minutes' sleep. Between stops, the clatter of the moving train represented peace and quiet compared with the bedlam that prevailed at stations, where the guards seemed to take a fiendish delight in manhandling the milk cans with a maximum of noise.

Suddenly, the train stopped dead in its tracks with the impetus of a runaway motor truck colliding with a brick wall. Although only half awake, I sat up involuntarily, put on my shoes, opened the compartment door and clambered down on to the permanent way. It was a false alarm. The Horror had merely stopped at a siding to enable the guard to launch yet another attack on a batch of milk cans. After the locomotive had been braked to a stop, the passenger carriage, the last vehicle on the train, had continued on its unrestricted way until all of the slack in the loose couplings between the wagons had been taken up.

Overall, those trains — named, misnamed and nicknamed — together with the other and unconventional modes of rail travel that I have enjoyed, endured or suffered, were an integral and in some instances nostalgic part of my nomadic railway life.

12 A Special Breed

It was the afternoon of Tuesday, 26 June 1951. I was on track inspection and called at Fisher, a gang camp 85 kilometres into the Nullarbor Plain — a spot devoid of any semblance of vegetation, and with a flat unbroken vista stretching 650 kilometres to the west, 85 to the east, 115 south to the Great Australian Bight and a similar distance north to the Great Victoria Desert. Six families lived there in isolation, their old three-roomed tent houses lacking electric light, reticulated water or sewerage. Their nearest neighbours were 22 kilometres to the east and 53 to the west and their only contact with the outside came when the Tea and Sugar train stopped for about 30 minutes twice each week, or when the roadmaster passed through on his weekly inspection.

When I arrived, I found an English woman and her two sons, aged about eight and three years, seated in the sun awaiting the gang's return from its day's work. All three were neatly dressed and their little tent house spotless. They were not sponsored migrants, and had arrived in Australia a few weeks previously. The woman expressed nothing but gratitude for the opportunities that this country offered, and said that they had come to Fisher to save money as a first step towards establishing themselves in their new homeland. Her only regret was that there were no schooling facilities for her elder son. We were able to correct this a short time later by transferring them to a school camp.

It takes a special breed of people to travel halfway across the world at their own expense, and then to settle uncomplainingly on the Nullarbor Plain.

But railwaymen are indeed a special breed.

They constitute a band of men who, with their wives, are prepared to accept the challenge of living and working on the railways in some of the most inhospitable environments on earth.

The very nature of the railway industry throws men together, particularly in remote areas where railwaymen and their families might constitute the entire population. It is an industry that enables the boss to get to know his staff personally. To be able to address them by their first names is both rewarding and good for the job. When one is isolated with them in a camp, or working round the clock alongside them on a washaway or derailment — and becoming just as tired and dirty as they are — all distinction seems to disappear, and in maintaining one's authority one has to exercise both tolerance and understanding.

My own railway career provided me with the opportunity to camp with railwaymen, live with them, work with them and share their harsh climatic conditions. These men and their wives lived and worked year in and year out in the back country, happy with their lot and, having succumbed to the fascination of the outback, stayed there for the whole of their working lives. They were truly indestructible.

It was at Widgemooltha, 84 kilometres south of Coolgardie, that, in 1931, I came to realise that the outback railwayman was something special. There, Owen Nazzari — a softly spoken Italian who, after the death of his wife, brought up his sons in a manner that was a credit to them all — was in charge of the permanent way gang. In the course of repairing the track after a minor derailment, one of his men — also an Italian — picked up an 18 foot (5.5 m) length of rail

Railway fettlers at Irrapatanna, Oodnadatta Railway, c. 1890 (*Photo:* Northern Territory Archives)

weighting 270 pounds (122 kg), and, holding it against his groin, carried it a short distance before letting it drop. When Alec Brown, who had been sent from Kalgoorlie to repair the derailed vehicle, suggested to him that he should not lift such a weight unassisted, the reply was short and blunt:

'Who's da boss; you or da ganger?'

Those railwaymen had diverse racial and ethnic backgrounds. Except for the inevitable strife that isolation is likely to induce, they lived and worked together — Europeans under an Aboriginal ganger, Australians under a migrant ganger, and former enemies living in comparative harmony,.

My personal favourites were truly cosmopolitan. Among them: Bob Henderson and Jack Gillies, white Australians; Bobbie Smith and August Baird, Aborigines; Edmund Turko and Owen Nazzari, Italians; Frank Sujkle, Yugoslav; Abdul Zader, Afghan; George Theodore, Greek; Dave Robb, Scottish; and Geordie Irving from Tyneside.

Typical of the mix was my engineering staff at Port Augusta. It consisted of six Australians, five Germans, two Czechs, a Dutchman, an Albanian, a Hungarian and two Poles. Of these, Max Zablonski was formerly of the Polish underground; Jan Slavoj and Jim Chernahorsky had left Czechoslovakia in some haste ahead of the Russian intervention; Jan Vreudenhil came to Australia from the Netherlands after completing

his national service in Indonesia; while one of the Germans, Fred Helriegel, first visited this country under duress — as a prisoner of war.

A number of those outback railwaymen had come here from Europe in the 1930s, intending to establish themselves before bringing out their families, but the war's intervention delayed the reunions by as much as ten years. Some started their railway careers as civilian internees.

One such man was Andy Aloi, an Italian internee directed to work with the Commonwealth Railways. In due course, he was given a D4 Caterpillar bulldozer — which he affectionately called his 'bulldog' — and left alone to live on the Central line, clearing watercourses and removing sand from the track.

When, in 1950, his wife succeeded in joining him, it was not without some trauma. Andy met her when her ship arrived at Fremantle, and they planned to travel by train to South Australia. When the Westland was brought into the Perth station, he left his wife — who could neither speak or understand English — on the platform while he boarded the train to locate their reservations. But the train departed while he was doing so, leaving Mrs Aloi lonely, desolate and incommunicado. Andy had no option but to wait until the Westland stopped at Midland Junction, 16 kilometres away, before he could detrain and rush back to Perth to reclaim his spouse. However, it was all resolved in the end and, their residence a converted railway van, together they lived and moved up and down the Central line, bulldozing contentedly,

Another was Edmund Turko — a mild, gentle Italian ganger at Rumbalara, 196 kilometres south of Alice Springs. The war also deprived him of the opportunity to bring his wife to Australia, but when this was eventually possible, her failing health prevented his doing so. Nevertheless, Edmund continued to support her in Italy.

Then there was George Theodore at Ilbunga, north of Oodnadatta, and the best gang cook on the line. He came to Australia from his native Greece prior to World War II to establish himself ahead of his family but the German invasion, followed by postwar political problems, delayed their joining him until 1953.

Had it not been for the displaced persons from Europe and, later, for the sponsored migrants, the Australian railways would not have functioned in the immediate postwar years. Most of them accepted their lot without complaint, but few stayed beyond their two years' bonded period.

In 1951, in an endeavour to overcome the critical labour shortage, the Commonwealth Railways, along with some of the state systems, recruited a number of migrants from Germany. At the time there was no migration agreement between Australia and the West German Government; consequently those who did come were contracted to repay their fares — and those of their families who followed 12 months later — over a period of two years. This imposition, together with the trauma induced by the isolation, the hot dry country and the equally hot dry climate — which no amount of explanation prior to embarkation could depict adequately — resulted in numerous defections, Indeed, in some instances, the shock of the new environment had psychological repercussions.

One who did stay was Charlie Walter, a well built blond Aryan who rose quickly to the position of ganger. Charlie was a conscientious worker, but he could not entirely free himself from the discipline that had prevailed in his native country. On one trip through Rodinga, I encountered the gang at lunch in the mess, with Charlie seated at the head of the table and nursing a rifle across his knees, It appeared that the men had disagreed with him over some mess activity — an attitude that he, as ganger, described as mutiny.

Later, sponsored migrants were recruited from Italy and Greece. Italians soon comprised the greater part of the workforces of both the Commonwealth Railways and the contractors on the construction of the Stirling North–Leigh Creek standard gauge railway. They settled in happily, one of their first actions being to establish a garden plot of green peppers, sometimes in the ground and at others in a kerosene tin. The men were distinguishable by their forage caps, skilfully fashioned out of brown paper.

The Greeks too seemed content, but we did have some quaint experiences with them. We sent four families to Ooldea, where a five roomed bungalow awaited each of them. But the four families wanted to share one house, one family to a room, and it took quite an effort on our part to convince them that each should occupy its own individual dwelling.

Then, at the 335 Mile camp, between Parachilna and Beltana on the Central Australia Railway, we encountered a different situation. The cottage allocated to one family was equipped with a wood burning stove and a kerosene-operated refrigerator. Obviously unfamiliar with such domestic refinements, they lit a fire in the backyard, over which they cooked their meals, using the aluminium trays from the refrigerator as cooking vessels. But they did not ignore the refrigerator entirely; they stored their clothes in it!

However, the origins of that special breed go back many years; to the men who were about during the hectic construction period that followed the gold and other mineral discoveries; to the men who challenged nature and pioneered the building of the first sections of the long dreamed-of north–south transcontinental railway; to those who built the Trans Australian Railway during World War I and who subsequently maintained it; and to those men who helped build and maintain the lines that were part of the development of the nation's agricultural industries.

A Special Breed
It was not until post-World War II that any mechanical aids were introduced into track construction and maintenance in this country.

Prior to that, the men had to rely entirely on hand tools, muscle power and a good eye.

Except on new construction, where an adzing and boring machine was used, dogspike holes in timber sleepers were bored by hand, using a jigger — a steel rod about 1.2 metres long, with a crank near one end similar to a carpenter's brace, and fitted with an auger at the other. Standing erect with one hand holding it near the top and the other on the crank, the operator would rotate the jigger and so drill the hole. It required superlative biceps power to do this through a 4½ or 5 inch (114–27 mm) hardwood sleeper. The dogspikes too were driven by hand, using a spiking hammer, a weighty tool with a head about 400 mm long and with a striking face only slightly larger that the head of the dogspike. An experienced permanent way man could swing a spiking hammer all day long with unerring accuracy, never once missing the head of the spike. They were the aristocrats of the gang. Unfortunately, lack of either confidence or skill has seen the almost total demise of the spiking hammer, and where mechanical spike driving machines are not used they have been replaced by large-faced sledge hammers.

Even the lifting and lining of the track was done by hand, using either a long timber lever or crowbars, the latter for making minor adjustments to the running top and for correcting the alignment. Ballast was packed under the sleepers with a beater — a pick with a hammer head about 50 mm long and 22 mm thick welded to one end — or a shovel.

Kneeling down on the formation with his eyes at rail level, and then standing well back and sighting the rails in perspective, a good railwayman could lift and line the track to a degree of accuracy not bettered by today's sophisticated track maintenance machines. One had only to observe Scotty Campbell's work on the sharp 10 chains (201 m) curves in Western Australia's south-west, or Bill Glasson's and Ken Beaton's lengths on the long straight to be convinced of this.

Another example of the permanent way man's uncanny eyesight was brought home to me by Dave Robb, at that time ganger at Southern Cross in Western Australia. A double compound — a set of points and crossings consisting of two tracks crossing at a flat angle of about five degrees, with switches and turnouts permitting straight through or diverging movements from either track — was due for renewal, and its replacement was not precisely to the same dimensions. The site was surveyed meticulously and the necessary pegs driven. Some time after the job had been done, we were again at Southern Cross and Dave came over to the survey van in which we were camped. In his unmistakable Scottish brogue, he said:

'You know that double compound? Well, your pegs were dead right.'

Of the many first class permanent way men that I have known, I would list the most outstanding as Jack Gillies, 'Geordie' Irving and Jack Dempsey. The greater part of Gillies' railway life had been with the SAR, where he played major parts in the construction of the Dry Creek and Port Pirie Junction marshalling yards, but it was as senior roadmaster with the Commonwealth Railways that I knew him and judged him. Jack had lived his own life fairly hard, but that did not stop him from taking a firm stand when someone under him exceeded recognised bounds.

I can recall three instances which justify my claiming him to be my top permanent way man. The first was in February 1950. Extensive washaways between Quorn and Marree made it necessary to drop the track off a bridge at Brachina into the stream bed and to construct a deviation. Without breaking the track — only loosening the fishplates — and calling the shots to a gang of men armed with crowbars, Jack Gillies managed to lift the rails, with the sleepers still attached, over the masonry buttresses of the bridge and down into the stream bed alongside. It was a masterly effort.

The second was some 12 months later, when a fast goods train was derailed on a low embankment over a salt pan between Pimba and Burando, about 220 kilometres west of Port Augusta. Passenger trains were banking up on either side of the derailment, and it became vital that the line be restored to traffic as soon as possible. The derailed vehicles were therefore moved clear of the track only far enough to allow for a minimum clearance. At the critical point there was an oblique gap of not more that four metres through which the track had to pass. This would have been difficult enough had the opening been square to the line, but, being askew, it was all but impossible. However, I told Jack that the line had to be threaded through this tiny gap; and, bearing in mind that it was on a narrow embankment over a salt pan with virtually no room for manoeuvre, it was a tall order. He looked at me quizzically but said nothing. He then went back about 200 metres, carefully pulled the track into two slightly reversed curves, and made it. It was a brilliant piece of track aligning. The clearance was so tight that, before allowing a train to pass through, we had to ensure that all windows were closed, lest some inquisitive passenger be decapitated.

The third demonstration of Jack's ability was when we started laying the rails on the Leigh Creek standard gauge railway. It was the first new railway in Australia — and possibly in the world — to be laid initially with long welded rails. With Milton Moore, the Assistant Chief Civil Engineer, Jack developed a technique by which a front-end loader with the bucket removed was used to haul a pair of long welded rails off the work train and down on to the sleepers. Tie bars were then attached to the rails to hold them to gauge before being spiked to the sleepers. This permitted the work train to move forward without delay. By today's standards, it was a crude procedure, but we did not have the benefit of straddle buggies and other sophisticated equipment. American experts who saw it were impressed.

'Geordie' Irving's nickname indicates his origins. During the worst days of the Depression, he battled his way to Port Augusta in search of work; and the address that he gave when applying for employment was 'The Pipes, Port Augusta'. Near the foreshore of Spencer Gulf, about two kilometres upstream of the town, were stacked several large concrete pipes, surplus from the construction of the Trans Australian Railway, which became the abode of many an unemployed man. One of them had been Geordie's temporary home.

During the next few years, he worked in various relaying and resleepering gangs, eventually progressing through the grades of fettler and ganger to roadmaster and, finally, to senior roadmaster. As roadmaster, he spent nine years at Cook, with his territory extending from the curves of the Barton and Immarna sandhills

to the long straight of the Nullarbor Plain. During those years there was no record of any trouble — either permanent way or domestic — in the district. Using his own methods, Geordie Irving used to solve problems almost before they happened. Despite his lack of education, he was an excellent officer, as well as a good companion on long inspection safaris.

I had less personal contact with Jack Dempsey, but saw enough of him to group him with Gillies and Irving. He was as at home on routine maintenance as he was on construction, and his years of outstanding service to the WAGR were well recognised by those who had the opportunity of working with him.

A classic example of someone who succumbed to the fascination of the outback was Bill Glasson, a relatively young man who went to Hughes on the Nullarbor, 86 kilometres west of Cook, rose to the position of ganger and maintained his 32 kilometres of track to a standard that would have compared with the best in the world. Bill carried his good housekeeping to the siding itself, where he planted a row of eucalypt trees in the limestone plain, watering them by hand from the limited supplies of water brought there each week by the Tea and Sugar. Preparatory work involved digging holes, about one metre square and over a metre deep, in the limestone, using only pick, shovel and spud bar. Then, after the holes had been dug, he had to fill them by scraping together what soil he could find on the rocky surface. This voluntary effort was typical of the man.

Of the many men that I had on the CAR, possibly the two most dedicated were Chris Kuhn and Pompey, both of whom spent years camped in the sandhills around Lake Eyre South where they worked horse-drawn scoop teams clearing away drift sand. Each man lived alone with three or four horses and his only contacts with the outside world were the twice weekly goods train that brought him water, fodder and stores, as well as the weekly visit by the roadmaster stationed at Marree.

Chris Kuhn had spent most of his life in the Lake Eyre country, and his leathery countenance attested to this. In fact, he raised his family there, sending his children to Marree when they reached school age. In the mid-1950s, Chris was drowned at Alice Springs when trying to cross the Todd

River, normally a dry stream bed.

Pompey was a fine type; well built, good looking, shiny black and always bare-footed. He had a daughter who had trained as a nursing sister, and of whom he was justifiably proud. Once, on inspection, I came across him still working well after normal knock-off time. When I mentioned this to the roadmaster he said that Pompey never worried about the clock; he just worked while there was daylight, even, at times, on Sundays.

At Marree too we had an excellent gang consisting almost entirely of men of Afghan blood, descendents of those brought to Australia 100 years earlier as cameleers. Abdul Zader, the ganger, was strong, hard-working and possessed an especially good eye, something essential when lifting and lining the old crippled rails that had been in the track since its construction in the 1880s. There was also one true Australian in the gang; an Aborigine, a giant of a man shown on the books as Sandy Sam.

Then we had Arthur Ah Chee, ganger at Alice Springs, a beautiful penman with strong traces of Oriental artfulness. Arthur was the offspring of a union between a Chinese man and an Aboriginal woman. In the early days of the Northern Territory, thousands of Chinese worked on the construction of the railway from Darwin to Pine Creek. During the war years, Arthur devised an attachment to the carburettor of his gang section car which effected a substantial economy in fuel consumption. Once too, while travelling with him at night, he retimed the section car engine in the dark using only a hand held torch for illumination. It seemed an unnecessary action, because the motor appeared to be performing admirably; no doubt Arthur did it just to impress me on this, our first meeting.

Strangely, and perhaps contrariously, I had a soft spot for Bobby Smith. An Aborigine in his twenties with a self-deprecating and hangdog demeanour, in his time he broke every rule in the book yet remained extremely likeable. He was a good worker and ganger, but the quality fluctuated in direct proportion to the level of his domestic harmony.

Although working in the single men's gangs between Oodnadatta and Alice Springs, Bobby had married a girl from Oodnadatta. For most of the time he lived in the gang mess while his wife and children camped nearby. That his family lived under those conditions was not the fault of the department; his wife chose to do so. We would have willingly stationed them at one of the married camps further south where a house would have been made available to them, but they wanted to stay in their own territory.

Especially during my track inspections on the Commonwealth Railways, I came to know and to admire those men and women who were prepared to accept the challenge of living and working on the railways under the most inhospitable environment on earth.

To those living in a town with every facility laid on, it is impossible to comprehend the conditions under which those who built and maintained the railways were forced to live and work; in virtual isolation and seeing no new faces save a fleeting glimpse of the crew of a passing train; hundreds of kilometres from medical help, a terrifying prospect for parents with children; in some instances without schooling facilities; lacking entertainment of any kind; devoid of water or soil suitable for gardening; subject to extremes of temperature; and relying on one grocery and two bread deliveries a week. Indeed, on the Pingrup and Sandstone lines in Western Australia they saw only one train a week; while for some years the Laverton line had only one a fortnight.

It may seem trivial to us, but, to those people a delay in the arrival of the weekly tobacco ration — something that applied well into the postwar period — was a serious matter. So too was a shortage of bacon, or a lack of variety in the jam supplied with the weekly grocery order. I saw it as my responsibility to resolve such matters, and to keep the men and their families as contented as possible.

Railway employees' cottages, Woolshed Flat, Pichi Richi Pass, Central Australia Railway (*Photo:* The Schiller Collection)

Single men's accommodation, Nullarbor Plain (*Photo:* Australian National)

Kurrawang Wood line, Western Australia. Main camp, 170 kilometres south of Kalgoorlie, January 1932. (*Photo:* the author)

The medical risk endured by these people was exemplified when, one night in 1949, Mrs Lloyd, wife of ganger Charlie Lloyd at Wynbring, 516 kilometres west of Port Augusta, suffered a stroke. The nearest doctors were at Port Augusta and Ceduna, the latter a flying doctor, but Wynbring did not possess a landing strip. Because of its inaccessibility, the nursing sister at Tarcoola undertook the 101 kilometres night-time journey to Wynbring by gang motor section car to do what she could, unfortunately to no avail. Following his wife's death, Charlie transferred to the single men's camp at Finke, on the CAR 228 kilometres south of Alice Springs, where, in charge of a happy and hard-working gang of Italians, he continued to render valuable service to the railways.

Another incident indicative of the privations endured by families stationed along the Trans line happened one Saturday evening in 1953. We were travelling from Tarcoola to Cook on the Commissioner's inspection train and, while descending the grade between Immarna and Ooldea, we came to a precipitate stop; it was obvious that an accident had occurred.

I alighted from the Commissioner's car at the rear of the train and walked ahead to the locomotive, to find that it had collided with a gang section car. On it were two men; the ganger from Immarna and one of his fettlers. Neither was injured, but the ganger was cradling a dead goat in his arms. So that he could give his children fresh milk, the ganger had bought the goat from an employee at Ooldea. But instead of seeking permission to transport the animal to Immarna — and surely this would have been granted — he decided to do so surreptitiously, neither informing his roadmaster nor seeking the train controller's authority to place the section car on the line. Consequently he was unaware of the running of the Commissioner's train. The goat was killed; the section car wrecked; and, sadly, the ganger dismissed.

Then, there was Johnny Tischek, a former displaced person who was a bundle of nerves and appeared to be in a perpetual state of fear. He was stationed in a number of gangs between Oodnadatta and Alice Springs, and could not be persuaded to take a holiday. He would even work during crib-time, holding a sandwich in one hand and a shovel in the other. Once, we got him as far south as Port Augusta for a few days. But there were washaways in the far north and Johnny joined the work train and travelled to Oodnadatta where, without seeking permission of anyone, he set himself to work. However, when it came to booking his time, he objected, claiming that he was still on holidays! In Johnny's case, the isolation and the anonymity of the Centre were just what he wanted.

However, those old-time railwaymen were not all uneducated navvies; indeed, some were well read. It was a revelation to observe the quality of the literature in Paddy Griffen's humble weatherboard cabin, set among the desert oaks in the sandhills at the 416 mile camp on the Trans line; while Ted Rycko, pumper at Bundooma and Ilbunga on the Central line, dabbled in writing and maintained correspondence with Darcy Niland and other Australian authors.

On a lighter note, the isolated living conditions probably accounted for the fact that, in the early days of the Trans Australian Railway, the Commonwealth Railways Provision Store, which acted as the providor for the employees along the line, was reputed to be the biggest retailer in

Loco crew's barracks at Cummins, Eyre Peninsula, 1923 (*Photo:* Port Dock Station Railway Museum)

South Australia of essence of vanilla (deemed to be a satisfactory substitute for liqueur) and extract of malt (the basic ingredient for home brew).

I shall always remember with affection working with those railwaymen; sharing their hardships and getting to know their wives. One sensed that they appreciated the fact that they were meeting the boss on their ground and not on his. At times too, they offered what hospitality they could.

Three times, at Widgemooltha and Boddalin in Western Australia, and at Barton on the Trans line, I returned to the siding to bed down as best I could after a long day's work on a derailment to be greeted by a hot meal prepared by one of the fettlers' wives.

At other times — at locations as far apart as halfway between Meekatharra and Wiluna in Western Australia and at the 950 Mile camp just west of the Nullarbor — I have been offered morning tea or supper by the ganger's wife. In each case it was apparent that the gesture gave them pleasure. On all of these occasions, the hospitality was tendered with dignity, and without any semblance of subservience; indeed, they rightly considered themselves as hosts of equal standing.

That hospitality was not, however, a one-way traffic. In the Depression years, the Lake Grace–Hyden railway was constructed under unemployment relief conditions. Each Friday night, when the men who had been stood down were about to join the train for the 430 kilometres overnight journey back to Perth, the Resident Engineer, Cedric Stewart, and his wife Nell would, without any trace of condescension, send them on their way with tea and scones.

Although enduring the greatest isolation and the toughest living conditions, the track forces did not constitute the only members of that special breed. The train crews in the days of steam should not be overlooked.

On the Eastern Goldfields, the Murchison and Eyre Peninsula, they were called upon to work on the footplate in the searing heat of summer, sometimes for more than eight hours, and then to retire to primitive barracks where, over a rest period often as brief as nine hours, they were obliged to prepare two meals from the contents of their tuckerboxes and to try to have some sleep before booking-on again.

The circumstances under which train crews rested away from home prompted Harold Clapp to observe to one of his departmental heads: 'Breeding Bolsheviks, are you?'

On the former CAR, two train crews worked the trains right through from Quorn to Alice Springs, each crew alternating between seven hours on the footplate and seven hours 'resting' in a rough-riding relay van at the rear of a long loose-coupled train. There, they were expected to snatch some sleep and refreshment, a rather futile expectation. The trip from Quorn covered seven such shifts, and on arrival at The Alice one of the crews was obliged to undertake another one on shunting duties.

Finally, I should refer to two men who worked with me on unemployment relief works in 1932–33; Tom Butler and August Baird.

Tom Butler was my powder monkey during the construction of the Wurarga reservoir. An old-time miner, prospector and station hand, he had prospected for gold over most of Western Australia, worked underground in the Kalgoorlie mines, and on cattle stations in Queensland. Grey haired, stooped and shuffling rather than walking, he seemed to be too old to be still working, but we asked no questions. Tom had lost all four fingers from his left hand in a mining accident, but that did not stop him from handling tools and explosives as expertly as the next man. Actually, he was somewhat embarrassed by his disability and resented anyone commenting on the proficiency with which he could use his fragmented hand.

Shortly before coming to Wurarga, Tom Butler had been working a promising gold prospect in the upper Murchison. For six weeks he had existed on a diet of damper made from plain flour, and of tea, the leaves doubling as tobacco after drying. Eventually it proved too much for him, so he gave up and went in to Geraldton. There, he received unemployment relief at the rate for a single man, namely 7 shillings (70 cents) a week. Proudly, he balanced his budget on this meagre sum, a feat which he claimed that his cousin Philip Collier, Premier and Treasurer of the State, could not do with many millions more.

One of my best workers on dam construction was August Baird. An Aborigine who, with his wife Petronella, had been brought up on a mission station in the Kimberleys, he sought work rather than rely on native welfare handouts. Unobtrusive and retiring, not only was he an excellent worker, but also, with his wife and two children, they occupied the tidiest camp on the job.

My respect for those construction men was not limited to the manual labourers; it extended to the resident engineers as well. With their families, they lived for years in the rather primitive houses that they took with them from job to job. For the most part, they were deprived of such domestic conveniences as reticulated water and electric light. Nor were there many avenues for social contact. The names of four men come to mind.

Both Alec McCullough and Cedric Stewart spent 11 years in railway construction camps spread over the entire spectrum of the WAGR; McCullough on the Busselton–Witchcliffe, Lake Grace–Newdegate, Hay River–Nornalup and Pemberton–Northcliffe railways; while Stewart was resident engineer on the Esperance–Salmon Gums, Meekatharra–Wiluna and Lake Grace–Hyden constructions, as well as the Kellerberrin–Bungulla deviation.

After working on such projects as the building of the Wyndham meatworks in the extreme north of the State, Stan Devine acted as resident engineer for eight years on the Norseman–Salmon Gums, Amery–Kalannie and Kulja–Bonnie Rock railway constructions; while Frank Carter, after a number of years with the Commonwealth Railways and on drought relief railway surveys in the Northern Territory, came to Western Australia to be engaged on the final stages of the Meekatharra–Wiluna construction, the pulling-up of the Meekatharra–

Horseshoe railway, the construction of the railway reservoirs at Meekatharra and Mullewa, and the deviation between Eradu and Northern Gully — a total of several years' service on the Murchison — before moving south to work for another five years on deviations between Collie and Brunswick Junction and between Merredin and Yellowdine.

Both McCullough and Stewart rose to the top of the Civil Engineering Branch, but Devine was killed near Northam in 1941 when his rail motor collided with a motor vehicle at a level crossing. At about the same too, Carter succumbed to cancer at a relatively early age.

Railways in the Blood

In October 1978 Westrail's Commissioner, Jim Pascoe, retired after 49 years' service. His father Dick had joined the WAGR at Mount Magnet in 1923, eventually becoming length runner between the 373 Mile camp and Bromus on the Esperance line, surely one of the loneliest runs on the system.

Jim, the second of eight children, was born at Lennonville, a small mining village near Mount Magnet. His early education was undertaken at one and two teacher schools in the Murchison, before being sent 357 kilometres to Geraldton — entirely at his parents' expense — for his secondary education. Joining the railways in 1929, and displaying outstanding promise from the start, he worked in every section of the Traffic Branch before becoming Chief Traffic Manager in 1965, Assistant Commissioner in 1968 and Commissioner in 1971.

Together, Dick and Jim Pascoe contributed 76 years to the railways in Western Australia. It was an outstanding example of that special father and son relationship that characterises the railway family, but it was not an isolated one.

Neal McCusker, whose father was a country stationmaster in New South Wales, was educated at one-teacher schools. But after joining the NSWGR as a junior porter he educated himself, not only in railway subjects but also in accountancy. His ability and diligence — particularly during the war years, when the railway systems on the eastern seaboard were on the verge of collapse — brought about rapid promotion. In 1956, aged 49 years, he was appointed Commissioner of Railways, possibly the biggest one-man job in Australia at the time. The joint McCusker contribution to the railways in New South Wales amounted to 99 years.

Pride of place, however, must go to the Walkers — grandfather Lewin, father Harold and son Neville — whose railway careers in Queensland notched up a total of 118 years. Lewin's 28 years' service included 11 in the Normanton–Croydon area, still Australia's most romantic and remote railway. Both Harold and Neville rose to the position of Chief Engineer for the Queensland Railways, their combined incumbencies in that chair amounting to 25 years.

In Western Australia, both Alec and Ian McCullough rose to become Chief Civil Engineer, Alec for ten years and Ian for five on his way up to Commissioner of Westrail; while Charles and Alec Holm totted up a joint figure of 27 years as Heads of Branches, the former as Comptroller of Stores and the latter as Chief Civil Engineer. The McCulloughs' combined service amounted to 81 years; the Holms', 87.

The Williams family—father and son — could claim a combined score of 64 years. Howard, the father, notched up 40 years with the WAGR, including one as Chief Civil Engineer, his occupancy of that position being cut short by his sudden death at the age of 58. His son Don's 24-year railway career was not continuous but included nine years as General Manager and four as Chairman of Australian National.

I can also claim, with pride, membership of this particular club. My father Harry served the WAGR for 42 years, mostly as a signalman, while I spent 22 years with its Civil Engineering Branch before moving to the Commonwealth and South Australian Railways. The Fitch tally amounted to 88 years.

My successor as South Australian Railways Commissioner, Murray Stockley, also qualified for membership. His father Thomas, whose 43 years' service ranged from porter to interstate ticket clerk, had the distinction of being stationmaster at Millers Corner in Jetty Road, Glenelg, during the days of the South Terrace Glenelg railway. In 1929, Thomas Stockley was given the privilege of giving the right-of-way to the last steam train to operate before the line was converted to an electric tramway. He was similarly honoured a few months later when the other railway to Glenelg —from Adelaide railway station through Mile End and Plympton — was closed down. His son Murray joined the SAR as an office junior during the Depression years, and after a thorough grounding in all aspects of traffic working became General Traffic Manager in 1968, Deputy Commissioner in 1972, and Railways Commissioner one year later. The Stockleys served the South Australian Railways for a total of 85 years.

Had they lived to see it, the fathers would have felt justifiably proud of their sons' successes. For my own part, I have been everlastingly thankful for my own father's words when, one day in 1926, after he had returned home from work, he said to me: 'The Railways are advertising for engineering cadets. You are putting in for one!'

The Brotherhood of Railwaymen

Some might call sleepers, ties; or bridges, trestles; or stations, depots; or guards' vans, cabooses; or guards, brakemen … but under it all we speak the same railway language. There exists a spontaneity between us, and we are indeed a worldwide brotherhood.

Overseas, one has only to mention that one belongs to that breed to be overwhelmed by friendliness and hospitality, and this irrespective of one's position on the status ladder. To the author, it has prompted invitations from enginemen and rail car drivers to ride up-front with them; to have been asked by a Union Pacific baggage handler to join him, his wife and daughter to dinner in the dining car when travelling between Seattle and Portland; to have a sleeping car conductor on Canadian National's Supercontinental introduce himself, sit down alongside me and talk railways; and to have knowledge of one's presence on long distance trains in North America and elsewhere passed by word of mouth from attendant to attendant — not out of subservience but as railwayman to railwayman.

At higher levels, I have been the guest at a luncheon in Washington DC, arranged in my honour by Dan McVey, Chairman of the Association of American Railroads; and to be received by W.H. Tucker, Vice Chairman of the United States Interstate Commerce Commission; and, over many years to have maintained personal correspondence and an exchange of valuable information with senior officers of other railway systems — in particular, with Jack Spicer, Executive Vice President of the Canadian National Railways, and with senior officers of British Rail.

Perhaps the most outstanding, and certainly the most unconventional, example of that freemasonry was given to me by Sir John Elliot. Formerly General Manager of the Southern Railway in England, after nationalisation he became Chairman of the Southern and the London–Midland Regions before, in 1951, being appointed Chairman of the British Railway Executive. In 1949 he was brought to Australia to report an the Victorian Railways, and on his arrival he made it plain to all that, as a railwayman himself, he intended to look at the problems from that angle. The outcome was an harmonious enquiry, and a report vastly different from some others made by persons unfamiliar with either railway practices or the political restraints that have gagged the industry in this country.

Sir John told me that, during his term as General Manager of the Southern Railway, he was called out in the early hours of the morning — as is the burden of railwaymen the world over — to attend to a disruption to traffic, this time resulting from enemy action. While motoring across London on his way to Waterloo station, he was booked by the police for speeding.

When he appeared in court, he pleaded guilty, but stated in extenuation that he was anxious to get to the incident as soon as possible. This seemed to anger the magistrate, who administered a severe reprimand to the defendant, making it quite plain that, just because he was the general manager of a railway, he was not endowed with unlimited licence to disregard the laws of the land. However, Sir John was dumbfounded when the magistrate fined him ten shillings, without costs.

Still under shock, he retired from the court, where he encountered the constable who had booked him and who greeted him politely, saying: 'Sorry sir'.

Elliot replied to the constable that he was only doing his duty, but added that he was astonished at the lightness of the penalty.

With just the trace of a smile, the constable remarked: 'Didn't you know sir?'

'Didn't know what?' asked Sir John.

'That the magistrate is an engine driver on the LMS' (London Midland and Scottish Railway).

Critics might have argued that, administratively and gauge-wise, the Australian railways consisted of seven separate islands, each operating individually in terms of its own mandate. However, operationally, commercially, technically, and from industrial relations and staff welfare points of view, they did constitute a closely knit voluntary federation. Together with the New Zealand Railways, it was designated the Australian and New Zealand Railways Conferences, and through it the individual systems regularly reached agreement on a multitude of matters.

In respect of staff welfare and morale, no better example could be found than that of the Railway Institutes. Fostered and encouraged but financed only in part by the administrations, they were managed by councils, predominantly elected by institute members, and with only nominal administration representation — the latter often senior officers happy to give of their time voluntarily — the Railway Institutes would have been the greatest contributor to staff welfare and contentment.

Such was the harmony and esprit de corps engendered by the Institute that, in the course of my inspections around the system, I was regularly entertained by local branches, not as Railways Commissioner but as one of them.

Sadly the semi-privatisation and the dismemberment of the formerly autonomous railway systems indicates that, at least in this country, there are signs of the demise of that brotherhood. However, it is a brotherhood of which I was proud to have been a member.

I concluded Chapter 1 with the following: 'I have been fortunate in having family members, teachers, tutors, coaches, supervisors, colleagues and friends who made substantial contributions to my upbringing, education and development, and to whom, together with my workmates of all grades and in all places, I shall be eternally indebted'.

It is pertinent to these reminiscences that I repeat those words, in particular, 'workmates of all grades and in all places'.

13   Mentors, Superiors and Colleagues

I was fortunate in my choice of mentors. Their influence and guidance extended from my formative years through to my academic, professional and sporting careers.

Reference has already been made to my parents and my brother. Of the others to whom I am indebted, some have already been mentioned and some have not. Encapsulated, their names and contributions were:

O.F. Blakey, for his teaching, consideration for the welfare of his students, and his continued close relationship with them long after graduation and until his death in 1952.

E.W. Morris, whose courageous return to work following his rail motor accident in 1941 was, to me, a shining example of unadulterated guts. Added to this was his encouraging comment after I, an inexperienced mistake-prone greenhorn engineer, had perpetrated yet another bloomer: 'Anyone can make a mistake, but it is a bloody fool who makes the same mistake twice'.

G.W. Fruin and C.R. Stewart, both my superiors with the WAGR, not only for their guidance while I was climbing up the engineering ladder but also for their demonstrations of humanity and humility; how to get on with people; and the fact that one does not have to ride the high horse to maintain discipline. Both of these gentlemen had a substantial influence on my approach to the job.

Apart from my father and my brother, W.J. Skipworth had the greatest impact during my formative years. I was fortunate to have been drafted into his 7th Standard (Year 8) class at Perth Boys' School in 1922. His influence on my development was pre-eminent, not only during my three years at that school, but also over the next 22 years, covering my secondary and tertiary studies and into my professional career. In addition to his teaching responsibilities, he gave freely of his own time conducting the school's gymnasium and coaching the swimming, lifesaving, athletics and football teams.

On a personal note, he guided and encouraged me both at school and in later years. Although I was only one of the hundreds of boys who passed through his hands, he never forgot me; and I shall never forget Bill Skipworth. His contribution to the character building of the many boys who passed through Perth Boys' over the years would have been on a par with that of Tommy Chandler, his headmaster at that time.

Indeed, T.C.Chandler, headmaster of Perth Boys' School from 1912 until his death in 1936, was the motivator behind the school's success in many areas.

Tommy Chandler not only looked on the welfare of every one of his pupils as his personal responsibility, but took the view that he should not lose interest in a boy's career after he had left school. Over the 12 years after I left school we kept in touch; and our last personal contact occurred only a short time before his death when, one morning, our trains and our paths crossed at Pinjarra on the Perth–Bunbury line. Tommy Chandler was a well loved headmaster who had his finger on the pulse of every boy under his care.

While Bill Skipworth had the greatest influence on my teenage sporting development, two others — John Leonard and Arthur Green, both regular state players during the 1920s and two names indelibly etched into Subiaco Football Club history — were my joint mentors during my short foray into League football. For the two years I played with the Jolimont Club in the Under 22 Years Football Association, Leonard was our coach. My hero worship of him, as well as his encouragement, prompted me to aim at higher things, and he nurtured me through my catastrophic initiation to league football.

However, it was Arthur Green to whom I owed most. After 14 years with the Subiaco Club, interrupted by two years' war service, he retired in 1928, and in 1929 coached the Club's Reserves team. It was here that, as a borderline A grade player, I first came into contact with him. In the following year he became coach of the League side, and it was then that Arthur Green coached, supported and encouraged me in every aspect of football. He went further, and entrusted me with tasks on the field which some of my critics

Arthur Green (*Photo: Subiaco Football Club*)

(*Left*) John Leonard (*Photo:* Subiaco Football Club)

considered to be beyond my capabilities.

Superiors

I served under five Railways Commissioners: Colonel H. Pope, E.A. Evans, J.A. Ellis, P.J. Hannaberry and J.A. Fargher.

The appointment of Harold Pope as WAGR Commissioner in 1919 might have been inspired by his distinguished career with the First AIF. Nevertheless, it would not have been possible to imagine one more enthusiastically welcomed by both the staff and the public. Moreover, the appointment was vindicated. Financially, his nine

years' administration would have been the most successful period in the system's history. In four of those years, a profit was recorded.

Born in Ealing, Middlesex, in 1873, Harold Pope started his railway career in 1889 with the Great Northern Railway Company. In 1895, he migrated to Western Australia, where he joined the WAGR.

In World War I his military career was meritorious. At the Gallipoli landing he was Lieutenant Colonel in charge of the 16th Battalion. Pope's Hill, scene of some of the heaviest fighting on the peninsula, is his everlasting memorial. Later, after commanding the 14th Infantry Brigade in France, Pope returned to Australia in 1916. However, he persuaded the authorities to permit him to travel to England in charge of transports. Once there, he was placed in command of the 52nd Battalion, which fought under him at Frommelles.

Harold Pope was admired and revered by his men. Arthur Read, my timekeeper on reservoir construction in later years, and who served under him at Gallipoli, often referred to the high esteem in which Colonel Pope was held by all ranks.

As Commissioner of Railways, Pope was able to inspire the same degree of respect and affection as he did as a military officer. He had the capacity, not only to get on with people, but also to get them to work with him. Of average build, and with a pleasing countenance topped by a receding hairline, his outstanding physical characteristic was his broad and perpetual smile. It was said that the smile broadened in direct proportion with his degree of displeasure.

When war-induced ill health forced his premature retirement in 1928 at the early age of 55 years, there were widespread and truly genuine expressions of regret. He saw the WAGR grow from less than 900 kilometres when he joined in 1895 to over 6000 kilometres at the time of his retirement. An outstanding soldier and railway administrator, it would be hard to imagine anyone in authority who could evoke greater affection and loyalty from those serving under him. As a humble and very junior engineering cadet, I had negligible personal contact with Harold Pope. Nevertheless, he made everyone in the service feel part of his team.

Pope's successor, E.A. Evans, was the very

Colonel H. Pope, Commissioner of Railways, Western Australia, 1920-1928

Mr E. A. Evans, Commissioner of Railways, Western Australia, 1929-1933

Mr J. A. Ellis, Commissioner of Railways, Western Australia, 1934-1949

Mr P. J. Hannaberry, Commonwealth Railways Commissioner, 1948-1960

Mr J. A. Fargher, South Australian Railways Commissioner, 1953-1966

antithesis of his predecessor. Born in Worcester in 1865, he joined the WAGR as Interlocking Engineer in 1896, from which position he progressed through that of Locomotive Engineer to Chief Mechanical Engineer in 1920. Perhaps it was unfortunate that his five years as Commissioner coincided with the worst of the Depression, but he did nothing to boost staff morale. Everlastingly dour and unsmiling, at times he turned social functions — normally a unique opportunity to promote esprit de corps — into wakes.

One such occasion was at the Civil Engineering Branch office picnic in January 1929, where Evans was the principal guest. In responding to the toast in his honour he concentrated on all things dismal. Office picnics are not appropriate places for despondent homilies. The day was sad enough without Evans' requiem. Earlier, Jack Ryder had lost the third Test of the Ashes series to Percy Chapman's all conquering side.

First as a student, and later as a young engineer, I had a fairly close association with J.A. Ellis. We young men owed him a great deal.

His appointment as Commissioner of Railways in Western Australia in 1934 coincided with a noticeable growth of confidence throughout the service that was by no means accidental. No man bore a greater stamp of competence and authority.

Born in Workington, Cumberland, in 1887, Joseph Arthur (Jack) Ellis migrated to Australia in 1910, where he immediately joined the Queensland Railways. The major part of his 16 years with that system was spent in the field on construction, and it was there that he first fostered the sporting and social activities among his staff that characterised his working life.

In 1926, only 39 years of age, he transferred to the Western Australian Public Works Department as Engineer for Railway Construction. Over the next four years he superintended the survey and construction of nearly 1000 kilometres of railway in locations as far apart as Wiluna in the north, Nornalup in the south and Bullfinch in the east.

Despite his comparative youth and his appointment from outside the department over senior men within it, he soon won them over. When, in January 1931, the railway Construction Branch was transferred from the Public Works to the Railway Department, Ellis became Assistant Chief Civil Engineer; and it was from this position that he was selected to succeed Evans as Commissioner. During the war, he occupied the position of Director of Locomotive and Rollingstock Construction with the Ministry of Munitions.

Jack Ellis was liked and respected on all sides. About 185 centimetres tall, of impressive physique and splendid carriage, he was able to maintain his personal dignity, and also that of his position, while at the same time mixing freely with his subordinates. He was especially interested in the welfare of the younger employees, following their careers closely and going out of his way to talk with them about their departmental and sporting activities. For many years, it had been the custom for the stores and civil engineering branches of the WAGR to hold a social cricket match during the Christmas–New Year period. Shortly after Ellis joined the Railway Department this was widened to include all five branches, as well as the Tramway and Electricity Supply Department. As Commissioner, he was an active participant almost to the year of his retirement.

Jack Ellis had a forthright and succinct, yet polite, way of expressing himself. Shortly after he became Assistant Chief Civil Engineer, one of his directives was questioned by Ted Hanley, a senior clerk. After telling Ellis that 'We always do it this way', Hanley asked: 'What do you think?'

The reply was short and to the point: 'I think that I would do as I was told.'

Two years later, Ellis went to Meekatharra with Charles May, the District Engineer at Geraldton, to inspect a ballast pit which, because of seams of solid rock in the gravel bed, had turned out to be a disaster. After looking over the pit, Ellis summed up the situation with: 'The best thing that you can do is to plant a weeping willow on this spot and forget that you ever had a ballast pit here'.

His 15 years as Commissioner of Railways — a record term for Western Australia — spanned difficult times: the latter years of the Depression, the war and the early postwar period, each with its own particular problems, and each of comparable severity. His administration was also subjected to a great deal of uninformed and unjust criticism, first by Minister H.S. Seward, who bore an undisguised malice towards the railways, and then by the Gibson–du Plessis Royal Commission of 1947 whose report deliberately overlooked the enormity of the problems facing the system.

However, the events of the decade that followed his retirement in 1949 — during which the WAGR suffered badly from the aftermath of Seward's actions — vindicated him entirely. His being awarded the CBE in 1963 was considered by those of us who knew him and owed him so much to have been long overdue.

The Commonwealth Railways had only four Commissioners — N.G. Bell, G.A. Gahan, P.J. Hannaberry and K.A. Smith, the last named becoming the first Chairman of the Australian National Railways Commission.

It was Hannaberry's appointment to that position in 1948 that created the vacancy of Chief Civil Engineer into which I moved in 1949. Patrick Joseph Hannaberry, who graduated in civil engineering at the Melbourne University, started his railway career with the Victorian Railways and transferred to the Commonwealth Railways in 1934, where one of his first jobs was that of project engineer on the construction of the Port Pirie–Port Augusta railway. Later he became Engineer for Way and Works, subsequently retitled Chief Civil Engineer. He was appointed Assistant Commonwealth Railways Commissioner some months before his predecessor retired.

Pat Hannaberry's energy and drive were prodigious; so too was his persistence. I have never encountered anyone less prone to accept the fact that something could not be done. In addition, he always did his homework, and in this he taught me a lesson on more than one occasion.

In May 1950, I accompanied him to Canberra to attend a conference in the Prime Minister's office in connection with the dispute that had arisen over the route to be followed by the new standard gauge railway to Leigh Creek. We arrived in Canberra at midday on a Sunday, the conference being scheduled for the following afternoon. We spent Sunday afternoon and evening, as well as Monday morning, going over all the arguments, even to the extent of seeking local analogies in respect of the terrain to be traversed by the line. Unaided, Hannaberry put on a magnificent performance before the Prime Minister.

In July 1953, returning from an inspection of the Darwin railway, he received word that an intensely irate group of pastoralists at Alice Springs wanted to meet him, alleging unsatisfactory service on the Central Australia Railway. Again, Hannaberry set to work assembling the facts, and single handedly answered every complaint thrown at him.

I had my baptismal experience of Hannaberry's impetuosity when on my first inspection trip with him to Alice Springs. At Deepwell, 77 kilometres south of The Alice, he walked into the gang mess, went straight to the kerosene operated refrigerator, opened its door, looked inside, slammed closed the door, turned round and said to the cook: 'You're sacked!' The cook and I, each of us novices to our jobs, were equally dumbfounded. It was an obsession with Hannaberry that refrigerators should be defrosted regularly. The one at Deepwell had not.

Pat Hannaberry and I did not see eye-to-eye in all things. Nevertheless, I had, and still retain, a respect for his ability, his directness, his drive and his energy. Despite any differences that we might have had, I never doubted his wholehearted dedication to the welfare of the Commonwealth Railways. His voluntary retirement in 1960, at the early age of 56 years, cost it its most dynamic Commissioner.

J.A. Fargher, who had been Assistant to the Railways Commissioner during R.H. Chapman's regime, became Acting South Australian Railways Commissioner on the latter's death in May 1953. Subsequently, he was confirmed in the position and retained it until his retirement in January 1966. My first contact with him was during the Royal Commission into the Leigh Creek standard gauge railway. It was perhaps the most fortuitous meeting of my railway life.

Jack Fargher, who was born on 14 January 1901, used to boast that he was born in, lived in and was educated in the Melbourne suburb of Carlton.

By virtue of his own assiduity, which resulted in his being awarded scholarships and exhibitions, in 1923 he graduated Master of Engineering at the Melbourne University. In November of that year, after a few months with the Victorian Railways Construction Branch, Fargher was engaged by the SAR to undertake the design of the new railway bridge over the river at Murray Bridge. It was here that he began his close association with Chapman. Three months later he was transferred to Adelaide, where, at only 24 years of age, he was made Design Engineer and placed in charge of all structural design. He held this position until, after a short period as Assistant Chief Engineer, he became Assistant to the Railways Commissioner in 1946.

Fargher was a brilliant designer. This was most evident during the war years, when the SAR undertook a great deal of work on behalf of the Department of Defence. Working day and night, he was responsible for the design of a number of munitions and other defence establishments. His output of plans during that period was phenomenal. At all times objective, Fargher's integrity was beyond question and his forthrightness a byword. Invariably, he told the truth as he saw it, which was not always appreciated. He applied his mathematical mind to the solution of railway problems, particularly those associated with the rating structure. Unfortunately, his colleagues did not subscribe to his views, or perhaps they did not understand them. Nevertheless, trends over the years since his retirement have entirely vindicated his line of reasoning.

Jack Fargher was an outstanding Railways Commissioner; yet I felt that his heart remained with engineering design. His continued passion for that discipline kept his engineering staff, both civil and mechanical, on their toes.

Colleagues

Of my brother commissioners, I shall not personalise, but I must say this: The century-old jibe about disunity that allegedly prevailed amongst the Australian railways — prompted no doubt by the tragedy of the gauges — was bereft of its barbs many years before my time in the chair. Common operating and commercial practices had applied for over 70 years; but, latterly, there emerged a strong unifying force, manifest publicly under the banner of the Railways of Australia; and this brought the seven individual

Mr C. G. C. Wayne, Commissioner of Railways, Western Australia, 1959-1967

Mr J. B. Horrigan, Commissioner of Railways, Western Australia, 1967-1971

Mr R. J. Pascoe, Commissioner of Railways, Western Australia, 1971-1978

Mr K. A. Smith, Commonwealth Railways Commissioner, 1960-1981

Mr E. H. Brownbill, Chairman of Commissioners, Victorian Railways, 1956-1967

Mr G. F. Brown, Chairman of Commissioners, Victorian Railways, 1967-1973

Mr N. McCusker, Commissioner for Railways, New South Wales, 1956-1972

Mr A. G. Lee, Commissioner for Railways, Queensland, 1962-1976

Mr C. E. Baird, Commissioner for Transport, Tasmania, 1951-1969

Mr G. T. Webb, Commissioner for Transport, Tasmania, 1970-1978

Mr A. T. Gandell, General Manager, New Zealand Railways, 1955-1966

Mr I. Thomas, General Manager, New Zealand Railways, 1966-1972

Mr T. M. Small, General Manager, New Zealand Railways, 1972-1976

The author when South Australian Railways Commissioner.

systems even closer together. Indeed, there was a unity of thought and objective probably unique in this country in an industry as large as that of the nation's railways.

Out of this, there developed personal friendships that have lasted into retirement. Sadly however, it would seem that current moves towards the dismemberment of the operational side of the nation's railways have inevitably led to the demise of that unity of direction and purpose.

To conclude, I would be remiss if I did not pay tribute to 'my workmates of all grades and in all places to whom I shall be eternally indebted'.

As young cadets and novice engineers too, we owed a lot to the men at the coal face; the chainmen who carried us on their backs during surveys; the inspectors and roadmasters who guided us through many a permanent way minefield; and the construction foremen who were saviours during our wisdom-teething years.

As Railways Commissioner, I directed that my inspection train should stop at every gang working along the track, something that I suggest no other person in the same position had deigned to do. I did not do so out of condescension, but rather as a token of acknowledgment. Those men might have been my employees, but they were also my workmates.

14 Reflections

On 30 March 1973 when, after 46 years on the footplate I started clearing leave preparatory to official retirement on the eve of my 63rd birthday, my active railway life ended. Hereditarily, I was not destined for any other career; nor indeed would I have been happy in any other.

Our first move was to Kingscote on Kangaroo Island, where Doreen and I enjoyed a sea change far removed from my beloved railways. Indeed, the nearest point to them would have been Victor Harbour, on the mainland and over 90 crow-fly kilometres over land and water. Nevertheless, a railway 'first' attached itself to our time on the island. Before retirement I stated facetiously that I intended appointing myself Stationmaster Kingscote, and that I would not countenance any appeals against it. When the time did come and we were accorded a valedictory farewell by the SAR staff, the opportunity was taken to confirm my self-appointment by presenting me with the official cap, complete with the SAR insignia. I retained that sinecuristic position for the next four years and, significantly, it has lacked an incumbent ever since.

Consequently, I can now claim three unusual firsts: the shortest pupilage at the Perth Modern School; collecting a black eye from the ninth delivery of the last over of the day; and being the only person to have held the position of stationmaster on an island lacking any trace of a railway.

Sitting back now in my proverbial rocking chair and reminiscing over my 46 working years — which witnessed the transition from pick, shovel and clydesdale construction to

Being confirmed as Stationmaster Kingscote, Kangaroo Island, South Australia, 23 March 1973 (*Photo:* South Australian Railways)

highly mechanised operations; and from coal burning steam locomotive, horse-and-buggy and primitive automobile transport to a diesel-powered locomotive, heavy road vehicled and jet aircrafted one — I would dare make the following observations.

Irrespective of their prima facie financial

Decorative poster at the Ralways Institute farewell function, 23 March 1973 (*Photo:* South Australian Railways)

losses, railway commuter services are socially necessary and must be retained, indeed improved. At the same time, however, realistic rather than lip service recognition should be given to their contribution to business and commerce.

Except for the mining industry, the phase during which the railways in this country were vital to its development has passed. Therefore, the railways should now be permitted to concentrate on those traffics for which they are best suited. Governments should have bitten the bullet years ago and rationalised their rail networks in line with those altered trends, something to which successive railway administrations had drawn their attention, sadly without effect. It had become apparent that our government railways had moved from being an instrument of national development into one of political expediency.

The transfer of the non-urban activities of the South Australian Railways to the Commonwealth in 1975 might well be interpreted as being an easy way out for the State Government, enabling it to avoid making its own decisions and to face up to change in the transport pattern. In taking such a step, it surrendered for all time its control over transport policy within its borders. Australian National, having no interest in anything but its own financial position, randomly closed lines and curtailed both the quality and frequency of services irrespective of the State's overall wellbeing.

The partial privatisation of the Australian railways has seen the demise of the railway family and, with it, the career paths and the loyalty that had marked it ever since our first railway in 1854.

The greatest tragedy of my working life was, when presented with a heaven-sent opportunity to achieve a unified rail gauge throughout Australia, interstate jealousy, parochialism, political intransigence and bureaucratic obstruction torpedoed the entire project. At the end of World War II we had, on the mainland, three gauges — 23 percent broad, 28 percent standard and 49 percent narrow — with a total of 13 breaks of gauge. Today, and after considerable expenditure on what was purported to be standardisation, we are still plagued with three gauges — 12 percent broad, 46 percent standard and 42 percent narrow — and still with 13 breaks of gauge, of which ten are operative and three inoperative. This final mess is to the everlasting discredit of those responsible. The chance to rectify it will never come again.

It would be appropriate at this juncture to offer some comment on the relationship between the government railways and the body politic. The senior public servant is a loyal person. He also has the obligation to tell the truth as he sees it, and to make honest recommendations to government, irrespective of its probable rejection or its clash with any prior expressions of opinion by the latter. However, having done that, he then has the obligation to carry out government decisions, even though they may conflict with his own views or recommendations. The moment that he feels unable to do so, he must resign.

But the problem goes further than that. From their inception in this country over 150 years ago, and until the latter part of the 20th century, the administration of and the responsibility for the railways were vested in the Railways Commissioners, who had been answerable to parliament but subject to direction only in matters of policy and finance. This left them substantially free from political interference, if not from political pressure. Fully conscious of their obligations, but at the same time also conscious of possible repercussions, the Commissioners had not been afraid to express their views, even when it was apparent that they would not be palatable. At the same time, they resisted political pressure when they felt that it was proper to do so.

In South Australia, the Railways Commissioner was deemed to be a body corporate who could sue and be sued. He also possessed wide powers, including those of staff recruitment and deployment, industrial relations and expenditure, the latter provided that it was in accord with the parliamentary estimates. On the other hand, he was subject to gubernatorial approval, or disallowance by Parliament, in such matters as the construction of or the pulling-up of existing railways, by-law freights and fares, and the letting of all but petty contracts. His financial performance was also subject to scrutiny by the Auditor General.

In a number of instances, however, attempts were made to coerce the Commissioner into making recommendations in keeping with the Government's preconceived or politically oriented ideas. On one occasion I was told quite bluntly, 'That is not the recommendation the Government wants', and on another it was intimated to me that the Government did not want to receive a controversial report. In neither instance did I abrogate my responsibility. To his credit, when I told my Minister that my job was to tell the truth as I saw it and that it would be no skin off my nose if the Government did not accept my recommendations, he expressed his appreciation of my attitude. Unfortunately, however, honest opinions are at times interpreted as obstructionism.

It had been apparent for some time that the politicians were out to strip us of our independence, to deprive the Commissioners of the level of autonomy previously enjoyed, and to intrude into matters far removed from those of policy. In 1971, the South Australian Railways Commissioner's Act was amended to the extent that, in effect, the Minister was empowered to bypass the Commissioner and give instructions direct to departmental officers or employees. Although this provision applied specifically to the SAR, its enactment coincided with an Australia-wide trend towards the erosion of the statutory authority of railway administrations.

The public railways in this country would constitute one of the nation's largest commercial and industrial undertakings, as well as being a vital contributor, not only to defence and development, but also to commerce and industry. Indeed, railway construction—the capitalisation of which could well represent more than 10 percent of the unimproved value of the land served by them — generally preceded agricultural development while freights and fares, which were subject to parliamentary approval, were often loaded in favour of certain industries. Consequently, the railway administrator was regularly faced with the problem of deficit budgeting and, with it, public censure.

At the turn of this century, the public railways in this country consisted of 35,000 route kilometres of track with a capitalisation of at least $50 billion, an annual traffic task of 500 million passengers and over 300 million tonnes of freight, revenue and expenditure of $7 billion and $6 billion respectively, and 115,000 employees.

During my 46 years' railway career, which encompassed three individual systems, I served under 13 different Ministers, whose trade or business backgrounds could be summarised as consisting of two gold miners, two farmers and one each of locomotive engineman, provincial tramway employee, licensee of a country pub, shearer, pastoralist, director of a retail carpet firm, tradesman printer, real estate agent and electrical tradesman.

How many, if any, of the 13 would have been qualified to act as a director of an organisation with capitalisation, level of activity, turnover and staff numbers of such magnitude? Moreover, would any of them have possessed the competency and experience to direct management in day-to-day matters, especially in the currently unregulated and intensely competitive transport market? Under such circumstances, decisions formerly made strictly on technical, economic or commercial grounds would be influenced by persons who, although skilled in the arts of politics and political survival, would lack both knowledge and experience in transport matters.

Constrained as they were to working within the financial parameters and charges laid down by government, as well as being obliged to operate services well knowing that, transport-wise, they were not economically viable, administrations paid particular attention to costs and efficiency. Yet, while doing so, they were subject either to condemnation for operating unprofitable services under government direction or public demand, or to outcries of protest when indeed they did take steps to eliminate them. Given a respect for government policy by railway administrations, and a reciprocal respect by government for the expertise and autonomy of those administrations, there should be no reason why the railways should not remain an instrument of national development and a source of support to commerce, industry and primary production.

On a personal and a happier note, and reflecting on the six objectives enunciated in Chapter 1, in retrospect, I feel that I can say that:

• As a 22-year-old greenhorn in charge of his first job — and moreover the youngest person on it — I very nearly had my spirit broken by my superior who, although located over 180 kilometres away and who inspected the job only twice in eight months, maintained by, telephone and written admonishment, a constant barrage of criticism. Fortunately, I survived more or less unscathed, but vowed never to succumb: a determination that I carried throughout the remainder of my working life.

• I endeavoured to tell the truth, perhaps adorned at times with a touch of poetic licence.

• My years of living and working under harsh conditions were the most rewarding, and, out of them, grew a lasting respect for the men and women who endured them for far longer periods than did I.

• I do not think it would be egotistical to say that I was able to establish a rapport with my staff. Out of this, there developed a number of friendships which have lasted into retirement.

• I learned very early in the piece to do my homework.

• My first encounter with a non-urban Aborigine taught me never to talk down to anyone, however humble.

I feel too that I can look back on a life that enabled me to learn and to love the outback; and to have been privileged to have been associated with, lived with and worked with such a band of dedicated men.

Those 46 years were in effect a long staircase which, as a 16-years-old engineering cadet, I never dreamed that I would ascend. Despite having stumbled once or twice, I would happily attempt such a climb again.

Reminiscing from that same rocking chair, this time on personal matters, I must say that the best thing that ever happened to me was to be sent to the little town of Williams in Western Australia. It was there that I met and fell inlove with the 19-years-old girl who became my wife, and with whom I spent 60 glorious years. Those 60 years were embellished by a family of which both of us were mighty proud.

If now I might philosophise for a moment, and at the same time speak from experience, I would urge every retiree to shun any inclination to vegetate. On the contrary, plan to do something that will keep your mind active. It does not have to be academic or difficult; just something that you want to do, in your own time and at your own pace.

The unexpected and somewhat embarrassing publicity that followed my PhD led to my being invited to participate in a seminar at the Australian National University titled 'Ageing Well: A Time to Reflect', and it might be pertinent if I reiterated some of my concluding comments:

'The encouragement that I received convinced me that there is a huge fountain of help out there awaiting the opportunity to be tapped and to assist any person who contemplates following the same path. These views of mine might appear to concentrate on the higher echelons of mental capacity, but they are not so intended. They could apply to almost any level.

I would like to say that I don't feel 93 years old, but 93 years young; and, if my happy circumstances mean anything, it is this:

- Think young and you will stay young.
- Do something, however basic, that will keep your mind active and will give you pleasure in doing.
- Couple with that mental activity some appropriate yet not too strenuous physical exercise.
- All of these things are good for your mental and physical health — and, in my case, good for my ego.'

That, I think, sums it all up, but, incongruously, my roseate memories and recommendations are tinged by two longstanding regrets: missing that goal in the 1933 football grand final in Kalgoorlie, and not being more proficient with the cricket bat.

Index

Long, Norman, 56
Long Straight, 19
Longreach, 179
Loongana, 117
Loveday, Ron, 164
Loxton, 156
Lunt, A.G., 43, 185
Lyndhurst, 119–20
Lyons, 119

MacArthur, General Douglas, 176
Mahoney, Jack, 124
Malcolm, 52, 72
Maluka, 214
Manjimup, 44
Manners, George, 33, 36
Maralinga, 118
Marble Bar, 9, 57, 64, 212
Marloo sheep station, 56
Marree, 110, 115, 117, 120, 132, 213
Marsland, Tom, 84
Martlow, Lindsay, 116
Maryborough, 170
Mashford, Max, 132
Mataranka, 124, 214
Matilda bay, 28, 30, 35
May, C.R., 44, 231
McArthur, Duncan, 14
McArthur, Mary, 14
McArthur River, 104, 124
McAuley, Fred, 128–9
McCarthy brothers, 99
McClelland, Ganger, 128
McCullough, Alec, 225–6
McCullough, Ian, 186, 226
McCusker, Neal, 14, 196, 201, 226
McIntosh, Malcolm, 137
McLarty, Ross, 50
McLean, Lance, 160
McLeay, George, 137, 181
McLeay siding, 119
McVey, Dan, 227
McWhinney, Bill, 79
Meekatharra, 12, 21, 45, 52–3, 57–8, 64–5, 68, 82–3, 93, 212
Meekatharra–Horseshoe railway, 58
Meenaar, 45
Melbourne, 108, 170, 174, 182, 183
Melbourne Road, 26
Menzies, 72
Menzies, R.G., 137, 180, 182, 191
Mern Merna, 115, 135
Merredin, 44–5, 72, 75–6, 170
Midnight Horror, 215

Miling, 44–5, 142, 144
Millar, C. and E., 103
Millicent, 187
Mills, Fred, 49, 51
Mistral, 208
Mitchell, Sir James, 44, 73
Moomba, 120
Moonta, 143–4
Moore, Milton, 96, 221
Moorine Rock, 72
Morgan (SA), 142, 144, 156, 159
Morgans (WA), 72
Morris, E.W., 56, 72, 75, 228
Morris, Milton, 198, 201
Mount Barker, 44, 215
Mount Christie, 112, 118
Mount Dutton, 124, 132
Mount Gambier, 144, 168, 187
Mount Helena, 45
Mount Magnet, 58, 68, 212
Mount Pleasant, 144
Mount Squire, 129
Mulga, 214
Mullewa, 45, 54, 56–8, 63, 212
Mundaring water scheme, 16
Mungala, 118
Munro, Don, 36
Murchison, 53, 57, 69
Murchison River, 57
Murdoch, Walter, 34
Murray Bridge, 159
Murrin Murrin, 72, 214

Nallan, 67
Nannine, 58
Naracoorte, 187
Narembeen, 44
Naretha, 117–18
Narrogin, 11, 49, 53, 76, 78
Nazarri, Owen, 217–18
Neales, 131
Nelligan, Joe, 163
New South Wales Government, 105
Newcastle Waters, 104
Newdegate, 44, 76
Niagara, 72–3
Nicholson Road, 19–20
Nixon, Peter, 165, 195
Noble, Vic, 116
Noongaar, 75
Nornalup, 44, 49, 76
Norseman, 14, 44, 52, 73
North Australia Railway, 103, 106–8, 112, 124, 214
North Dandalup, 14